The Reconstruction Justice of
Salmon P. Chase

LANDMARK LAW CASES

&

AMERICAN SOCIETY

Peter Charles Hoffer

N. E. H. Hull

Series Editors

HAROLD M. HYMAN

The Reconstruction Justice of Salmon P. Chase

In Re Turner and *Texas v. White*

UNIVERSITY PRESS OF KANSAS

Published by the University Press of Kansas (Lawrence, Kansas 66049), which was
organized by the Kansas Board of Regents and is operated and funded by Emporia State
University, Fort Hays State University, Kansas State University, Pittsburg State University,
the University of Kansas, and Wichita State University

Library of Congress Cataloging-in-Publication Data

Hyman, Harold Melvin, 1924–

The reconstruction justice of Salmon P. Chase : In re Turner and

Texas v. White / by Harold M. Hyman.

p.   cm.

Includes bibliographical references and index.

ISBN 0-7006-0834-6 (alk. paper). — ISBN 0-7006-0835-4 (alk.

paper)

1. Chase, Salmon P. (Salmon Portland), 1808–1873.   2. Judges—

United States—Biography.   3. Slavery—Law and legislation—United

States—History.   4. Afro-Americans—Civil rights—History.

5. United States—History—Civil War, 1861–1865.   I. Title.

KF8745.C45H95   1997

342.73'087—dc21   96-54819

British Library Cataloguing in Publication Data is available.

Printed in the United States of America

10 9 8 7 6 5 4 3 2 1

The paper used in this publication meets the minimum requirements of the American
National Standard for Permanence of Paper for Printed Library Materials Z39.48-1984.

TO FERNE,

FOR ALL THE GIFTS OF FIFTY YEARS, MUCH THANKS,

AND TO JERRY RUSH,

WHO IS MISSED, ALSO THANKS

CONTENTS

Editors' Preface *ix*

Acknowledgments *xi*

Introduction *1*

1. Preparation *13*

2. Practice *25*

3. Politician and Attorney General for Runaway Slaves *37*

4. Down the Slippery Slope to Secession *54*

5. Civilizing America's Civil War *72*

6. Means and Ends in the Union's Evolving War Aims *81*

7. Matters Momentous and Mundane in Reconstruction *94*

8. Freedom's Meanings: States' Wrongs and Citizens' Rights *107*

9. *In Re Turner:* Its Hour Come 'Round at Last *123*

10. *Texas v. White:* National Motto or Final Solution? *140*

Epilogue: Fulfilled and Unfulfilled Pledges *151*

Conclusion *166*

Bibliographical Essay *170*

Index *175*

EDITORS' PREFACE

The American Civil War wrought a revolution in American constitutional law. Driven by the winds of war, the federal government assumed powers that before had been reserved to the states. Amendments to the Constitution ended slavery, defined citizenship, and impressed upon the states that they not deprive any person of life, liberty, or property without due process of law or deny to any person within their jurisdiction equal protection of the law. Under a series of Civil Rights Acts federal courts were obligated to aid petitioners whose rights were abused by state officials. Gone with those same winds were the secessionists' claims that the Union was neither perpetual nor indissoluble and that the federal Constitution was nothing more or less than a public version of a private contract whose parties were the sovereign states. The defeat of the Confederacy had confirmed Pres. Abraham Lincoln's contention that the Union had never been broken.

But the defeated Confederates had left behind them a legacy of public and private legal arrangements that were not so easily disposed of during the Reconstruction period. The way in which one federal judge used the new constitutional doctrines to dismantle the machinery of slavery and Confederate government is the subject of Harold Hyman's moving and swiftly paced account. *In re Turner* and *Texas v. White* were relics of slavery and rebellion that Justice Salmon P. Chase heard in the years immediately following the war. They raised questions of the rights of the former slaves and the status of the Confederate states. Chase's opinions demonstrated that the Civil War had fundamentally altered the nature of both private and public law.

In re Turner was what today would be called an employment law case. American employment law had undergone its own small revolution in the first half of the nineteenth century. As Robert Steinberg demonstrates in his *Invention of Free Labor* (1991), early American contract laborers who left their jobs before completion of the contracted duties were subject to fines and imprisonment. By the middle of the century, however, the punishment for such breaches of contract was no longer personal. One simply could not collect wages if one left a job before it was done. Indeed, in some states, the laborer could obtain a portion of the agreed-upon payment for the work that he had completed. Labor was now truly free, but not for slaves, whose status as personal property (chattel) denied them not only the right to make contracts for their labor but also all legal identity as people. If the Thirteenth Amendment or, as in wartime Maryland, a state statute, ended slavery, was the former slave free to bargain for his or her services and free to breach that bargain when it was patently unfair? That was the question in *Turner*.

Turner was a private law case—the parties were individuals. *Texas v. White* was a public law case, for although the defendants were private individuals who happened to be the "holders in course" (the people who purchased Confederate war bonds from their original owners), the underlying question was the legality of the acts of the Confederate state of Texas. Could Confederate states issue bonds whose buyers could demand payment after the war was over from the reconstructed state governments? Not if the Confederate state had no legal existence. Once again the issues raised reflected an explosion in the use of state debentures (bonds issued by a state upon its own credit) to fund capital improvements and to underwrite private enterprises in the antebellum years. In the 1840s and 1850s, as Mark Summers documents in *The Plundering Generation: Corruption and the Crisis of the Union, 1849–1861* (1987), cities and states issued bonds to support the construction and operation of canals, railroads, and corporations. Some of these ventures were public, but others were wholly private. All were subject to corruption and some succumbed to that disease. Politicians were among the worst offenders in the plundering of the state treasuries. Thus *Texas v. White* not only raised issues of the legality of the actions of Confederate governments; it also recalled an era of blatant partisan misconduct.

Justice Chase welcomed these difficult cases. A man of personal probity and public virtue, he saw the federal courts as the instrument of moral as well as legal judgment—or more precisely, saw that the two worlds were not separated from one another. A Republican who had early and often urged his president to move more swiftly against slavery, Chase saw in his chief justiceship a rostrum for reform. And most important, he envisioned, as few did among the leadership of either party, a time when race would not matter in America, if only law and the decisions of law courts could speed the arrival of that day.

ACKNOWLEDGMENTS

James Charlton's *Writer's Quotation Book* (privately printed, 1981), p. 5, attributes to Blaise Pascal the perception that "the last thing that we find in making a book is to know what we must put first." I must put first my awareness of the half-century-old endlessly reincurring debt I owe to Henry Steele Commager and the late Allan Nevins and Richard B. Morris, my doctoral mentors at Columbia University in the early 1950s. From then to the present my own graduate students have educated me further about the pains and delights of research, thinking, and writing. A long list of librarians and archivists across the country, but, concerning the present volume, especially those at Rice University and most especially Ferne B. Hyman, made available to me essential printed and manuscript materials. Even deep wounds heal, and I am grateful that an editor of the series in which this book appears, an editor who is also a treasured friend, Peter Hoffer, offered his famously frank estimates of every draft. Irene Zisek patiently transformed the drafts into a form that Melinda Wirkus and others of the able production editorial staff of the University Press of Kansas made into the book before you, and I thank them. Rice University's diverse supports were generous and consistent, and I acknowledge them gratefully. I am indebted also for F. M. Cornford's advice in his *Microcosmographia Academica: Being a Guide for the Young Academic Politican* (London: Bowes and Bowes, 1908), p. 3, not to be "ashamed to study men's weaknesses and prejudices." And, I add, their strengths.

Readers will find direct quotations not specifically attributed, locatable in relevant sources cited in the bibliographical essay.

INTRODUCTION

We shall not cease from exploration,
And the end of all our exploring
Will be to arrive where we started
And know the place for the first time.

T. S. ELIOT, "LITTLE GIDDING"

"There is the orator, Mr. Lincoln," recalled Salmon Portland Chase in May 1866. Lincoln's secretary of the treasury from 1861 through 1864 and since earliest 1865 the chief justice of the United States, Chase was previewing a now-famous painting by the artist Francis B. Carpenter. Inspired by participants' accounts of a pivot-point in America's history, the artist had recreated the dramatic scene in the White House four years earlier. It was the moment during the Union's darkest hours of the Civil War when, without warning, Lincoln announced to the bemused cabinet heads his determination to do what Chase, among only a few there, had been advocating so strongly and persistently that it frequently irritated the harassed president.

Commander-in-chief Lincoln had at last agreed with Chase about the necessity to exercise the nation's war powers and by an executive order to emancipate slaves in the states that were still actively rebelling. Depending on the outcomes of battles the new policy, if effective, might transform and elevate the war aims of the Union. Until then the nation's announced goal was to restore the prewar union of states, presumably with the rights of most slave owners intact, including that of taking slaves into the federal territories and, by implication, into free states. Thereafter, Lincoln's decision to emancipate the rebels' slaves elevated the Union's war aims to that of reconstructing a Union greatly improved by the end of slavery in the states where armed resistance persisted and in all the federal territories.

During that brief, single-topic, momentous session of 1862, Lincoln explained to the cabinet his justifications for the decision to emancipate. They thrilled Chase. As the treasury secretary had done, Lincoln, before deciding on military emancipation, had reexamined intensively the Constitution's clauses on the nation's powers and duties during wars and other crises. Combined with the depressing effects of a year's accumulation of battlefield reverses and stalemates, Lincoln's prayerful study had brought him finally to agree with Chase, that his duty as president and commander-in-chief was to do everything "necessary and proper" to maintain the Union. And so Lincoln "promise[ed] . . . to myself . . . and to God . . . that this thing should be done."

The trinity of Constitution, law, and religion were as precious to Chase as to Lincoln. Little wonder that Chase, his recollections sharpened in 1866 by Carpenter's portrait, recalled vividly how he and the other cabinet officers had responded to Lincoln's announcement. They had sat quietly, silenced by the immediate significance and longer-range implications of what they had just heard. Chase praised the artist for having captured not only the cabinet members' facial expressions but also the essence of each man's inner response, their jubilation and fears on hearing of Lincoln's determination. Likening the scene to one portraying an attorney's courtroom pleading, Chase wrote: "There . . . is the great act; the [Emancipation] Proclamation [that Lincoln had] just read; and there are the witnesses, the [cabinet] Heads." With them Chase sat mute and immobile, yet with inner feelings boiling; he remembered "thinking of what they had just heard, and the future it opens."*

That future had many pasts. For Chase, the path to emancipation in prewar decades had involved him and Lincoln with a brave minority of antislavery lawyers who since the early 1830s had tried, largely unavailingly, to impose legal, constitutional, and political barriers to slavery's immense westward spread from the Mississippi River to the Pacific Ocean's shore by 1860. Later, as president, Lincoln would acknowledge that Chase was foremost among the people who had influenced him to pursue these seemingly hopeless antislavery struggles and then to risk emancipation. Lacking pacific alternatives, in 1862 Chase and Lincoln had agreed fundamentally about the essentiality and timeliness of incorporating the moral imperative of prewar antislavery into America's war aims if the Union was ever militarily to overpower the Confederacy. The two high officials agreed also about the Constitution as an adequate source of authority to justify military emancipation.

That was the past. But Chase correctly perceived the greater potentialities for America's future in the president's announcement of 1862.

---

*Thomas F. Schwartz, "Salmon P. Chase Critiques *First Reading of the Emancipation Proclamation of President Lincoln, Civil War History* 33 (March 1987):84–87.

Lincoln's decision to emancipate basically thawed and redirected long frozen public policies involving the destinies of whole races, policies that had heavily favored slave owners. With those policies changed, the Union, if it survived the Civil War militarily, must reimagine both its immediate and more distant racial futures. Arising from the Union's desperate military needs, emancipation both mirrored the past that slavery had inflicted on America and inspired visions of an improved future. As of 1862, Lincoln's emancipation expedient, if successful, unlike many earlier federal policies that favored the slave states and slave owners, might result in a contraction of areas open to slavery in postwar America.

Treasury Secretary Chase would help to shape that immediate wartime future. Then, as chief justice, in deciding *In re Turner* (24 Fed. Cas. 337 [1867] 14, 247) in 1867 and *Texas v. White* (74 U.S. 700 [1869]) in 1869, Chase would again perceive and seize the opportunities those lawsuits offered to give longer-range form to this militarily reunited, now totally free yet still racially diverse, postwar federal Union.

Neither case was on Chief Justice Chase's docket in 1866 when he saw Carpenter's painting, although *In re Turner* would be filed soon after. What Chase took with him when he previewed the painting was his privileged insights into "the future that emancipation opened," insights that infused his positions in both *In re Turner* and *Texas v. White*.

Those insights included the fact that on January 1, 1863, three months after the cabinet meeting when Lincoln announced his decision to emancipate, he had greatly extended the significance of the Emancipation Proclamation in a manner that would fundamentally alter the Union's war aims and postwar composition. Again enjoying Chase's emphatic support, Lincoln had authorized the recruitment of blacks into the Union army through volunteering and conscription.

The great majority of blacks were slave residents of the southern states. Both Lincoln and Chase were able lawyers and had steeped themselves for decades in state and federal laws concerning slavery. They knew that arming blacks to kill whites was a statutory crime, a felony, in every seceded state. Further, Lincoln and Chase were aware that elevating blacks through federal policy to the status of white soldiers transformed them, whether former slaves or ever free, into people whose clear display of allegiance imposed claims on the nation's protection and conscience. For example, if captured by Confederate troops, black Union soldiers and their officers needed every protection their loyalty to the Union could afford against prosecution or other retribution by rebel authorities.

This immediate wartime concern by 1865 shaped the near future in ways almost unimaginable before the Civil War. Since the 1862 cabinet meeting, vast battles had finally brought the Confederacy to defeat. Ultimately nearly 200,000 black soldiers, enlisted after Lincoln implemented his policy on emancipation, had reinforced the Union army's weary Billy Yanks. Most of the black reinforcements were from southern states. Expectations were that they would return there.

But they would not return as individuals whose skin pigment automatically identified them as legally inferior slave or "free negro" members of the most degraded categories of southern civil society. For more than two centuries state laws and customs had confined generations of blacks to these disesteemed levels. Then, almost simultaneously with Lincoln's murder in mid-April 1865, at Appomattox, both white and black Union soldiers in effect had ratified the pending Thirteenth Amendment to the federal Constitution well before its formal ratification and adoption by the number of states required to make it part of the supreme law of the land.

The Thirteenth Amendment is brief, seemingly simple; yet in terms of race relations, federalism, and many common private contracts, it is potentially revolutionary:

> Section 1. Neither slavery nor involuntary servitude, except as a punishment for crime whereof the party shall have been duly convicted, shall exist within the United States, or any place subject to their jurisdiction.
> Section 2. Congress shall have power to enforce this article by appropriate legislation.

At the least, the Thirteenth Amendment nationalized and constitutionalized emancipation from sea to shining sea. It was a universal prohibition against any action by national, state, or local officials or by private persons that reduced other parties to slavery or, except for crimes, to involuntary servitude, that is, to civil conditions of life and labor not agreed to by all parties. Until 1865 the Constitution, the nation's supreme law, had recognized two classes of Americans, free and slave (Native Americans composed a category to which Chase, like most antislavery crusaders, remained almost totally oblivious). And slavery had just been obliterated. As far as it lay within the power of a justice, even a chief justice, of the

United States to do so, especially in *In re Turner* and *Texas v. White*, Chase would undertake the burden of ensuring that the universal freedom called for by the Thirteenth Amendment and its sequels was not demeaned by coexisting involuntary servitude, however disguised in seemingly irrelevant state laws. In his decisions in the two cases he would try also to stipulate that though state-centered federalism remained the basic reality of the restored nation, the national government possessed a core interest in defining basic characteristics of that federalism.

Unlike many of his comrades in antislavery efforts, Chase never forgot that despite the two centuries of accumulated customs and unjust laws on race, in the Civil War black Americans had rallied zealously to the Union. By their so doing, antislavery activists' prewar hopelessness had been transformed into realistic war aims and postwar goals. Because blacks contributed so notably to the Union's final military success, as Chase saw matters the nation retained a duty to shield all blacks, not only former Union troopers, against southern states' racially bigoted state criminal laws and civil customs.

As still another aspect of the future that emancipation opened, the Thirteenth Amendment was not race-focused. Whites were not slaves. Convicted felons aside, however, many whites were in voluntary servitude, as apprentices, for example (the latter was the status of the appellant in *In re Turner*). But what of whites or blacks, males and females, who claimed actually to be in involuntary servitude, that is, a condition so like slavery as to be a differentiation without a difference?

Answers to this question could move America far beyond even the complete abolition of slavery, to steps toward equalizing the legal civil rights of both races and genders as free labor under the laws of the reunited nation and of all the states. In 1865 Chase, Lincoln, and other proponents of the pending Thirteenth Amendment had assumed and hoped that it could insulate freedom from possible postwar erosion or even reversal by contrary-minded majorities or officials of the states or nation and that freedom and involuntary servitude were incompatible.

Chase's reflections of 1866 included his concerns about President Andrew Johnson's overly precipitate (as Chase and many other persons were measuring matters) resurrections of all-white southern state and local "provisional" governments. Disquieting questions were rising about white residents in the former slave-owning states who were evading the new amendment's ban on involuntary servitude. These evasions were tarnishing the future that Chase had imagined in 1862 and that he had assumed was ushered in by Appomattox, the more decent, purer, freer future that visionary abolitionists had sought since the 1830s. Therefore as 1866 ended and through much of 1867, an even more turbulent year, Chase seized an opportunity to reenhance that future to conform to his sense of the meanings of the past.

While on his Maryland circuit (circuit-riding was then a duty of federal Supreme Court justices) in October 1867 Chase received a habeas corpus petition from a young black woman, Elizabeth Turner, a recent slave perhaps still in her teens. Turner wished to be released from the apprenticeship contract to which her mother, also a former slave of the same master, who may have been Elizabeth's father, on her minor daughter's behalf, had committed Elizabeth under terms of a relevant Maryland statute. The contract required the daughter to serve the erstwhile master, now her employer-mentor, for several more years. His responsibility under the Maryland law was to teach her certain vocational skills and to provide specified minima of food, clothing, shelter, and pay. She claimed, however, that since contracting he had kept her to rote menial tasks hardly differing from her lot as a slave. Further, he had failed to meet his obligations about the physical facilities due to her under the apprenticeship contract. His delinquencies were encouraged because the state's law discriminated against black apprentices, her lawyer asserted. That law specified lower minima and fewer protections for them than for whites. Last, through her attorney Turner claimed that she suffered the substance of involuntary servitude not only for those reasons but also because her mother had committed her to the apprenticeship.

Did Elizabeth Turner deserve the nation's protection against her unwelcome and allegedly servile status that, claimed her counsel, was forbidden both by the Thirteenth Amendment and by its implementing statute, the new federal Civil Rights Act of 1866 that defined blacks as citizens of the United States? Chief Justice Chase would answer this question.

Meanwhile it should be noted that in the 1860s few white women, much less a young black woman so recently a slave, then or for decades to come presumed to seek legal remedies for a white male's breaches of a civil contract. Turner must have been very courageous and determined and her lawyer quite inventive and alert to opportunities on behalf of his client.

Furthermore, Chase's decision concerning Turner reflected the fact that in his opinion emancipation had immediately opened a future for her in which Turner could do what until very recently had been unthinkable. If needing to defend by means of a lawsuit her economic self-interests as an employee, she and all Americans, regardless of race and gender, could seek in federal courts an equitable remedy for the defects in marketplace situations like hers, caused both by employers' unfair advantages and remissness that had been nurtured by a state's discriminatory public policies.

Almost precisely ten years before Turner appeared before Chase, the majority of the Supreme Court, speaking through his predecessor, Chief Justice Roger B. Taney, in deciding the *Dred Scott* case, had held that even in its own territories the nation could not constitutionally bar slave owning, a legitimate form of private property in some states but not in others. Taney held also that American blacks, whether slave or free, were never citizens and had always had virtually no civil rights that whites were bound by law or custom to respect. Further, five years before Turner filed her plea, in the same Baltimore courthouse where Chase heard it, Taney had decided John Merryman's petition to be released from Union military custody where his prosecession activism had placed him in the hectic earliest days of the Civil War. In Merryman's case Taney held that even in a civil war the nation's self-defensive remedies against actual—not theoretical—disloyalty were so tightly limited to those of a formal, declared, international war as to be irrelevant in the existing situation. As suggested by his willingness even to hear Turner's petition, in Chase's hands the amended Constitution might be less a Taneyesque web of constraints, that is, if the Civil War had really resulted in more permissive legal and constitutional doctrines of the sorts championed in the politics of mid-nineteenth-century America, especially by Republican party spokesmen including Chase and Lincoln, in place of those doctrines Taney had advanced.

Chase presented his solo *Turner* opinion on circuit, in the hope that it would help to lay to rest one increasingly troubling issue arising from emancipation in the former slaveholding states, but it was an issue of national importance both politically and otherwise. That issue was the legal status and marketplace rights of one among the millions of emancipated slaves to bargain and contract with employers for wages and other conditions of labor, on a parity with white workers. In legal theory both the employers' capital and the workers' labor constituted forms of private property. Therefore both parties to employer-employee contracts had property (or, in contemporary usage, civil) rights. If they conflicted, as Elizabeth Turner alleged had occurred in her case, and were unresolved, labor relationships could be destabilized not only throughout the former slave owning states but also in all the other states. And so Chase agreed to decide the rights of this single and singular young black working woman.

The very status of the former Confederate states was the other politically incendiary issue that in 1867 had already thrust its way onto the Supreme Court's docket. Chase had with him in Maryland, when Elizabeth Turner appeared before him in 1867, the adversary attorneys' briefs in *Texas v. White*, a case that the whole Court would decide in 1869. Those turbulent two years were marked by the imposition by Congress of Military Reconstruction, the ratification of the Fourteenth Amendment to the Constitution, the impeachment of Pres. Andrew Johnson (over which Chase presided), and the 1868 presidential elections, in which he was passionately involved as a would-be but frustrated presidential candidate. Notwithstanding all distractions, Chase studied the *Texas* briefs with unusual intensity yet with his usual ability quickly to master complex information.

Texas v. White originated in the Confederate state government's seizure and sale of prewar U.S. bonds. The rebel government having become defunct, the successor Texas government and private claimants asserted ownership of the securities and inspired the lawsuit.

In many instances before the Civil War the U.S. Supreme Court had decided property rights questions arising from contending parties in diverse states. In rarer instances the justices had defined states' rights in the federal system, even decreeing the existence of limits on certain state powers. But as a body the Court had never cared or dared to assume to decide which of two contenders was the lawful government of a state, that is, to decide what constituted a state.

Fortunately rarely posed, this fundamental question of federalism had come, however, to the prewar Supreme Court in *Luther v. Borden* (48 U.S. 1 [1848]) in 1849. It resulted from contested elections after a mini–civil war in Rhode Island, the so-called Dorr Rebellion. In an adept evasive maneuver, Chief Justice Taney propounded a "political question" doctrine. By its terms the popular branch of the national government, that is, the Congress, not the Court or the president, properly determined the legitimacy of state governments when election results were disputed. Congress could evidence its determination by admitting one or the other contending delegations to representation.

{ *The Reconstruction Justice of Salmon P. Chase* }

In the far different postwar Reconstruction context, with few exceptions Republicans employed Taney's political question doctrine to justify Congress's exclusion of southern states' delegates-elect and, combined with carryover war powers, of Military Reconstruction legislation. Denying the applicability of the *Luther* precedent, postwar Democrats resurrected states' rights doctrines as the heart of a healthy federalism. Thus, adverse positions on the rights of black individuals in states, the issue of *Turner*, and on the very existence of a state that had once declared itself seceded, the heart of the *Texas* matter, were debated passionately outside the Court during the impeachment proceedings and the 1868 election campaigns.

In re Turner and *Texas v. White* posed novel problems of both political and legal nature. Some federal judges and Supreme Court justices were as anxious to avoid them in the latter 1860s as Taney and his colleagues had been twenty years earlier. Except by the accident of their professional practice before they became justices, almost no members of Chase's Supreme Court were experienced in what has become known as "free labor" contracts, like the one in Turner's case, or in pondering the justiciability of the essential nature of a state in the federal Union, the central concern in *Texas v. White*.

More than any of the brethren, Salmon Portland Chase had relevant experience. He had long wrestled with both theoretical and practical aspects of race-driven labor law and with legal and constitutional theories of state-based federalism. And as a perpetual politician, moral ethicist (at least in his self-perception), pragmatic practitioner of law, and Supreme Court justice, Chase tried to accommodate these divisive and passionate issues in this constitutionally bound yet dynamic federal system of economic capitalism and popular democracy.

For understandable reasons *Texas v. White* enjoys landmark case status in America's constitutional history, yet *In re Turner* is all but ignored. Texas' lawsuit reached the Supreme Court. Elizabeth Turner's case did not, largely because her former owner chose not to appeal from Chase's circuit court ruling. More important, by implication *Texas v. White* involved the legal status of every one of the former Confederate states, not of obscure individuals; yet a decision by the justices also must necessarily affect black residents of Texas and of all the states. Issues in *Texas v. White* far transcended the original claim to the ownership of prewar government bonds that, even as Chase decided *In re Turner*, had already added *Texas v. White* to the docket of the U.S. Supreme Court. Yet, by himself defining the status and rights of black individuals in *Turner* and by the Court's defining the status and rights of a state in *Texas v. White,* Chase in the former lawsuit and all the justices in the latter were touching intimately the basic and primary problems of American federalism.

Striving bloodily for answers to these questions, hundreds of thousands of Americans, both black and white, had suffered in body and purse during four years of civil war, the longest, costliest conflict fought anywhere in the Western world since Napoleon's downfall in 1815 until the agonies of World War I began in 1914. *In re Turner* and *Texas v. White* were the linked and essential elements of a legal-constitutional compound that, once implemented politically, Chase hoped would both dissolve the Reconstruction knot in ways decent for all parties and elevate all Americans' civil rights to equality under federal and state laws.

Events would prove him wrong, more about politics and racism than about law or constitutionalism. Yet the political, legal, and constitutional aspects of both *In re Turner* and *Texas v. White* were indeed inextricably interwoven, and Chase's decisions in both lawsuits reflected his own prewar and wartime career as premier antislavery attorney and political activist.

Like America's postemancipation future, Chase's decisions in Turner's case and in *Texas v. White* had roots in his and the nation's histories. For three frustrating prewar decades Chase, like Lincoln, as private lawyer, political gadfly, and public official had helped greatly to keep the legal strategies, moral bases, and constitutional dogmas of the antislavery impulse alive, at least enough so that Lincoln could add them to reunion as the Union's desperate, hazardous, yet ennobling war aim. When Lincoln decided on emancipation as an exercise of the commander-in-chief's war powers, Chase understood that it was then only an aim, one that, like reunion itself, along with other aims including inexpensive homesteads and federal aid to education, was still far from being achieved. The *Turner* and *Texas v. White* lawsuits suggest also that even in 1867 and 1869 those aims had not yet become realities. Only when they did would the repeatedly destabilizing issues of race and federalism be erased from the nation's political and constitutional agendas, Chase believed.

His decisions in *Turner* and *Texas v. White* were rooted in his personal history. From the early 1830s through the Civil War and the constriction of Reconstruction in the early 1870s, Chase, in addition to private lawyering, held increasingly important elective and appointive public offices on

{ *The Reconstruction Justice of Salmon P. Chase* }

every level of the federal system. He was a Cincinnati city councilman in the 1830s, a U.S. senator from Ohio from 1849 to 1855, and governor of that frequently pivotal state from 1855 to 1861. Then Lincoln appointed him to be secretary of the treasury and, as 1864 ended, chief justice of the United States, the position Chase filled until his death in 1873. He invested his prewar private lawyering and the high public offices he filled, including those during the Civil War and after Appomattox, with widest public significance. These offices profoundly influenced his views in *Turner* and *White*, and through his opinions in those cases, he remade American law.

Chase's prewar careers as private attorney and Ohio public official nurtured an antislavery impulse that persisted through decades of frustrating political and juridical reverses. His bold and humane principles fit the Union's wartime needs and derivative policies about biracial coexistence in a postwar United States. True, others' intransigence ultimately frustrated Chase's vision of a nobler postvictory America. He yearned for a reunified and free nation in which the 1787 Constitution, including its long-minimalized Preamble, would be redefined as part of public law in terms compatible with the equalitarian essence of the Declaration of Independence and with the negatively phrased but positive protective purposes of the Bill of Rights and by the Emancipation Proclamation and its progeny, the Thirteenth, Fourteenth, and Fifteenth Reconstruction amendments. Chase hoped to elevate all Americans' minimal rights to equal legal protections against both federal and state wrongs, including racial and gender wrongs, committed against individuals either by officials or by private persons acting under or unrestrained by some public authority. That elevation required a beneficent revolution in nation-state federalism that, he hoped, might become a first step toward a diminution of racism and other bigotries.

This was a future that Chase envisioned in 1862 when Lincoln announced his emancipation decision. Chase yearned still to realize that vision in 1866 when viewing the portrait of the announcement to the cabinet. And in 1867 and 1869, this eminent prewar antislavery lawyer and political activist who had become chief justice of the United States, tried, in his *Turner* and *Texas v. White* opinions, to imbed his dreams and hopes for that future into the nation's constitutional law in a manner to evoke obedience from all individuals in all the states.

From the early 1870s well past the vital center of the twentieth century, less lofty visions than Chase's would dominate public policies and frustrate his aspirations. Then, in our time, "second reconstruction" concerns about equal justice under law revived discourse about ideas of the sort he advocated and inspired renewed attention to his career. Chase's significant successes and tragic frustrations concerning his goals suggest the wisdom of Sophocles' instruction to historians and biographers 2,000 years ago in *Antigone:*

> You cannot learn of any man the soul, the mind, and the intent,
> Until he shows his practice of ... government and laws.
> For ... who controls the state,
> And does not hold to the best plans of all,
> But locks up his tongue through some kind of fear. . . .
> He is the worst of all who were or are.

In his "practice of government" Salmon Portland Chase, many of his contemporaries assure us, never "locks up" his tongue or pen "through some kind of fear." Was he, however, as numerous commentators imply, because of his ambition for ever-higher public offices, "the worst of all who were or are"?

CHAPTER 1

Preparation

Chase was born in 1808, a year before Lincoln. In young Chase's New England his extended family enjoyed a relatively elite social status that contrasts sharply with Lincoln's mudsill heritage. Named after an uncle who had died in Portland, Chase was one of the ten surviving children of a once-wealthy New Hampshireman. Successively and sometimes simultaneously, his father farmed, kept a tavern, manufactured glass, and filled minor elective local public offices, a pattern of livelihood similar to that followed by the several Chase uncles living nearby, except that most of the latter achieved election to higher stations. However else they earned their livings, Chase's father and uncles were also practicing politicians.

Young Chase counted among the uncles a later Episcopal bishop who would profoundly influence his young nephew, a U.S. senator, and several lawyers, including one who became Vermont's chief justice. The often passionate and simultaneous interests in politics, religion, and law displayed by both male and female Chase adults helped to define Salmon's youth and maturity.

So did the fact that his father died, bankrupt, in 1817, when the boy was nine years old, just when a severe panic, or economic depression, was constraining the nation's economy. The indomitable and pious widow continued instructing her bright son at home in religious matters. Through efforts that Harriet Beecher Stowe, who knew the Chases, understood to be infinite economies and unknown exertions, Salmon's mother scratched up the money to pay tutors and schools for his secular education. But by the early 1820s the younger children also needed schooling, and she was too physically exhausted and financially straitened to accommodate both their costs and his. She then prevailed on her brother-in-law, Philander Chase, the Episcopal bishop of Ohio, to be the youth's guardian.

Meanwhile, Salmon had edged awkwardly toward his teens. He was a thin, gawky, shy adolescent, increasingly aware of his immediate family's economically depressed, poor-relation status that local bullies mocked and that contrasted humiliatingly to the status of his successful uncles. In order to ease his mother's financial burdens, in 1820 the boy left New Hampshire to join the bishop in the latter's combined home, church, school, and farm located in a hamlet near Cincinnati.

In the Ohio near-frontier of the early 1820s, a bishop's life, at least as Salmon's uncle chose to live it, involved few amenities and no luxuries. Possessed of an impressive physique, Bishop Chase was a workaholic. Accustomed to having his own way, he accepted deference as his due. He preached enthusiastically that young people derived essential benefits from hard physical farm labor, strictly disciplined schoolwork, and sustained attention to Christianity's moral preachments and salvational promise, and he enforced his views on everyone in his charge.

Still hurting from his family's fallen fortunes, the impressionable young newcomer began to emulate his forceful uncle's domineering ways. If only overtly they commanded respect. In time, the imitative mask of ponderous self-righteousness that young Chase adopted, perhaps to fend off further hurts, hardened into its own reality.

Bishop Chase assumed that his bright nephew-ward would share his assumptions both about the character-building benefits of labor and a calling to a priestly career in their church. In addition to the formidable roster of field chores that he imposed on the boy he required Salmon to read and recite daily in Latin and Greek and to master exercises in mathematics and Christian theology.

The resulting strains on the nephew evidenced themselves in a lisp. As a young adult he exorcised this speech impediment by rigorous elocution exercises. Chase's hard-won triumph required him to regain, and throughout his life to retain, tight control over his facial muscles. Contemporaries would read his massively composed features as indicating a vain and stubborn indifference to views other than his own, an estimate that was by no means a total misreading of the cast of mind behind the mask. Salmon emulated also his uncle's religiosity. But once grown he evidenced his piety in secular as well as in religious matters.

During his years with the bishop Salmon's heavy physical workload muscled his growing but still-spare frame. Like Lincoln in neighboring Illinois, he soon surpassed six feet in height, unusual for that generation. The bishop's duties included missionary circuits of the state, and Salmon frequently accompanied him as wagoner, porter, and acolyte. Once they arrived at the homes of congregants or possible converts into which the peripatetic pair were invited, at the bishop's bidding young Salmon read from the Bible or from morally suitable classics, often also leading mealtime and evening prayers.

These occasions delighted the boy, and the bishop's backwoods audiences were deeply impressed by his precocious erudition, sly humor, and despite the lisp, loquacity. Combined with his often-resentful admiration for his fearsome uncle, the praises the maturing boy received for sermonizing and reciting encouraged him further to imitate the bishop's mannerisms. In later decades Salmon Chase would seem to many contemporaries to be a self-righteous elitist, a pious snob who, like the bishop, spouted Scripture when challenged by facts leading to views adverse to his own. "Chase is a good man, but his theology is unsound. He thinks . . . [that he] is a fourth person in the Trinity," quipped Benjamin F. Wade, Chase's fellow-Ohioan and that state's U.S. senator in the 1860s.*

As a youth Chase proved that he was at least a superior student. At Cincinnati College, then little more than a struggling, debt-ridden, church-related prep school despite its loftier label, Salmon swiftly outpaced the ability of the faculty, including his now less fearsome uncle, to teach him. Disaffected from pursuing either a priestly or a farmer's career, Chase discerned in higher education the key to a better material life. His father's bankruptcy still stung. He desired, however, that material success must harmonize with his militant and evangelical Protestantism, although such harmony proved to be elusive.

His goal—to learn more than either the bishop or Cincinnati College could teach—was easier for Salmon Chase to arrive at than to finance. In order to save money to cover the tuition charged by better institutions, during Cincinnati College's midyear recesses he endured wintry stints as a rural schoolteacher. Teaching then and for a long time to come would remain a common fallback job for America's tiny elite of classically educated or, as in Chase's instance, half-educated, aspiring young white gentlemen suffering from pocketbook poverty. By combining his scant savings with gifts and loans from his family, in 1824 Chase left Ohio and, returning

*Frederick J. Blue, *Salmon P. Chase: A Life in Politics* (Kent, Ohio: Kent State University Press, 1987), 246.

to New England, enrolled in Dartmouth College. It granted him advanced standing and in 1826 he graduated Phi Beta Kappa—but without a job or a firm sense of commitment to a career.

Chase's talents, interests, and education predisposed him to a place in the "chattering classes," then thought of as composed chiefly of journalists, lawyers, politicians, and ministers. But Chase disesteemed the last and, temporarily as matters worked out, his younger siblings' economic needs diverted him from the others. And so the new college graduate again resorted to rural schoolteaching.

And again he hated this vexing choice. His pupils were inattentive and unprepared. To Chase and his status-conscious family, bucolic schoolmastering was at best only a minimally respectable dead end, one ranking socially little higher than a house servant or petty storekeeper (notably, the last category attracted rather than repelled young Lincoln). But after weighing alternatives Chase despaired; schoolteaching was the only option that his expensive education had prepared him to undertake. And so, after borrowing the money needed to outfit a classroom, he again undertook that work, but now in the more urban setting of Washington, D.C., the nation's capital city. It would prove to be a step that would start him on the road leading eventually to the chief justiceship of the United States and to the *Turner* and *Texas v. White* cases.

Still heavily flavored by southern ways wafting from across the Potomac, in the mid-1820s the national capital was emerging from its villagelike origins and from the effects of the British army's incendiary visit during the War of 1812. When Chase arrived there Washington City, as most mail was then addressed, was enjoying more adequate if still-thin urban amenities. More immediately important to Chase was the fact that long-service congressmen, other government officials, private practitioners of several professions, and merchants were bringing their families, including school-age children, to live in the federal district. But Chase worried about the stiff competition among schoolmasters for their custom and tried to hedge against risks. He asked another uncle, by then a U.S. senator, to tout to colleagues the availability of this new schoolmaster in their midst and also to find him a back-up sinecure on some federal bureau's payroll, a favored cocoon for unpublished authors and undiscovered artists. Like his brother the bishop, however, the senator was dedicated to self-help doctrines and declined to aid his nephew.

Despite the school's early if modest financial success, Chase remained unhappy, sometimes even despondent. Though profitable, schoolteaching imposed heavy emotional strains on him from which he prayed for release. Especially when Congress was in session, the seductively glittering Washington society swirled around this ardently ambitious young man but ignored him. He associated with other transplanted, self-conscious sophisticates like himself, young men with high expectations but low immediate prospects who were Chase's fellow-tenants of a cheap and seedy boardinghouse that also lured laborers and transient unemployed men, some barely distinguishable from vagrants, who gambled away the Sabbath. Chase thrashed particularly noisome, drunken tenants, he boasted to an intimate.

Chase continued to read about and yearn for invitations to the White House and to the elite residences, clubs, and embassies where congressmen, high civil and military officials, and diplomats gathered to dine and dance. But increasingly he feared that his unrespected livelihood, schoolteaching, condemned him permanently to exclusion from the elite social circles he assumed to be rightfully his because of his family's eminence in New England and Ohio and his privileged education.

Ironically, Chase would case off what he described as his dual yoke of poverty and teaching through the agency of some of the very students he privately looked upon as a collective burden. The pupils at his school included a son of Henry Clay and a son of William Wirt, and the latter boy interested his father in schoolmaster Salmon Chase.

Then in his twelfth year as the attorney general of the United States, Wirt engaged Chase originally only to tutor his son after school hours. But soon after Chase accepted the moonlighting job, he began to use the front door to Wirt's palatial residence rather than the servant's entrance usual for menials, including tutors. Gossips noticed that though a mere teacher, Chase was frequently a guest at the formal dinners, dances, and recitals that made the Wirt home a Washington social hub. It was also a center where political tacticians, influence peddlers, and favor-traders gathered. Chase was soon conspicuously present at these closed-door caucuses of Wirt's important political friends. Without Wirt's patronage Chase probably would not have gained or kept access to the high society or to the intimate political discussions that he had so yearned to enjoy. But Chase's own qualities of personality and promise kept him there, drawing him and Wirt ever closer in ties of mutual respect and affection.

Invited frequently by Wirt to the latter's splendid residence, Chase happily accepted and soon thought of marriage with each of the several lovely Wirt daughters in succession. Their father, however, directed their attention to other, already established spousal choices. Chase's frustrated romantic notions did not mar his relationship with Wirt. And Chase found in Wirt an appealingly warm and supportive father figure that his uncle, the bishop, could never be. When Wirt and Chase met, by contemporary standards the former, born in 1772 and thought of by a younger generation as a child—or perhaps a relic—of the Revolution, was inching into old age. He and the tense young schoolmaster were individuals of strikingly dissimilar personalities. Ever sprightly in carriage and amiable in discourse and expression, Wirt seemed to be unquenchably youthful, Chase prematurely old.

Long a resident of Virginia and then of Washington, Wirt was a noted raconteur, poet, playwright, musician, and popular author. His biography of Patrick Henry and his tribute to Thomas Jefferson and John Adams, who both died on July 4, 1826, linked him with the already gilded age of the nation's Founders. A hard-drinking, slave-owning extrovert, Wirt had scant respect for religious orthodoxy. His wordly ways seemed to separate him unbridgeably from Chase. Yet in essential ways the two disparate men understood each other, and understanding blossomed quickly into friendship.

Commonly accounted to be one of the best lawyers in the country, Wirt maintained an erratically remunerative private law practice during his long service as top government lawyer. The latter duty included his participation as counsel before the Supreme Court and other high tribunals in most—170 by one scholar's estimate—of the major constitutional cases of those formative decades. As examples, Wirt was counsel in the treason proceedings against Aaron Burr and in the *Dartmouth College, McCulloch v. Maryland, Cohens v. Virginia, Cherokee Nation,* and *Charles River Bridge* cases that made Chief Justice John Marshall's long incumbency (from 1803) as head of the Supreme Court so significant in the nation's history. Yet Wirt's formal preparation in the law had been sketchy.

As Chase's patron, Wirt was the younger man's conduit into the polite society he so prized. Awareness grew that Chase was an eligible bachelor with a socially and politically powerful sponsor, and leading hostesses invited him to formal dinners, dances, and receptions, including those at the White House. Happier now than at any time in his life, he was no longer visibly melancholic. When he estimated that occasions or companions warranted the effort, Chase was a stimulating conversationalist. Washington's hostesses planning formal parties tended to include the young man because, taken together, his social assets and connections and, Wirt implied, his political prospects, offset his shriveled finances and humble schoolmastering trade. As a result, Chase began to define himself and his aspirations less by the austerity of his New England boyhood and Ohio adolescence than by his present situation and prospects for the future.

But as Andrew Jackson's star waxed in the latter 1820s, Wirt's status waned. Despite his lofty title and intimacy with the mighty, Attorney General Wirt was on the way out. By opposing Jackson's election to the presidency in 1828, Wirt had to relinquish the attorney generalship and face figurative exile as a disfavored political manipulator.

Well before then, however, this virtual foster father to the long-fatherless Chase had become his adviser about career choices and his mentor in the law, the profession Chase chose to pursue. Wirt illuminated for the long-confused younger man the desirable aspects of the law as a professional alternative to the ministry or pedagogy. Justifiably confident that Chase understood how politics worked, Wirt then advocated what he would later counsel Chase to avoid: a career like Wirt's own combining politics and law. As represented by Wirt's way of life rather than by the advice he offered Chase, a mix of legal practice with political activism could be intellectually engaging, economically enriching, and socially contributive. Therefore Chase decided to become a lawyer, one like Wirt, he hoped. He sold his interest in the school and apprenticed himself to Wirt, a situation that though intrinsically unlike Elizabeth Turner's forty years later, perhaps predisposed Chase to interest himself in her plight.

As the 1820s advanced Chase studied law under Wirt's tutelage. An often-repeated judgment is that the dilletantish Wirt was an exceedingly undemanding preceptor, and that instead of applying himself diligently to learning the law, Chase continued primarily to circulate in the high society that Wirt's sponsorship had opened for him. An extension of this view is that Chase performed very poorly on the examination that the local bar required before licensing a new attorney to practice. Two factors allegedly altered the examiner's initial decision to fail Chase. One was the latter's tie to the much-admired Wirt. The other was that Chase told the examiner that he had decided to practice law in Cincinnati, not Washington, since Wirt's political clout was ebbing. The examiner, according to a scholarly consensus, concluded that a professionally deficient lawyer was adequate for the inhabitants of the Ohio wilderness and licensed Chase.

It is improbable that Wirt, who consistently inveighed against inadequately prepared attorneys, would have allowed his favorite, Chase, to exit unprepared from his apprenticeship. To be sure, Wirt kept Chase grinding away at humble legal chores throughout their five-year association. His scrawly handwriting notwithstanding, Chase, like the vast majority of law apprentices and clerks, copied an unceasing flow of legal documents, delivered necessary papers to clients and court clerks, and saw to the cleanliness and order of Wirt's office. Many lawyers taught their minions little or nothing, merely profiting from the juniors' labors and pocketing the fees. Apparently Wirt did teach Chase, yet he accepted no money from him. Instead, serving as Wirt's only apprentice, Chase enjoyed special advantages over most of his peers. In addition to Wirt's direct tutelage, Chase, without competition from other apprentices, as time permitted could and did exploit his mentor's unusually well-equipped library. It boasted a full range of the profession's acknowledged basic texts, a category that was then widening. Prominent Illinois attorney Isaac Arnold, in *Recollections of the Early Chicago and Illinois Bar,* quoted famed U.S. Supreme Court Justice Joseph Story's comment of 1821 that a "perfect avalanche" of legal treatises, case reports, and law periodicals was issuing from presses, requiring large sums for a lawyer to house "in a single [law] library." David Hoffman's *Course of Legal Study* had been available since 1817. Court reporters Alexander Dallas and William Cranch were making U.S. Supreme Court decisions and opinions since 1789 regularly and reliably available. Would-be lawyers across America, including young Lincoln in Illinois and Chase in Washington, still unknown to each other, were poring over St. George Tucker's 1803 edition of William Blackstone's *Commentaries on the Laws of England,* John Goodenow's 1819 *Historical Sketches of the Principles and Maxims of American Jurisprudence,* Thomas Sergeant's 1822 *Constitutional Law,* James Angell's 1824 *Watercourses,* and Joseph Chitty's 1826 *Practical Treatise on the Law of Contracts.* By 1830 New York chancellor James Kent's four-volume *Commentaries on American Law* would also be in print, soon followed by Story's parallel treatises. Wirt had them all, and more.

Lincoln had to search for copies to borrow and read. Chase had them at hand, plus an unusually complete rank of other professional publications, especially those by writers who were advocates of making the law more "scientific," or at least more systematic. These advocates included

Richard Rush, St. George Tucker, and Wirt himself, whose publication of his official opinions as attorney general typified this approach to law reform. Combined with his studious habits Chase's privileged access to Wirt's unusually rich and up-to-date law library helped to shape his interests and career. Chase found particularly engaging James Kent's and Joseph Story's preachments in their treatises and case opinions about a dynamic branch of American legal practice known as equity, a branch that Wirt stressed in his mentoring.

Equity supplemented but did not displace the more formal rules of civil procedure and standards of proof governing contracts and other civil legal relationships between individuals and authorities. Contract law was itself in swift evolution as production, transportation, and finance technologies developed dramatically across the growing nation. Despite these changes, however, contract law tended to focus intently on formal agreements' stated terms. By commanding strict performance of contract commitments, certain judges and legal writers helped to stabilize market relationships, they argued. And most contracts were held to strict or specific performance.

By contrast, attorneys claiming equitable remedies usually wanted their clients to be freed from meeting contract obligations, the opposite of specific performance. More rarely, an equity plea was for a judge to issue an injunction ordering third parties to stop or to start certain behavior before future injuries to purse or person resulted. An attorney pleading in equity thus had to convince a judge to widen the law's sensitivities from the documentable past to the present and even to an imagined future.

Aiming to touch the conscience of the judge, a lawyer might claim in equity, for example, that misrepresentation or duress in the negotiations preceding the commitment to a contract prevented a client from comprehending fully the obligations he was shouldering. Alternatively, equity arguments might be that natural disasters, wars, or innocent errors thwarted honest attempts at fulfillment. Equity pleaders prophesied increasingly that clients would suffer undeserved detriments to themselves and that society at large might be injured should contracts complained of be enforced. In one situation judges approved for reasons of equity a state charter for a new bridge company to build a structure paralleling and, therefore, making obsolete, an earlier toll bridge whose builders had been promised a monopoly by a public charter or contract. The growing republic required the creative voiding of property rights in the original contract.

Equity seized the imagination of young lawyers like Chase and Lincoln who before long in their careers would take up some form of the antislavery cause. Generally, all attorneys, including these two, venerated the rights to state-defined private property as the source from which all other rights flowed. Although like all lawyers they assumed that virtually all private contracts and public charters required specific performance, they came to except contracts involving slaves, at least those who reached free states. Keeping in mind Lincoln's statement of 1862 about his promise to God concerning emancipation of slaves and Chase's theologically weighted upbringing, it is not surprising that these two otherwise disparate young attorneys worried about immoral and wholly evil contracts that, though lawful, injured persons and society.

Though eager especially in their early years as practicing lawyers to serve any client who opened their doors, both these beginning attorneys made ethical exceptions based on their discrete senses of religious convictions. Both men granted that by action or inaction a state could sanction a private property and, through courts and other institutions of law, provide ways for individuals to protect their property rights. But both men also worried that majorities of voters were too susceptible to passions that resulted in immoral and evil properties—a category that for Chase soon included slavery and liquor—enjoying protection by the public laws of relevant states and, for slave owners, also by their states' congressional delegations. Even before Chase left Washington for Ohio, his respect for the state bases of federalism and for state-defined private property rights mixed uncertainly with his ardent Christianity. The latter humbled all men (including Chase, presumably) before God and necessarily required consideration of the derivative divinity possessed even by black slaves. These elements of Chase's upbringing, education, and professional training stirred further his growing concerns about election verdicts by popular majorities.

By definition, few prophets are held to hard evidence. Imaginative attorneys seized opportunities that equity offered to exploit judges' sensitivity to ethical and moral elements in clients' special circumstances that might justify modifying or even voiding contracts or prohibiting imminent actions while avoiding destabilizing the larger society. Because ethics and morality were central concerns of this literate and pious young apprentice lawyer, for four decades Chase would resort to equity pleadings when defending runaway slaves and their benefactors and, as judge, when deciding *In re Turner* in 1867. And his concerns about the need for law to constrain state power when the latter became runaway by reason of majority votes, so central in his *Texas v. White* position, had roots in Wirt's sadness at his own decline in political significance as the Age of Jackson dawned.

As Chase feared, the Jacksonian era heralded the end of Wirt's long tenure as attorney general. Once inaugurated president, Jackson replaced Wirt with one of his spoils system supporters, and Wirt returned to private practice in Baltimore. With his mentor's departure Chase lost the many reassurances about his own future employment that he had been enjoying from their treasured daily contacts and from Wirt's political connections.

Leaving Washington, Wirt designated Chase as caretaker of the Washington residence of which both men were deeply fond, an unfortunate assignment for this moody, twenty-one-year-old youth. Chase contrasted the mansion's melancholy silences with the lively daily banter, streams of distinguished and influential visitors, and frequent gracious entertainments that the house had harbored recently. Like Wirt's deteriorated residence, the decline of his influence and of Chase's own prospects, plus much else that seemed to be wrong in America, was Jackson's fault and that of the increasingly southern-dominated Democratic party that had touted the war hero, Chase concluded.

Causes even worse than Old Hickory underlay the nation's malaise, in Chase's unhappy estimation. Wrong-thinking majorities, especially those in the East Coast's raucous cities and in the trans-Appalachian western states, had voted the unlettered Jackson and all that he represented into the White House and his minions into control of the national government and of many states. Errors of this magnitude perverted elections into essentially baleful, near-lawless mockeries of a mythic nobler time. Therefore, as Chase viewed events, the majorities' policies needed to be questioned and tested by the higher authorities provided by law and morality.

In addition to sorrow at his mentor's reverses, Chase's fears for his own future prompted such dour misapprehensions. If a giant like Wirt fell prey to multitudes of minnows, what chance did Chase have? None, in light of the unfortunate changes that in his view were wrenching American political life in potentially tragic directions. These tendencies must be substantially reversed, Chase asserted, so that worthy individuals could garner appropriate rewards independent of the party affiliations of essentially lawless majorities. His fear that law and order were up for grabs resurfaced frequently and intensely throughout his lifetime.

By 1830 when Chase left Washington, his self-serving repugnance at what he discerned as democracy's excesses had become part of his enduring indifference and, often, hostility to consistent party loyalty. He soon found the cure for the first and the substitute for the second in his religion's preachments about original virtue, the sinful fall from grace, and the promise of redemptive leadership. A young lawyer just starting out in professional life and a new citizen of a still-malleable city and state, Chase offered himself as a moral leader in activist politics, a leader who, careless—no, contemptuous—of party regularity, would educate the credulous masses about the proper legal and moral bases of public policies that affected private property rights.

CHAPTER 2

Practice

The young French aristocrat Alexis de Tocqueville, touring America about the time Chase left Washington to begin practice, observed that attorneys were the popes of this society. Aimed more at his own countrymen than at Americans, his comment still might have been relevant in the 1820s and 1830s to the most elite lawyers in the nation, men like Wirt or Webster. Although many lawyers kept lifetime honorific titles of "squire" or "judge," most attorneys led fear-haunted professional lives and had an ambivalent social status quite unlike that enjoyed by their profession's stars.

Almost all attorneys practiced solo or in two-man partnerships that were usually temporary. Partnerships spread the risk of too few incoming clients. Attorneys commonly formed several different partnerships, often simultaneously, in as many rural county seats or cities, a technique soon facilitated by the quick spread of early toll roads, bridges, railroads, steamboats, and telegraph communications and by referrals among colleagues leading to split fees. Nevertheless, early private practice for most young attorneys mixed patience with fear and made all but mandatory a need to serve whatever clients first came through office doorways.

If only because of the inevitable, depressing intervals between clients, many younger lawyers, especially those already trained in oratorical aspects of litigating, drifted into politics. Such drifters learned quickly to find moneyed backers to subsidize the placards, parades, and lyceums that reflected the democratizing effects of early Jacksonian America on political styles. If elected to a local, state, or federal office, incumbents enjoyed a minimum subsistence while still practicing law, plus a kind of free advertising about their presumed influence with contemporary movers and shakers of the dynamic society and economy. And incumbents in many elective offices dispensed patronage. Every hamlet required a federal postmaster, every lighthouse a keeper, every tavern in some states a permit, and every would-be West Point cadet a nomination by his congressman.

Spirited expansions of agricultural, commercial, industrial, and economic infrastructures were under way. Swelling in population from both native born and the inpourings of immigrants, in unprecedented volume Americans were building roads, canals, bridges, factories, housing, aqueducts, mills, and, predominantly outside the slave-owning states, schools. Most of these ventures were privately financed. Others, including the important Erie Canal, Chicago wharves, Cincinnati warehouses, and New Orleans levees, mixed private and public funds, banking practices, and authorities in legally novel ways. However contrived in legal terms, these essential assets of an expanding society required attorneys to arrange contracts for land sales, condemnations, rights of way, purchases of materials, and, sometimes, workplace conditions and to defend against damage claims for injuries on the job or from the use of a client's product or service.

On the face of it, lawyers' centrality in these exciting yet often socially uncomfortable transactions should have quickly afforded them equivalent high status in their communities. For some it did. But as Wirt's long service, yet humiliating dismissal, reminded Chase, even elite attorneys were ultimately destined to remain subservient to the prosaic farmers, bankers, real estate developers, and mill operators among their clients unless financial independence was achieved quickly. Therefore, his elitist predispositions notwithstanding, for near-penniless beginners like Chase, politics combined with legal practice seemed to be the way to wealth, a way perhaps eased by a fortunate marriage. A lesson learned well during his years with Wirt, to young Chase making his way westward meant also a need to antagonize no one wherever he began to practice, to keep his office door open for any and all potential clients, and to generate a reputation for assiduity, competence, and connections.

Yet however clearly beginning lawyers like Chase and Lincoln understood and obeyed these precepts, neither man proved able wholly to divorce the moral imperatives derived from their upbringings, educations, and social attitudes from their professional lives. As Tocqueville observed, lawyers were indeed becoming the popes of American society because of their central roles in lubricating the economy and the political machineries. Some attorneys, however, would keep reminding society that in their view popes should search for better, more ethical human relationships and through both law and politics expose those links that were unethical or even vile.

Then and since, a well-advised beginning lawyer chose a community for his first flight into professional practice only after carefully considering alternatives. Baltimore, where Wirt lived, attracted Chase, as did a commerical center developing at aptly named Lockport, New York, along the still-new Erie Canal, where a younger brother practiced law. But Chase selected Cincinnati despite warnings that the city was already oversupplied with attorneys. Even so it was more familiar than forbidding to him. Ohio had been Chase's home during his formative adolescent years. Reports were proliferating in the East of the state's growing commercial vitality along both its northern Great Lakes flank and its southern front on the Ohio River, at Cincinnati. Already enamored of creature comforts from his years with Wirt, Chase was attracted to Ohio by the prospect of establishing in a substantial city a new practice that might not require him to endure years of penury.

Most new lawyers starting practices in large population centers found them to be already overinhabited by established attorneys who had monopolized the available legal trade. As a result, many novices suffered a seemingly inevitable kind of second apprenticeship when, to escape a market dominated by established practitioners, a substantial majority of beginners moved, as Chase did, from the cities where they were trained to rural hinterlands or even to frontier communities. The beginners' interstate mobility was facilitated by the prevailing ease of gaining permission to practice in their new communities. Where it existed, licensing to practice was a function of a county or city bar association rather than a uniform statewide requirement. New lawyers in a farming hamlet or frontier community had commonly to survive primitive living and office conditions possibly for a number of years. Then, if good luck escalated demands for local products with the resulting need for formal contracts, or if conflicts arose from inadequate early boundary surveys or from businessmens' disputes, striving young lawyers might redeem their early investments of patience. Chase set out for the West—Ohio—not because he was inadequately trained to practice in the East but because the problems new lawyers faced in the West contained the promise of quicker future rewards.

Already the largest city west of the Appalachians, Cincinnati's waterborne economy was booming and rail links soon further enhanced its trade. By reputation its lawyers were hustlers. But Chase decided in his already immodest manner that few attorneys there had his educational advantages.

He knew that the newish city lacked some urban amenities, but he hoped that its very crudities would encourage neighborliness among the business and social leaders of its unusually diverse and swiftly enlarging population (in 1830 roughly 25,000 people lived there. That total would grow to 45,000-plus by 1840 and ten years later to 115,000). A newcomer might find both a quick welcome and, even if more slowly, prosperity.

Slowly, indeed. Chase had hoped to earn ten dollars in his first three months in practice, forty in the next three, and eighty the next. But only two clients sought him out during the early weeks. One paid him four dollars for a legal service, the other a half-dollar for drawing up a simple deed, then, a week later, borrowed it back and never repaid it.

Patiently waiting for clients was endurable. Idleness was not. To pass the time Chase read religious tracts and reviewed Ohio law, of which no compilation existed. Irritated by but sensing opportunity in the lack, he began preparing one. Published in 1835, *Chase's Statutes,* as it was known, in three volumes covered all Ohio ordnances from 1778 through 1833. It brought Chase little revenue. But preparing it made him an expert in the laws of his adopted state, and favorable reviews by national legal luminaries, including Joseph Story and James Kent, inflated Chase's stature in the region's commercial and legal communities.

Added to Wirt's letters of introduction, Chase's enhanced professional reputation and family status opened doors for him to the homes and offices of the leaders of Cincinnati society, business, and law. In 1831 Tocqueville visited Cincinnati, collecting information for what would become his *Democracy in America,* still studied 150 years later. Among the people he interviewed, Chase, already a civic booster, spoke frankly about the reciprocations between the city's soaring commercial pace, his increasing law practice (by 1835 he employed junior partners, one of whom, Flamen Ball, would maintain the Chase & Ball office in Cincinnati until Chase's death forty years later), and his hectic social whirl.

The last brought Chase a bride. In 1834 he fell in love with, courted, and married local heiress Catherine Jane Garniss. The Reverend Lyman Beecher, president of Cincinnati's Lane Seminary and Harriet Beecher Stowe's father, officiated at the wedding. Soon after the birth of a daughter a year later a disease killed Chase's wife. He fell again into dour reflections on his own unworthiness. But he had his infant daughter to raise and so, as was common for widowers, especially those with small children, Chase soon wed again, another wealthy woman, Eliza Ann Smith. But she, like Chase's first wife, also died from disease, as did Sarah Laidlaw, his third spouse. In a graveyard tally heavily disfavoring women and children that was too common then, from 1834 to 1852 Chase buried not only three wives but also all the offspring of these unions except two daughters. One, Catherine Jane, later better known as "Kate," would play an intermittently significant and, some said, a notorious role in Washington politics and society. After burying his third wife Chase remained a widower, lonely and in harmony with the spirit of religious melancholy then prominent among American Protestants, perhaps desperate to fill his life with meanings congruent to his religion that controlled him, he believed, and with secular purposes that he hoped to control.

Earthly purposefulness was essential to Chase. He was unattracted by other-worldly appeals ranging from varieties of Transcendentalism, Roman Catholicism, and Mormonism that intrigued many of his contemporaries. Chase would exhibit both a lifelong fondness for the secular comforts to which his mentor Wirt had exposed him and an increasing Calvinist-like itch born of his religious upbringing to be his brother's keeper in matters of private morals and public law and policies. His need to monitor and to oppose what was unworthy might hinder his secular ambitions. But not if Chase could help it.

Such personal qualities suggest why from his first years in Cincinnati, Chase added law-related writings like *Chase's Statutes* to his legal practice and plunged ardently into civic, cultural, social, and political activities. Partly by accident as well as by design, his political work would subsume the rest.

By resettling in Cincinnati, Chase placed himself in an eye of the Jacksonian whirlwind that, sweeping across the expanding nation, reshaped its politics. Among other effects, the "revolution of 1828" was shattering the East Coast's domination of national politics. By 1830 nine new states were added to the original thirteen; by 1850 seven more. Only two, Maine and Vermont, were eastern. Most states further democratized suffrage. Feeding fears about King Mob rule, constitutions in states old and new increased the number of elected public officials, including judges. Thereby, many lawyers fretted, voters politicized both the offices and the legal processes that protected private property from inequitable diminutions by private persons and from arbitrary seizures by public authorities.

Profoundly altering party and power relationships in Congress, the states, and most localities, the newly fluid politics destroyed Federalist remnants. Uncertainties ensued about party purposes. Successor Whig organizations struggled to survive. They competed for supporters with both exuberant Democratic party rivals and with ultimately temporary special-interest political groups, especially the Anti-Masons, the antiliquor temperance groups, and later, the anti–Irish Catholic Know-Nothings. Jackson Democrats representing primarily coalitions of western and southern farm interests and eastern urban workers seemed, however, to be invincible. They initiated local, then statewide, political party organizations that kept operating between elections as well as during campaigns and then met in national nominating conventions to replace the elite caucuses such as Wirt's in Washington. Shadowing every level of the federal system, Democrats' city, county, state, and national party echelons' year-round operations made politics a full-time trade. Party loyalty became its central theme. Raising funds, selecting candidates, devising platforms, and conducting election campaigns, politicians used patronage to reward supporters and to punish defectors for behavior spotlighted by open voting.

During Wirt's turn-of-the-century heyday, most attorneys mixed lawyering with politics. But by the time Chase hung out his shingle many were being displaced, as Wirt had been, by a new breed of full-time politicos. Nevertheless, many aspiring younger venturers into politics such as Chase and Lincoln felt it necessary to retain their legal practices, if only as safety nets should fate at the hands of the fickle public oust them from whatever places of influence or profit they had gained. Losers like Wirt rationalized their oustings by grousing that the befouled political arena no longer deserved their participation except as voters, and, often, as voters for or candidates of one or another evanescent, often special-interest third party. In 1832 Wirt, for example, became the Anti-Masonic party's presidential candidate. He died two years later.

Matching Wirt's advice to Chase, a growing consensus among the pace-setting authors of the legal treatises, commentaries, and articles Chase read held that lawyers should avoid politics' sullying effects. The legal profession's heavyweights forcefully and repetitively advised colleagues, especially beginners, to be full-time practitioners. They reasoned that an attorney must defend clients' interests by the best legal techniques even if he and the clients disagreed. Candidates for political offices, however, must surrender legal professional principles to party regulars' mercenary needs and to mass voters' transitory moods.

Logically, Chase's increasing family demands and his social views should have encouraged him to heed such advice from Wirt and from local lawyers, politicians, and relatives. But those concerns did not affect his oscillating political allegiance as a voter. Reacting to the contemporary fluidity in party politics, Chase, in his early years in Cincinnati, described himself as an independent Democrat. Yet except for supporting Wirt in the latter's hopeless 1832 presidential race, Chase voted like a Whig. For example, he supported his friend William Henry Harrison in 1836 as a better presidential candidate than Jackson's Democratic heir, Martin Van Buren.

Yet Chase was advised to refrain from activist involvements in politics beyond voting. Wirt emphasized Chase's particular need to insulate himself from interests unrelated to his professional advancement because he was a new attorney only recently settled in Cincinnati, a riverport city that was the overland gateway to the fluid new West and the riverborne bridge to the Deep South.

Cincinnati was already notorious for its hard-drinking, sometimes riotous industrial and port workmen, many of whom had immigrated recently from the Germanies. Prosperous from slaking stevedores' thirsts, local brewers wielded important political clout. Chase should court them, he was advised, because their substantial legal needs could ease his fledgling years in practice. Instead, already a contrarian about some matters, Chase, soon after arriving in Cincinnati, volunteered to teach in a local Episcopal Sunday school, quickly becoming its superintendent. He volunteered also to offer a lyceum lecture. In it he advocated temperance as a step toward forcing Ohio, through politics, totally to prohibit alcoholic beverages as a necessary and proper policy, even though limitation, much less prohibition, diminished the property rights of brewers and saloon owners and their customers' long-accepted social behavior. The moral end justified the drastic means, Chase asserted.

Temperance sentiment was gaining strength then, especially among spokesmen for salvational religions. Chase's piety never diminished. If risky for a beginning attorney, neither a Sunday school superintendency nor a lyceum lecture was a call to revolutionary political barricades. Perhaps his decision to teach piety and to tout temperance reflected both his loneliness and his shrewd perception of an opportunity to advertise himself to the local respectables—few brewers or saloon owners yet rated the label—

whose children were his Sabbath pupils and who themselves patronized the lyceum's educational offerings.

Whatever his reasons for entering the temperance arena, Chase chose to emphasize a secular facet of the antiliquor theme that would later reappear significantly in his criticisms of the slave trade and slavery. His early theme was that drink destroyed the inebriates' work ethic and fueled the increasingly bawdy lawlessness, private licentiousness, and public disorder that, he asserted, were visibly eroding the moral and legal bases of orderly Cincinnati society. Chase may have intended his expressed concern about religion and public order as a thinly veiled criticism of local Jacksonians. But the enthusiastic reaction of the lyceum audience indicated that he had hit the target.

For lawlessness was a hot topic in Cincinnati, one encouraging political exploitation. Overall, Chase benefited professionally by doing just that. In the early 1830s issues including temperance, state chartering of public taverns and private banks, a state-run lottery, and deteriorating race relationships tempted political activists and leading businessmen, clerics, and attorneys. They insisted that liquor, unstable banks, and gambling adversely affected workers' productivity, private morality, family stability, and marketplace prosperity and that voters' wrong decisions in such matters fed public disorder. The warnings impressed Chase. But initially he decided that except for temperance these other subjects were too controversial for prudent handling, and he skirted opportunities to commit himself on them.

His straddling on such sore regional topics except temperance were practical for a young and ambitious lawyer who was anxious to avoid offending anyone important. Thus his swift plunge into the most dangerous public policy whirlpool—the one involving the public law of slavery and race relationships—is even more remarkable. No issue a freshman lawyer faced in that place and time offered larger hazards.

During the latter 1820s on at least three major occasions white mobs had assaulted hapless residents of Little Africa, the Cincinnati slum where city ordinances laced with racial prejudice forced blacks to live. In 1829, a year before Chase reached the city, a peculiarly savage, unprovoked, and unpunished mass attack by white rioters on residents of the black ghetto inspired hundreds of despairing black Cincinnatians permanently to emigrate to Canada. Ill feeling continued to fester between blacks remaining in the city and many passionately racist whites. Fears grew among the Cincinnatians Chase courted that more lawless, race-centered violence impended, to the detriment of commerce, legal procedures, religion, and public order, which were essential to morality, as Chase and many others had come to define that elastic term.

Like many white contemporaries, Chase worried less about blacks' recent injustices and sufferings than about whites' impending hurts from renewed lawlessness. On the one hand, Chase's compilation of Ohio's statutes praised the slavery exclusion clauses of the 1787 Northwest Ordinance. On the other, Chase, without deploring the fact, acknowledged also that the state's laws and community customs denied black Ohioans the ballot, jury service, and public education. Chase's work on Ohio's statutes taught him additionally that in 1804 Ohio's legislators had enacted "black laws" to discourage fugitive slaves from increasing the state's black population. Among other topics, the laws included requirements that new black arrivals in an Ohio county warrant their free status and post a burdensome bond before settling in. The bond's alleged purpose was to guarantee blacks against destitution; its real purpose was to protect white taxpayers against providing for destitute blacks. As *Chase's Statutes* implied, however, this qualified freedom was better than the hopeless slavery most black Kentuckians endured—a proposition affirmed by Kentucky slaves who preferred white Ohio's conditional liberty.

Ohio was especially surly as the 1830s began because neither its black laws nor Cincinnati's bigots deterred Kentucky blacks from voting with their feet, fleeing to Ohio and other free states, commonly at awful personal risk. This influx raised among unhappy Ohio whites the question of further steps. Chase's answer was one common among whites during the first half of the nineteenth century; colonize blacks somewhere abroad. A perennially resurfacing reaction to race problems, colonization appealed, for example, to President James Monroe in the early 1820s and to President Abraham Lincoln from the early 1860s to early 1865. Indeed, at one time or another virtually every important white critic of slavery was also procolonization. And in the early 1830s this theme enlisted Chase's support for the work of the Ohio Colonization Society.

This reaction was considered eminently appropriate civic activism by almost all whites' standards. But Cincinnati's boundaries for acceptable civic voluntarism were hardening, and whites' racial prejudices were ossifying. The city's 1829 race rioting had revived painful memories of the heated nationwide debates resulting in the 1820 Compromise and of the 1822 and 1831 revolts, led by South Carolina slave Denmark Vesey and Virginia slave

Nat Turner. Yet perhaps to emulate Wirt, but also almost as if he aimed perversely to attract unfavorable local notice, in 1831 Chase, in another lyceum lecture, praised Great Britain's antislavery leader Henry Brougham. Then in July 1831 Chase published his lecture on Brougham in the *North American Review,* America's most widely circulated and prestigious secular periodical.

Perhaps most offensive to Cincinnati lawyers with clients whose economic interests in Kentucky and elsewhere down the Ohio and Mississippi rivers to New Orleans were linked to slave-produced commodities, Chase's praise of Brougham underscored the moral ambiguities that slavery intruded into contract law. Brougham "went to the bottom of the merits of the case and denied utterly the fundamental principle of slavery, that man may be the subject of property," Chase stated admiringly. Slavery was an immoral property. It denied bondsmen the ties of marriage, sundered parents from children, exposed female slaves to sexual assault, countenanced bastardy, and demeaned religion. Chase quoted Brougham: "There is a law above all the enactments of human [law] codes; . . . it is the law written by the finger of God upon the heart of man; and by that law . . . , while men despise fraud, and loath rapine, and abhor blood, they shall reject, with indignation, the wild and guilty fantasy that man can hold property in man!"

Chase's position seemed to ally him firmly and publicly with the unquiet students of Cincinnati's Lane Seminary, an institution as young in the city as Chase himself. It was presided over by Lyman Beecher, a Presbyterian minister who, like Chase's Episcopal bishop uncle, combined teaching and pastoral duties. After her marriage to Lane faculty member Calvin Stowe, Beecher's daughter Harriet would electrify America with her writings about slavery. Long before her popularity, a man Chase's contemporary in age, Lane theology student Theodore Dwight Weld, afire from the evangelical revival then sweeping the country, transformed the seminary into a temperance and antislavery center. By combining their shared convictions about the duties evangelical Protestants owed to society to achieve temperance, Weld encouraged Chase's second absorbing concern, to erode slavery.

In the critical year 1833, South Carolina defiantly nullified a federal tariff law because it threatened the profitability and therefore the stability of slavery. Almost simultaneously Weld organized a Lane chapter of the new American Antislavery Society. Written by young firebrand William Lloyd Garrison, the abolition association's Declaration of Sentiments paired the

Declaration of Independence and divine revelations as adverse to slavery. This dualism, one that Chase would soon adopt as a lodestar of fundamental law, suited the zealous millennialism of the time. But in the early to mid-1830s, he continued openly to support colonization and was still to be convinced that slavery was both a legal and constitutional wrong and a sin. Thereby, in a division typical of the antislavery advocates' seemingly incurable tendency for schisms, then and for decades to follow Chase felt able to deny that he was an abolitionist and insisted instead that he opposed only the further territorial enlargement of slavery, thus marking himself off from Garrison's and Weld's more militant and encompassing immediatism.

By spring 1834, town-gown tensions in Cincinnati were severe. Defying President Beecher's advice that they soft-pedal criticisms of Ohio's racist folkways and of slavery everywhere, Lane students held classes for local blacks. Weld enlisted Kentuckian James G. Birney as a champion of the causes the students advocated. An able attorney, Birney was a wealthy former slave owner converted by Weld first to advocacy of colonization for his slaves, whom he set free, and then, inspired by a mystical religious experience, to total and immediate abolitionism. Birney's and Chase's lives soon intersected.

In late 1834 Weld led the Lane students in a prayerful revolt against President Beecher, who had ordered an end to campus antislavery activities and a softening of public criticisms of slavery. Weld's refusal initiated his dismissal, which triggered a large secession of other Lane students. Chase provided them with the free use of a large vacant house owned by a relative. These events persuaded Birney to publish an antislavery newspaper in Cincinnati, the *Philanthropist.* Begun in 1836, it attended closely to the events at Lane and to abolitionist developments everywhere. On a mid-July midnight a mob, including several high city officials, looted the *Philanthropist*'s office and destroyed its presses, then rampaged through the black ghetto, beating hapless blacks they encountered.

This awful, visible breakdown of law, this contempt for persons and property, this corruption of public officials responsible for order, revolted Chase. But he did not share the reactions of more radical antislavery evangelists to these events. Some found religious doctrines favoring secular anarchy a necessary prelude to the imminent kingdom of God on earth. Others favored early socialist doctrines that were infiltrating America through European immigrants. These solutions required the curtailment or even the termination of private property, seen as the source of all sins, including slavery. But Chase tempered his disgust with his unswerving respect for all state-sanctioned private property except slaves, liquor, and gambling. He had found satisfyingly moral justifications for his own continued participation in politics. Could he also continue as a wealth-seeking private lawyer?

CHAPTER 3

Politician and Attorney General
for Runaway Slaves

In her survey of important men of those times, Harriet Beecher Stowe wrote of almost all Cincinnati attorneys and most of their deepest-pocket clients, that their "whole secret instinct . . . was to wish that slavery might in some way be defended because Cincinnati stood so connected with it in the way of trade, that conscientious scruples on this point were infinitely and intolerably disagreeable." But, she added, exceptions existed.* Stowe placed Chase at the head of the thin company of lawyers who dared publicly to criticize slavery.

Nevertheless, in the 1840s and 1850s the even smaller cadre of radical abolitionists who were attorneys excoriated Chase and others like him who daringly professed distaste for slavery yet denied that they advocated somehow abolishing that economically, politically, and constitutionally impregnable state-defined private property. It required the Civil War to shift Chase and adequate numbers of other Americans to sustain a change from antislavery to abolitionism. But that wartime swerve—and only the war's imperatives—would realign constitutionalism and law so that *In re Turner* and *Texas v. White*, concerning the rights of individuals and the nature of American states, could occur. Until the events of the Civil War prompted Chase into advocacy of total abolitionism, he stubbornly retained an increasingly public role as a critic of slavery in only two of its manifestations.

Slavery was first revealed to him by the exposure of its evils inside slave states. These accounts were written primarily by white ministers, journalists, and other travelers through the South. As an Ohio attorney, however, he could not touch the institution in terms of law in any slave state. Slave owners' property rights were impregnable from outside their own states. The U.S. Constitution specifically protected slave owners' state-defined

*Harriet Beecher Stowe, *Men of Our Times* (New York: J. D. Denison, 1868), 253.

property rights in ways not enjoyed by owners of any other form of private property, a fact giving rise to a popular label for slavery as the "peculiar institution." The Constitution and enforcement laws provided that without trial or other due process runaways be returned to owners from any free jurisdiction that fugitives reached.

As Chase and others frequently but futilely pointed out, a skewed federalism had resulted from the need of the Constitution's Framers in 1787 to pay the price for union demanded by the slave states. The result of the "great compromise" of 1787—misnamed as Chase saw matters—was that southern states' laws on human bondage had a bridge on which to cross into free states via the federal Constitution. But free states' laws forbidding slavery could not use that same bridge to enforce antislavery laws in slave states.

This perception motivated Chase to ask questions to which he would give answers under the vastly changed circumstances surrounding *In re Turner* and *Texas v. White*. Was this a Union of equal states possessed of equal rights or one in which the slave states were privileged? What *was* a state, only a geographical entity or a political construction? Or was a state all of its residents? If the last, were a state's people subject only to that state's policies and customs, or, as inhabitants of both their state and nation, did every dweller in every state necessarily enjoy all protections for their persons and property, including property deriving from the fruits of their labor, of the dual governments constituting this federal system? A bar to antislavery activists, federalism and the Constitution were open roads for slave owners, Chase came to realize.

Black runaways from slavery, especially from Kentucky just across the Ohio River from Cincinnati, provided the second source of Chase's knowledge about slavery, federalism, constitutionalism, property, and public morality. Always an apt pupil, Chase learned quickly and exploited this knowledge both in law and politics. Carving the second route, one far more graphic, direct, and intimate than the first, slaves who assumed the terrible risks of running away from their owners and who managed to reach southern Ohio were to find in lawyer-politician Chase an ardent champion, although rarely a successful one in the resulting lawsuits. For Chase, however, his pro bono defenses of runaway slaves and of Ohioans, white and black, who aided the fugitives, taught the lawyer how deficient America's constitutional arrangements were in provisions relevant to the protection of individuals' rights against states' wrongs—the future central issues of both *In re Turner* and *Texas v. White.*

Ohio's politics as well as courtrooms offered Chase alternative forums from which he criticized slavery in the states where, until the Civil War, criticisms from a free state might gall slave owners but rarely actually touch their property rights. For twenty years before the Civil War Chase fed both his ambitions for esteem and his desire to gild his profession with his own sense of ethics and religion by criticizing slavery from successive Ohio and federal offices to which he won appointment and elections: U.S. senator, 1849–1855; governor, 1855–1859; and again U.S. senator, 1859–1861.

But in the 1830s and for a quarter-century to come Chase felt that it was essential for his professional reverence for private property and for his own spiritual comfort to maintain the increasingly artificial distinction between antislavery and abolitionism. Even the unpunished attack on Birney's newspaper by a Cincinnati mob estimated to number 5,000 whites did not shift Chase from his centrist position into a commitment to seek through law and politics the destruction of slavery in every state.

Successive eruptions of unpunished lawlessness continued in Cincinnati and elsewhere. These brutal excesses deeply troubled the introspective and often still-melancholic man and also affected him personally. Antiabolition Cincinnatians identified Chase's sister Abigail and her husband Isaac Colby as Birney supporters. Fearing that the same vigilantes who had attacked the *Philanthropist* would assault them next, his relatives essentially became frightened refugees from their own neighbors, taking shelter in Chase's residence.

His law practice only recently flourishing, Chase yearned still for the community to turn to decorously genteel ways. Many local merchants and bankers looked sourly on lawyers who destabilized commerce with slave owners. Nevertheless, Chase organized a meeting of business and professional leaders to protest local lawlessness and publicly condemned the mobs' actions against Birney and other critics of slavery as insupportable violations of the First Amendment. Probably neither he nor his audience grasped the manifold implications for an altered federalism in Chase's early link between the First Amendment and the imminent failure of law and order in his state and city because of unpunished vigilantism on behalf of slave owners. Later, as in the *Turner* and *Texas* cases, he would transform the negatives of the Bill of Rights into a positive duty for the nation to protect individuals against unjustified actions or failures to act by national, state, or local officials.

As if to mock Chase's moderate purposes of the 1830s, proslavery activists disrupted the meeting he had called, then besieged Birney's hotel hideout. Rushing there, at considerable personal risk Chase interposed himself in the hotel doorway. Finally out-shouting the crowd's leaders, he helped to convince its members to disperse. Slavery-connected external events would not disperse, however, for Chase or the nation. Adding to the effects of these events, his inner imperatives, transcending his lawyerly devotion to all private property, kept driving Chase toward an initially partial yet ultimately significant juncture with abolitionism.

Among midwestern antislavery activists, Birney continued to play pivotal roles, including running as the presidential candidate of the new, antislavery, minority Liberty party in 1840 and 1844. Meanwhile, Birney involved Chase in other roles that further educated both men about ways to criticize slavery through legal procedures, and, less successfully, to inhibit the returns of fugitive slaves to masters, ways needed because hopes were dim that voter majorities would ever agree to change the law.

Represented by Chase, Birney sued in a state court for damages done to his press and shop by the easily identifiable violent intruders and won. Victory was simple over persons committing assaults, breaking and entering, and similar traditional offenses in state law. But successes over slave owners were far less easily achieved or as often recorded.

In 1836, Matilda, a slave (and daughter) of a Marylander who was moving from Maryland to Missouri, escaped from their riverboat moored to a Cincinnati wharf. Hidden by an Ohio underground local that abetted runaway slaves, she became Birney's housemaid. Then Matilda's master-father hired a private detective who specialized in recapturing runaways; he discovered and seized her. At Birney's request Chase tried to win her freedom and simultaneously propagated antislavery doctrines.

He petitioned the presiding judge of the state's court of common pleas, a low-level tribunal of original jurisdiction, to issue a habeas corpus writ requiring her return to Ohio jurisdiction. In support of the petition, Chase's multilayered brief covered broad constitutional and legal horizons that he, ahead of almost all other antislavery attorneys, was already able and willing to explore, touching on every level of authority in the federal system that affected her status.

Matilda was no fugitive from slavery, Chase contended. No other offense than seeking liberty was alleged against her. Slavery could exist only by the positive law of a state and locality. Otherwise freedom—"freedom national"—prevailed. Therefore liberty was Matilda's by natural law, and, a peaceable person, she was subject to no police authority by any level of government. Certainly, he insisted, no Ohio magistrate had a duty under the federal Constitution to enforce the nation's fugitive slave law against an inoffensive sojourner in that free state (a position soon to echo in the U.S. Supreme Court in *Prigg v. Pennsylvania*). Instead, because freedom, not slavery, was the natural condition for Americans, according to Chase, Matilda's recapture violated the prohibitions against unreasonable searches and seizures in the Constitution's Fourth Amendment and the Fifth Amendment's requirement that defendants enjoy due process. In again raising the Bill of Rights against other provisions of the Constitution, Chase was once more a pioneer.

Chase granted that Matilda was brought involuntarily to Ohio. But, he argued, the man claiming to own her had come there as a voluntary sojourner. Ohio was a state as sovereign as Maryland. States' rights did not allow one state's wrongs to intrude into another state. Matilda's master was a master only in Maryland. He knew that slavery was forbidden in Ohio by the "self-evident... axiom that all men [and women] are born 'equally free,'" a maxim enshrined in the Declaration of Independence, the Northwest Ordinance, and the state's constitution and laws, a maxim meaning that slavery could not exist in Ohio. Therefore, by touching the state's soil, Matilda was freed.

Ideas like these were coursing through America's legal communities. In Massachusetts, for example, the chief judge, Lemuel Shaw in 1836 (the same year as Matilda's case in Ohio) gave those ideas pungent expression in *Commonwealth v. Aves* and in other opinions. The basic point common to Chase and Shaw was that a slave became free who was brought voluntarily by a master into a free state. Shaw differed from Chase, however, when the legal question involved the return from a free to a slave state of a runaway slave. To Shaw that question was answered by the federal Constitution's clauses and implementing laws requiring the return of fugitive bondsmen. Chase wholly rejected that last point.

Instead, he took a position that free soil freed all people, including runaways who reached free jurisdictions. Destined to be repeated endlessly by him and by many antislavery advocates from the mid-1830s through the early 1860s, Chase's advanced freedom national views arched back to the 1772 decision in Great Britain in Somerset's case and applied to Matilda, as he insisted in 1836. His basic argument was that slavery could exist only by those laws of the slaveholding states and that slavery was unmentioned in the Constitution. It had become a cancerous aberration demanding cauterization by restricting it to the states where it then prevailed. Equity required this conclusion, Chase insisted. The nation had nothing to do with that particular private property.

Ohio's judge hearing Matilda's petition appreciated Chase's zeal in refining and presenting the argument but decided against Matilda, who remained a slave. But her brave flight had inspired Chase to craft a legalistically and politically comfortable way to reconcile otherwise clashing concerns about property, morality, and federalism.

Chances are that if events had not pressured him further, by the latter 1830s Chase would have slowed down or even stopped participating in antislavery efforts through lawsuits or otherwise. He lost some clients who disliked the kind of publicity he generated in defending Birney and Matilda or who felt themselves to be economically vulnerable to retaliation by their customers in slaveholding states. Additionally, a precipitous national economic downturn began in 1837. Soon several of Chase's investments failed. These matters and the awful mortality rate of his family most likely preoccupied him. In any event, in terms of his constitutional views Chase, though holding to the ideas concerning sojourning and fugitive slaves on free soil, was content then with his midroad freedom national position: owning slaves in the states where it existed by terms of the national compact was a legitimate and untouchable property right; the coin's opposite face was a presumption that freedom was the condition of all residents of free states. States' rights deserved equal respect, Chase asserted. Means and ends had joined—if matters remained stable.

William Wiecek and other scholars have noted that Matilda's case was one of several crossroads for persons of antislavery opinions. They differed sharply among themselves about means and ends, pace and purposes, timing and tactics. The most radically searching among them, like Garrison and Wendell Phillips, gave up the Constitution, they and other abolitionists damning it as a covenant with death and a league with hell. In so doing, radical abolitionists essentially accepted the most doctrinaire southern view, that the Constitution's Framers had indeed especially protected slavery. In giving up the Constitution, antislavery radicals were also abandoning politics to slavery's accommodationists, who formed a significant element of the Democratic party, and, worse in Chase's view, to slavery's most ardent, alert, and advantaged defenders, the southern phalanx among Democrats inspired by South Carolina's John C. Calhoun.

Chase never sought a retreat from antislavery lawyering or politics, a steadfastness he shared with Lincoln and others despite the discouragements over antislavery reform that succeeded one another in the ensuing decades. But to Chase, the despairing radicals like Garrison had a basic redeeming quality. They perceived even black slaves to be humans possessing a divine promise of salvation and the commitment to equality set down in the Declaration of Independence, much of the Constitution, and the Bill of Rights, that is, if only the Constitution worked properly.

Determined to see that it did not work, southern spokesmen and their northern Democratic party counterparts were refashioning the Constitution into an instrument that could work neither of itself nor by the political efforts of transient majorities adverse to slavery. Insisting with increasing success that only the formal text of the body of the Constitution, not the Declaration of Independence or the Preamble, governed questions of slavery and much else, Calhoun, for example, perfected a vision of the Constitution as a fixed machine of government that must permanently protect slave owners' property rights. This seemingly simple and politically attractive formula appealed to many segments of a nationwide voting population that was worried about disturbances to the economy, race relations, or other disequilibrating changes.

To his credit, Chase, along with other moderates (but a number far too few and scattered to determine the outcomes of elections or jury trials), retained faith in a view of the Constitution as a changeable, evolving instrument of popular will. Chase saw his role as that of a teacher. He and others of like views must stubbornly educate the public about this dynamic Constitution through political action, lawsuits, and moral suasion.

Chase's depiction of himself as the natural mentor to the masses was elitist by more recent standards. But it resonated also with faith that majorities, once educated about slavery's intrinsic inequities to blacks and innate hazards for whites, would do the right thing.

With Chase now mentoring him on these constitutional, legal, and ethical positions, Birney accepted the presidential candidacy of the new Liberty party in 1840 and 1844. Both men knew that his chances to win election were nil, but they used the campaigns to broadcast Chase's position that the federal Constitution nowhere validated slavery and that it was a flexible charter of individual freedom as well as of all states' rights, a charter that included the Declaration of Independence, the Preamble, and the Bill of Rights.

As vigorously as Calhoun, but for opposite purposes, Chase deified the Tenth Amendment as a bulwark of free states' rights and duties as well as of slave states' property laws. In the mid-1830s Chase was already edging toward a vision. If by these means slavery might be contained within its existing boundaries, its eventual diminution and even extirpation were imaginable, the latter, however, only in some remote future time. By this reasoning the troubling derivative issues of former slaves' constitutional status, legal rights, and social standing could be left to posterity for solution. No one in the 1830s could foresee how soon solutions would be needed or that Chase would provide relevant ones in his *In re Turner* and *Texas v. White* opinions.

In the 1830s Chase's prophetic vision quickly attracted persons of midroad antislavery views who found the more urgent exhortations of Garrison or Phillips politically implausible at best, and at worst, socially destabilizing. A more patient approach than theirs toward the attainment of nationwide freedom, Chase's alternative, though workable only if blacks continued in servitude for some undefinable period of time, merged antislavery's moral and constitutional goals into a politically feasible if slow-paced unity. It combined ideas about rights deriving from God with those emanating from the Declaration of Independence and the Constitution, including the Preamble and the Bill of Rights, the very trinity that Calhoun and other proslavery champions vehemently denied.

Chase polished these ideas, using Scripture and Jeffersonian emphases on every person's equality before God and political equality with other men, and applied them politically, eventually on every level of the federal system. In the U.S. Senate, for example, he later spelled out his antislavery republican political religion in evangelical terms, insisting that antislavery was "embodied in the self-evident truths of the Declaration of Independence . . . and in the Golden Rule of the Gospel—nothing more, nothing less."* Although consistent in his argument that antislavery efforts were essential to the task of redeeming America, for as long as he could Chase

* *Congressional Globe*, 33d Cong., 1st sess., App. 138.

clung to his relatively moderate, even conservative, constitutional stance expressed on behalf of Matilda: that both free and slave state could coexist in the federal union so long as neither transgressed on the other.

Matters did not stand still. Jubilant at the outcome in Matilda's case, local opponents of Birney now sued him for having sheltered her, an offense under Ohio's black code. Convicted, Birney had Chase appeal to the state's supreme court. In deciding *Birney v. State* (1838), the judges reversed Birney's conviction but only on a technicality rather than on the broader front that he and Chase had hoped for. The court ruled that Birney lacked prior knowledge of guilt in what he did (in law, *scienter*). Matilda's servile status—the very point Birney and Chase denied—and her illicit flight when Birney employed her, were unknown to him because under Ohio's laws skin color provided no presumption of a servile legal status. The last point was a thin half-loaf for runaway slaves who managed thereafter to reach Ohio.

Chase was disappointed that Ohio's judges chose not to consider his extended constitutional assertions in Matilda's case. Points he had raised in her defense about sojourners and other matters, especially about involuntary servitude that was so close to slavery as to make distinctions less than a difference, boosted him to a prominent position among antislavery legal strategists. Several free states enacted personal liberty laws. They strengthened antikidnapping penalties and requirements for habeas corpus and jury trials, thus improving procedural safeguards. Still, reverses exceeded gains.

In 1842, a half-century after the Constitution's adoption, when deciding *Prigg v. Pennsylvania* (41 U.S. 539 [1842]), the Supreme Court defined for the first time the meaning of the runaway recapture clause (Article 4, Section 2) and the legitimacy of the fugitive slave law implementing it. Both this clause and the statute were central to Chase's and Calhoun's opposite positions.

Prigg was a professional slave catcher, a breed whose livelihood depended on slavery's continuation. The widow of a Marylander hired Prigg to return to her the slaves whom the deceased master had let live for years in Pennsylvania, yet without freeing them formally by a written statement of manumission. Under Maryland law the blacks remained slaves. But in 1826 Pennsylvania, like other states, especially those bordering slave states, had enacted a personal liberty law. It aimed primarily to diminish kidnappings of black Pennsylvanians by requiring formal trials of alleged runaways, not to obstruct the operations of the federal fugitive rendition law. Instead of cooperating in a Pennsylvania trial for the accused runaways, Prigg hustled them back to Maryland and slavery, whereupon a Pennsylvania grand jury indicted him for kidnapping.

Complicated negotiations between the two states evoked an extraordinary procedure whereby the Pennsylvania Supreme Court convicted Prigg, sustained the validity of the state's personal liberty law, and hastened his appeal to the U.S. Supreme Court. It reversed Prigg's conviction, a heartbreaking blow to Chase, because an opposite decision by the Court by implication would have sustained Chase's freedom national view that free states' rights were as precious as those of the slave states.

The complex issues in *Prigg v. Pennsylvania* had so torn the justices that seven separate opinions emerged. Chase's disappointment over the dominant point of decision, that the 1793 fugitive slave law was constitutional, was intensified because Justice Joseph Story, whom he had revered, spoke for the majority in so deciding.

Story's judgment undercut Chase's freedom national stand, that free states need not class as slaves runaways who reached free jurisdictions. Further, Story reaffirmed Congress' sole authority to return fugitive slaves, a blow to pure states' rights theories that Calhoun's followers nevertheless applauded. The Court's decision invalidated state personal liberty laws and removed doubts about the lawfulness of the rugged techniques of slave catchers like Prigg, though those techniques lacked procedures called for in state antikidnapping laws and in the federal Constitution.

As Chase feared, slave owners, whether in person or through agents, could now even more confidently enter free states and redeliver supposed runaways to owner-claimants without the inhibitions of trials, witnesses, or documentary proofs. Antikidnapping statutes endured, but the *Prigg* decision weakened them. Henceforth state officers were unlikely to inhibit returns by interposing relevant state constitutions, bills of rights, personal liberty laws, or customary common law requirements for evidence. The only bright spot in the *Prigg* decision for Chase and other antislavery attorneys was Justice Story's observation, echoing implications in Chase's pleas for Matilda, that, though morally bound to do so, a state's officials need not enforce federal laws, another obeisance to the primacy of states in the federal system.

Prigg settled neither questions of law nor morality. In 1842, the year of the *Prigg* decision, Chase took on John Van Zandt's defense. Formerly a slave-owning Kentucky farmer, Van Zandt, Stowe's model for John Van Trompe in *Uncle Tom's Cabin,* had obeyed a religious imperative to free his slaves. He then moved to southern Ohio and made his new home a safe retreat for runaway slaves from across the river. But his home proved not to be safe. They and Van Zandt were vulnerable to the long reach that, especially as sanctified by the *Prigg* decision, the federal Constitution afforded slave owners. As on the Atlantic Coast, their offers of rewards for the return of runaways had nourished the growth of a minor slave-catching industry along the Ohio River borders between slave and free states.

When harboring runaways, Van Zandt and his hapless charges fell afoul of local, raffish, fee-earning slave catchers who, without the formal procedures called for by Ohio laws, returned the refugees from Ohio to Kentucky. Chase encouraged Ohio to initiate kidnapping charges against the agents, who, however, remained outside that state. But the outraged Kentucky slave owner, Wharton Jones, sued Van Zandt for damages under the 1793 federal fugitive slave law, claiming that he had abducted the reenslaved blacks.

Chase defended Van Zandt in his trial before U.S. Supreme Court Justice John McLean, on circuit in Cincinnati in mid-1842. In his extensive plea, Chase, in addition to repeating much of the substance of Matilda's defense, added technical legalities, especially those of equitable remedies, and wider issues of morality. The 1793 federal law did not specify sufficiently what constituted adequate notice that alleged runaways were slaves, he insisted. No citizen of Ohio should be considered a violator of law unless that person knew, by receipt of specific notice, that the particular individuals he was feeding and sheltering as acts of Christian charity were the named, identified runaways. But Justice McLean instructed the jury adversely to Chase's arguments, and the verdict awarded Jones $1,200, a huge sum to the aged and ill Van Zandt.

Renouncing fees, in December 1846 Chase, joined by New York's governor William H. Seward, another able lawyer, on Van Zandt's behalf appealed to the U.S. Supreme Court. Chase's lengthy brief in *Jones v. Van Zandt* (46 U.S. 215 [1846]) made four points. In the first he restated his lower court stand on the need for precise notice under the 1793 fugitive slave law. Second, Chase underscored that law's inconsistencies with the 1787 Northwest Ordinance. In the third he dealt with the imprecise meaning of harboring or concealing in the 1793 fugitive recapture statute. And in freedom national terms, in his fourth point he argued that the 1793 law was repugnant to the Constitution.

In phrases that quickly became ammunition in antislavery activists' armories, Chase insisted again that slavery existed only as a product of positive local law: "The government of the United States has nothing to do, directly with slavery." The Constitution dealt only with states and persons and clothed the latter "with those highest attributes of personality which belong, of right and equally, unless the Declaration of Independence be a fable to all men. It knows no slaves."

Antislavery commentators hailed Chase's effort. But he had to report to his dying client the justice's dismissal of his arguments and reaffirmation of the *Prigg* ruling that the 1793 federal recapture law was constitutional. The two men took what comfort they could from another of Chase's assertions made to the Court: that the fundamental issues before the justices were of a "moral and political nature, [and] the judgment even of this court cannot be regarded as altogether final."

Indeed not. It was not final for stubborn Chase, and through the tenacity of persons like him, not final for millions of slaves and their owners, or for the nation. Despite the *Prigg* and *Van Zandt* decisions, arguments like Chase's were echoed by other attorneys involved in sojourner and fugitive recapture lawsuits. Elizur Wright, for example, ignored the 1823 U.S. Circuit Court opinion in *Corfield v. Coryell*, by Justice Bushrod Washington, which gave an extremely narrow definition of an American's privileges and immunities that the federal Constitution's Article 4, Section 2 supposedly protected. And Chase continued to deride the 1833 Supreme Court decision in *Barron v. Baltimore,* that the federal Bill of Rights applied only to the nation, not to the states. Chase's core position remained that slavery was unknown to the Constitution and that all persons enjoyed the Fifth Amendment's prohibition against deprivation of life, liberty, and property without due process of law.

In sum, by 1850 lawyer Chase's pro bono efforts for the Ohio Antislavery Society, the publisher of the *Philanthropist,* Matilda, Van Zandt, and the founders of a black orphan asylum gave him heroic status in Ohio ghettos and nationwide eminence among antislavery activists, including those lawyers involved in the myriad associations of the diverse Protestant sects. Virtually no pressures existed on attorneys then to provide indigents with free services or at low rates. Already wealthy from the fees he had earned from his many commercial clients and from his shrewd investments, Chase did so, preparing deeds, arranging bail for and otherwise defending blacks accused of crimes, and, echoing his Matilda arguments, representing other runaway slaves and their abettors. While continuing to add to his commercial law practice, he used every legal maneuver he could contrive on behalf of fugitives from slavery and those people who aided the runaways. Still, few verdicts favored his clients.

If motivated only by self-interest, Chase would have served himself far better economically and politically by resolutely ignoring the moral imperatives that slave owners' champions were thrusting into political discourse, thereby themselves illuminating their favored standing under the federal Constitution. Exploiting their large advantages, slave owners' increasingly aggressive spokesmen kept thrusting.

Concerning proslavery spokesmen's political advantages, Chase had not anticipated adequately the parliamentary skills that southern congressmen such as Calhoun had developed during their long tenures resulting, often, from unopposed reelections. Southern delegates to Congress formed weighty, stable blocs with northern Democrats. By contrast, many free state congressmen had to accommodate diverse constituent interests, shorter incumbencies, and party vehicles destined for brief lives. Antislavery advocates among the nation's lawmakers tended toward schisms. Weak and unstable party organizations were a consequence of their party-jumping. Therefore, few antislavery congressmen accumulated the seniority and experience in parliamentary maneuvering or backdoor dickering exhibited by many southern legislators.

And with respect to the advantages in the law enjoyed by the defenders of slave owners' rights, with the relatively few exceptions among truly radical antislavery lawyers, a category from which Chase excluded himself, American attorneys considered all legitimate private property to be sacrosanct, especially in light of antiproperty class unrest that rocked Western Europe in 1830 and again in 1848. Here, however, not Fourier or Marx but Blackstone and like commentators guided lawyers. In American legal communities the Lockean axiom that property rights safeguarded all other rights was entrenched. Chase's contemporaries among American attorneys accepted Blackstone's insistence in his *Commentaries* that anyone, who "either by fraud or force," dispossessed a rightful owner of a property of his rights, "is guilty of a transgression against the law of society, which is a secondary law of nature."

Agreeing, Chase and other antislavery lawyers nevertheless objected that by classifying blacks as property, whites dehumanized and excluded them from the procedural and equitable protections of laws and constitutions, from participation in capitalism's competitions for property, and from Christianity's salvational, ethical, and moral emphases. Such objectors, however, were frustrated by the state bases of American federalism, at least as interpreted in the *Prigg* and *Van Zandt* rulings of the Supreme Court, a fact pressuring Chase and others of like concerns into politics.

In politics as in law slave-owners enjoyed impressive advantages over critics of their peculiar institution because each state defined through its political institutions what was and was not legitimate private property. When defending Matilda and Van Zandt, Chase acknowledged what few lawyers even with antislavery convictions then denied: slaves were rightful property in the states allowing racially defined hereditary servitude. Despite accepting this view, Chase denied that the federal Constitution's fugitive recapture clause and the implementing statute required either the nation or free states to enforce slave state laws. He thus rejected the idea that the 1787 Constitution was a one-way bridge across which slave state law could enter free states but free state law could not apply in slave states.

This idea was to become central in the views of other antislavery lawyers who, like Chase, were exploring political ways around the inexorable fact that in law each state defined property. By 1840 his practical political education was well advanced. Chase understood that politics, like law, paralleled American federalism's essentially state bases; as a later politico expressed it, here all politics are local. In the fluid context of the Whig party's declining fortunes, Chase exploited the resulting political instabilities by enlisting defecting Whig and Democratic voters into new antislavery third parties. By so doing, in the 1840s and 1850s Chase would help greatly to organize, successively, the Liberty, Free-Soil, and Republican organizations.

They had in common a political strategy that reflected Chase's basic premise. It was that without violating the bedrock state right to define private property, through politics and moral exhortations escalation of antislavery goals was possible from the states to the nation. Coalescing across party lines, free states' congressmen might win through federal policies the victories that lawsuits were not achieving, especially the containment of slavery to states where it then existed.

Energized by the publicized sufferings of Birney in Ohio, the murder of Illinois abolitionist Elijah Lovejoy, the decisions in the Matilda, Prigg, and Van Zandt cases, the violence and publicity attending slave "revolts," and some spectacular fugitive slave recaptures, antislavery activists including Chase dared to dream further. When, for example, proslavery congress-men contrived procedural gags against antislavery petitions, this limita-tion on debate inspired former president John Quincy Adams, then a con-gressman, relentlessly to argue the merits of unfettered speech. Chase was alert to the possibilities that the gag-rule arguments could portray pro-slavery aggressiveness as a threat to all free state residents. Many if not most whites, like Chase himself, were unsympathetic to advocates of racial equality except with respect to legal rights to person and property. But free state opinion was becoming increasingly receptive to Chase's arguments that slavery imperiled everyone's rights. Chase reacted shrewdly to opportunities presented by the gag-rule controversy, by the heated arguments about ending the noxiously visible slave trade in the District of Columbia, by the increasingly stringent enforcements of the federal fugi-tive slave law, and above all by slavery's further expansion into the nation's territories.

Defenders of southern interests were also alert. They objected to every antislavery tactic and goal. "Intermeddling" by free states with slave states' property laws was impermissible, Calhoun asserted (a point with which Chase concurred so long as it worked both ways). Continuing, Calhoun argued that the original federal constitutional compact between the states forbade watering down the fugitive slave recapture law or limiting slavery in the federal District or territories (points with which Chase wholly dis-agreed). In Calhoun's view, which was wildly popular in the South and in national Democratic party councils, efforts to set such limits "would be a direct and dangerous attack on the institutions of all the slaveholding states."

Even accident frustrated antislavery advocates. Two of Chase's personal friends, the Liberty party's Birney and the Whigs' William Henry Harrison, both Ohioans, had run for president in 1840. Birney never had a chance to win. Harrison won easily but died within weeks of his inauguration, the first death of a sitting president. President John Tyler, a Virginian and a Calhoun disciple, then accelerated the political whirligig by returning to Democratic party allegiance, thereby adding significantly to its clout. Despite Chase's and others' efforts, however, most Whigs remained disin-clined to echo his antislavery stand on fugitive slave recaptures, slavery in the federal District, or its further extension into federal territories.

And so in 1841 Chase formally embraced the infant Liberty party. He reiterated his conviction that the Declaration of Independence infused—

or should have infused—antislavery doctrines into the Constitution. Those doctrines, he repeated in a refinement of his arguments for Matilda offered at his party's 1844 national convention, required the total and unqualified divorce of the national government from slavery. A creature only of local (that is, state) law, slavery could not transcend its state borders in the form of individual runaways or by becoming entrenched in the national territories, those states-in-the-making, or in the Republic of Texas, that would-be instant state.

Chase always acknowledged that America was in fact a hybrid federal society so far as slavery was concerned. Slavery existed because a state's positive laws specified that it did, but that historical fact did not, he argued decade after decade, fix the federal Constitution in a permanent proslavery mode. The basic thrust of Chase's position was for a future in which slave ownership somehow, by statute, constitutional amendment, or Supreme Court decision, would be kept within the old southeastern region, stopping at the Mississippi and at the Gulf, and going no farther.

But as it had since 1787, in the latter 1840s slavery again transcended state boundaries and in a grand manner. America's victory in the Mexican War added to the Union a new trans-Mississippi western empire including slave-owning Texas' vastness and the seemingly boundless acreages from there to the Pacific, and ultimately from the Rio Grande to the Canadian border. The subsequent great debates of 1850 concerning slavery's place in the nation's now transcontinental destiny won some antislavery goals, such as the prohibition of the slave trade in the federal capital. But Chase's pleasure in this victory was soon overshadowed. The southern states' primacy in defining national policies exhibited itself again in the enactment of a notably more stringent federal fugitive slave law. Its passage mocked Chase's freedom national formula and further eroded antislavery spokesmen's fragile alliances.

Chase concluded that the underlying solvent had been working since 1787. Compounded from constitutionalism, politics, racism, and property law, it catalyzed the advantages that slave owners enjoyed in courtrooms and Congress for their special interests. Yet whenever he could Chase exploited southerners' very arguments about states' primacies in the federal system in a manner that would make him, as major scholars maintain, the most successful antislavery politician. In 1850 and for a decade to follow, however, that success was only dimly apparent.

Notwithstanding all frustrations, by the latter 1850s Chase was increasingly important in the national councils of the infant Republican party, the successor to the earlier antislavery political organizations. His essentially midroad antislavery position alienated the more radical antislavery activists such as Garrison, who abandoned politics, litigation, and the Constitution. Chase had made his moral choices, however, and he continued trying through law and politics to transform them into public policies, a goal requiring that antislavery factions stop their endless sniping at each other and instead play politics effectively. And in the future toward which America was rushing, the moral choices Chase made in the decades from 1830 to 1860 would remain vital and manifest themselves again in his *Turner* and *Texas* decisions.

CHAPTER 4

Down the Slippery Slope to Secession

From the late 1830s through the 1850s party loyalty was as unimportant to Chase as it was to many thousands of voters, especially in the free states. The political parties, like many other private associations, were in flux. Shifts like Chase's in party allegiance were common and destined to remain so. His generation of activists treated the legal, moral, and political aspects of antislavery with utmost seriousness but party affiliations as almost beneath notice. So too the proslavery militants, except that the great majority of the latter, who were southerners, tended to remain Democrats because increasingly they dominated the national levels of that once-liberal party and were transforming what had been the vehicle of Jeffersonianism into one of Calhounian reaction. Southern Democratic party leaders tied their supporters into powerful alliances of interests with groups in the most urbanized northeastern commercial and industrial states. By exploiting whites' fears of uncomfortable changes in their privileged positions in legal, political, and social relationships, Democratic party spokesmen added to the deep reservoirs of racism that repeatedly overflowed violently in Cincinnati, Baltimore, and elsewhere.

During those decades such fears were expressed in a rigidly static constitutionalism that underlay the Democrats' political agendas. Negations on many seemingly racially unrelated functions of government, including subsidies for transportation and public education, were necessary, asserted purveyors of racial fears, because such policies might lead to future changes. Exceptions to the web of negatives were the southern states' police functions, justified by rare, bloody, but inherently doomed episodes such as John Brown's call for a slave uprising in Virginia and the alleged duty imposed on the nation by the original compact, the Constitution, to return fugitive slaves to masters and to keep its territories open to slavery.

By the early 1850s the southern states were virtually one-party domains of the Democrats. Everywhere the erstwhile Whig opposition was futile or it simply disappeared. Anti-immigrant (meaning, essentially, anti-Catholic) Know-Nothings and Anti-Masons managed only localized successes. And antislavery politics of Chase's sort had no realistic national party base at all.

Although Chase persisted in politics, he searched for less futile ways to resist the proslavery onslaught. Not surprisingly, he hoped that the law's procedures and the tenets of his less static, evolutionary constitutionalism might yet imbed themselves into the agenda of a political party that in realistic terms could resist Calhoun's proslavery juggernaut.

As the 1850s began Chase considered the demise of the Federalists and the Whigs and the limited voter appeal of the Anti-Masonic, Know-Nothing, and other would-be successor parties. He knew how high the odds were against either the Liberty or Free-Soil organizations attaining nationwide status. Therefore in the 1848 presidential campaign Chase and other Free-Soilers encouraged Ohio "Conscience" Whigs to defect and vote against that party's candidate, Zachary Taylor, a slave owner. Taylor's victory reflected both the innate political advantages enjoyed by the defenders of slavery and antislavery's political marginality.

But the marginality did not affect Chase. Although he continued to lose lawsuits on behalf of slaves and their benefactors, his successive elections to public offices suggest that as an individual his essentially moralistic positions on the law and the constitutionalism of slavery and freedom paid off. He won elections as rewards for his activism and because he understood early the need to match existing means with antislavery ends. Correlation was essential with other individuals like himself who had voter appeal and with whatever political organization that was relevant to their purposes, else efforts to match public policies with antislavery principles were futile.

And so Chase, an indefatigable scribbler, corresponded endlessly with a large network of like-minded individuals whom he cultivated across the troubled country. It included religiously motivated persons like himself and secularly focused, politically prominent converts to the antislavery cause such as Massachusetts' U.S. senator Charles Sumner. Like Chase, Sumner was already widely known as an apostle of many reforms and Chase welcomed him in the Senate. New York's governor William Seward had been co-counsel with Chase for defendants enmeshed in the constraining webs that slavery and racism had woven around Americans, white and black. Closer to home, Kentuckian Cassius Marcellus Clay, a picaresque, outspoken antislavery newspaper publisher, and former Whig one-term Illinois congressman Abraham Lincoln frequently exchanged views with Chase about slavery-focused politics.

Combining piety and politics, they mourned the potency of the Democratic party, exhibited starkly, for example, by its aggressive successes in achieving the Compromise of 1850 and, four years later, the Kansas-Nebraska Act. By repealing relevant clauses of the by-then-hallowed 1820 Missouri Compromise, the 1854 Kansas-Nebraska Act opened vast areas to slavery that were conduits to the West and that since 1820 had been dedicated to future free state status. The proliferating lawlessness of Bloody Kansas and John Brown's raid followed, in which both proslavery and antislavery police, militia, and vigilantes substituted violence for the procedures of law and politics that Chase revered.

In the Western world the United States was the only nation where, during the half-century of Chase's lifetime, the resident slave population and the extent of territory open to slavery grew, and, considering the Texas and Kansas additions, grew by imperial measures. The shame Chase felt because of this fact would mix with his increasing anxieties about the viability of political democracy and its coexistability with law and morality. His anxieties greatly increased when, in 1857, the Supreme Court issued the *Dred Scott* decision.

In 200 years perhaps no other Supreme Court ruling, including *Brown v. Board of Education* (347 U.S. 483 [1954]), on race-blind access to education, or *Roe v. Wade* (410 U.S. 113 [1973]), on women's abortion rights, so inflamed public reaction as did the *Dred Scott v. Sandford* (60 U.S. 393 [1857]) decision. It encouraged serious efforts to legitimize slavery even in free states, inspired violence, and, as Chase viewed matters, led to the ultimate near-anarchical lawlessness of states' secessions and civil war. In sum, the Court's *Dred Scott* decision destabilized the very political institutions and processes that its majority justices aimed to insulate as permanently as possible from dynamic majority views by making constitutional law of Calhoun's arguments about the original constitutional compact.

A slave, Dred Scott had traveled with his peripatetic master, an army surgeon, in federal territories decreed by the 1820 Missouri Compromise law to be free and that had since become free states. Then Scott returned with his master to Missouri, that slave-owning salient into the trans-Mississippi West. Scott's subsequent owner held antislavery views. With fees provided by abolitionist donors, prominent attorneys sued for Scott's

{ *The Reconstruction Justice of Salmon P. Chase* }

freedom in the state and then in the national appellate courts. Other front-running lawyers sustained Missouri's right to perpetuate Scott's servile status. Perceptions proliferated that decisions in this case might affect the legitimacy of the Missouri Compromise statute, the enforceability of the even more ancient federal fugitive slave law in its reinforced 1850 guise, and the legal status and rights of blacks in free as well as in slave states.

If, as his lawyers claimed, Scott was a federal citizen, a status wholly undefined since 1787, then every slave, whether a runaway, a sojourner with his master in a free state, or a resident in a slave state, could demand trial by jury. Slave owners' spokesmen worried that runaways or sojourners so tried in a free jurisdiction would win verdicts that might encourage other blacks, and white lawyers like Chase who were trying to aid them, to initiate other troublesome lawsuits. Resulting verdicts might effectively erode Supreme Court rulings such as the one in *Prigg v. Pennsylvania* and even nullify the fugitive slave law.

Worse in such nightmares was a possibility that misled voting majorities might one day elect a president and a majority in Congress that would reconstitute the Supreme Court. Resulting legislation and judicial decisions might then hold that citizens of any free state were also citizens of the nation. But despite their obeisance to the original compact, Democratic leaders detected a lurking menace in the Constitution's Article 4, Section 2 "comity" provision, that "the citizens of each state shall be entitled to all privileges and immunities of citizens in the several states."

What slave owners feared as a menace offered hope to Chase and other antislavery lawyers, and they sorely needed hope. Therefore they paid close attention to Dred Scott's lawsuit as it progressed from state to federal appeals courts, tracking it especially by means of correspondence with antislavery individuals and committees, a technique in which Chase excelled. He and other freedom national advocates lamented the South's repugnance to the idea of a biracially inclusive citizenship. They did not, however, foresee the passion of high jurists to exclude as perpetually as possible from both politics and law moralistic goals like Chase's for slavery's ultimate destruction through majoritarian political action leading to its territorial containment.

The prominent attorney and premier constitutionalist, Marylander Reverdy Johnson, sensed these winds swirling in the Supreme Court better than the antislavery attorneys. On behalf of Missouri, Johnson asserted in the Supreme Court that Scott had never been a citizen and that in 1820

Congress had overstepped the Constitution by prohibiting slavery in the Missouri Compromise area except in Missouri itself. Extending Johnson's premises, Chief Justice Roger B. Taney gave the Court's ruling, he and every justice then adding separate concurring or dissenting opinions.

Taney's dominating position was that contrary to major precedents, Scott remained a slave despite his free-soil sojournings. Only states, not the nation, then created citizens. The murky phrases of the comity clause left the matter of citizens' privileges and status to each state. Continuing in phrases that spelled doom for the hopes of all blacks and of every anti-slavery white to achieve race-blind equal justice through law or politics, Taney asserted that blacks had never, in any state or federal territory, been citizens or had rights that whites were bound to respect. Therefore blacks had no standing to sue in a federal court.

Taney was twisting history. The Constitution not only required all states, and by implication the federal government, to give all persons the privileges and immunities enjoyed by citizens of any state, but it also re-quired states to give "full faith and credit" to the public records of other states, a requirement that "Congress may by general laws prescribe" (Ar-ticle 4, Section 1). Blacks had been and were citizens in some states that had long been race-neutral or nearly so in matters of their citizens' formal legal, constitutional, and even political rights. Taney's distortions ignored the fact.

Having denied jurisdiction by reducing all blacks to legal invisibility except as slaves, or as free persons devoid of rights, Taney could have stopped there. But he was determined to take out of politics and law as many slavery-related questions as possible, including those deriving from the nation's authority over slavery in its territories. After politically rend-ing debates, in the 1854 Kansas-Nebraska Act the Congress had already repealed the 1820 Missouri Compromise law on which Scott's appeal partially depended. Taney exhumed the corpse of the 1820 statute only in order permanently to rebury it. His formalistically static interpreta-tion entombed every midroad freedom national, free-soil position that for twenty years Chase and other antislavery moderates had contrived. Calhoun's compact theory was now constitutional law.

Not only was Scott still a slave, Taney asserted. In 1820 Congress had violated the Fifth Amendment (of the Bill of Rights!) by unconstitution-ally excluding slave owners' human property from major areas of the Loui-siana Purchase. The Constitution conferred on Congress only the power and duty to protect owners' property rights. By Taney's lights all branches of the national government were obligated to defend slave-owners' private property rights regardless of voting majorities' contrary desires to limit those rights. His decision proscribed future change toward that end through ordinary politics. Indeed, Taney aimed the direction of probable changes backward, not forward.

Two dissenting justices, Benjamin R. Curtis and John McLean, disagreed at length with every point made by the chief justice for the majority. The more important of the two dissents, Curtis's, stressed the fact that since 1789 several states had made blacks citizens and that in the Northwest Ordinance the Congress, including then numbers of the Constitution's Framers in its membership, had regulated slavery in the national territories even to the point of excluding it. A black's legal condition according to the laws of his state of residence did not necessarily strip him of his rights (however undefined and unimplemented they were) under the federal Constitution, including the right to sue in the nation's courts, Curtis continued. To be sure, since 1789 U.S. citizenship and state citizenship had been synonymous, for Congress never defined the former status. Nevertheless, the Constitution required comity.

In many ways Curtis's dissent meshed neatly with Chase's freedom national position. In comparison with Taney's overextended views, the dissenting justice and the antislavery attorney advocated humane, enlightened, and historically valid alternatives. Yet neither Curtis's nor Chase's propositions transcended the notion that blacks whom states recognized as citizens retained standing in federal courts. Further, Congress' authority to bar slavery from the nation's territories violated neither the Fifth Amendment nor other provisions of the Constitution. But however valid, Curtis was in dissent and Chase only one of numerous prophets in a wilderness bereft of constitutional comfort.

In immediate terms Taney's opinion for the majority threatened altogether to knock the props out from under Chase's hopes that his freedom national ideas could ever become the core agenda of a political party capable of swaying events. A new organization, by the mid-1850s calling itself the Republican party, was then sprouting from northeastern and midwestern remnants of the several former fragmenting organizations and also attracting support from a new generation of young voters. Appealing especially to a congeries of often-inharmonious interests wanting, among other future-directed policies, publicly financed improvements in communication, education, and banking, low-cost homesteads in free federal territories, tariff protections, and other marketplace advantages for domestic producers, the Republicans, however otherwise disparate, did agree on means and ends. The means: the Constitution, defined by Republicans as adequate, despite *Dred Scott*, to sanction such positive public-sector economic interventions while embracing the moral imperative of denying access to slavery in the territories; the end: a nationwide free capital and labor market.

Chase was not enchanted by Republican proposals concerning banking. His experiences with revamping banking in Ohio disinclined him from meddling with economic ebbs and flows, especially in light of the distressful consequences of the panicky nationwide depression that began in 1857 and threatened to continue. But the southern-dominated Democrats were even less attractive.

If Chase was disheartened by the immediate political implications of *Dred Scott*, that decision's awful foreshadowings transcended mere gloom. For, buoyed by implications in the *Dred Scott* decision, Democratic party leaders wondered pointedly if the 1787 Northwest Ordinance was as defunct as the illicit (in Taney's views) 1820 Missouri Compromise law. Perhaps, despite contrary constitutions, laws, and customs, free states must honor sojourning slave owners' rights to take, sell, or buy slaves there.

In the form of lawsuits built on *Dred Scott* implications, such ambitions emerged as frighteningly impending realities. Soon after *Dred Scott*, Massachusetts judge Lemuel Shaw decided *Betty's Case*. A slave, Betty accompanied her Tennessee master on a trip to Massachusetts, where antislavery activists sued for her release. Despite Betty's own desire to remain a slave with her "family," Shaw, while reaffirming views similar to Chase's freedom national views, acknowledged also that he was defying Tany's *Dred Scott* judgment. Massachusetts had authority to refuse to consider any resident a slave. But, he concluded, as a mature individual Betty had a right to decide her own fate and she chose to continue in servitude. Abolitionists then denounced Shaw, once their hero, as a conscienceless turncoat.

They should have attended also to Shaw's expression of concern in *Betty's Case* about the dark shadows *Dred Scott* was casting over free states' rights, shadows deepened by implications in *Prigg* and other Supreme Court cases that free states' constitutions and laws notwithstanding, slavery could yet have legal existence in all the states. At least this was Justice Samuel

Nelson's clear suggestion in his opinion in *Dred Scott.* Concurring with Taney's primary views, Nelson had noted:

> A question has been alluded to, on the argument, namely: the right of the master with his slave of transit into or through a free State, on business or commercial pursuits, or in the exercise of a Federal right, or the discharge of a Federal duty, being a citizen of the United States, which is not before us. This question depends upon different considerations and principles from the one in hand, and turns upon the rights and privileges secured to a common citizen of the republic under the Constitution of the United States. When that question arises, we shall be prepared to decide it.

As if responding to Nelson's hint, in 1860 another lawsuit was making its way to the U.S. Supreme Court. It threatened to create what Lincoln worried was "another nice little niche" from which slave owners' rights would emerge to take priority over antislavery states' rights.

Lemmon v. . . . New York (20 New York, 562 [1860]) arose from the sojourning of Virginians, with slaves, in New York City from where the owners intended to board ship for Texas, there to sell their bondsmen. Complaints by New York blacks inspired the slaves' release on a state habeas corpus writ. Successive New York courts, including the state's highest tribunal, upheld the validity of the release, whereupon the Lemmons appealed to the nation's Supreme Court, still composed of the *Dred Scott* majority justices. The *Lemmon* appeal was on the Court's docket when the Civil War began and was never decided. But its potentialities were part of the volatile mix that, for Chase, included fear of an unstoppable spread of slavery.

It is little wonder that these momentous questions involving the legal status and constitutional rights of blacks and of the states of the federal Union should have made such lasting impressions on Chase and on many of his contemporaries. His sensitivity to these questions sharpened by events that transpired in the 1850s, in the late 1860s he refocused on these issues and in *In re Turner* and *Texas v. White,* sitting in Taney's place, offered answers diametrically opposed to Taney's and Nelson's in *Dred Scott.*

His focus suggests also that unlike other veteran antislavery activists, Chase, *Dred Scott* fallout notwithstanding, never despaired that further political action was fruitless because slaveholders and their allies controlled not only the slave states but also the free states' major political organizations and, therefore, the national government, including the president, Congress, and the Supreme Court. In 1859 this conviction of domination by the "slavocracy" inspired the messianic John Brown, a participant in the Kansas bloodlettings that followed the ill-fated Kansas-Nebraska Act, and his little coterie of supporters to seize the Harpers Ferry federal arsenal in Virginia and call for slaves to rise against their masters.

To Chase, Lincoln, and many of their correspondents and constituents, these events were unhappy continuums from the earlier lawless assaults against Birney and Chase's relatives in Ohio and the murdered Lovejoy in Illinois. They confirmed judgments that slavery both legitimized lawlessness committed in its defense and spawned counterviolence. To Chase, such lawlessness threatened the stability of all democratic society, especially one organized constitutionally in a federal union based on the Declaration of Independence and the Constitution. Also at risk were the law's stately procedures, the primary protection for property rights that were the source of all other rights.

Despite their increasing discouragements throughout the 1850s, Chase, Lincoln, and others who shared their inherently optimistic views persisted stubbornly in efforts to infuse antislavery's ethical and legal principles into both politics and law. Chase and Lincoln cooperated in building first Free-Soil and then Republican party local and statewide organizations. Lincoln adapted to Illinois situations the constitutional and legal points that Chase's freedom national concepts had pioneered. In 1858 Chase stumped for Lincoln in the latter's campaign against Stephen Douglas, a major author of the Kansas-Nebraska Act, in their contest for a U.S. Senate seat that Lincoln lost.

Both Chase and Lincoln adhered implicitly and explicitly to Locke's and Jefferson's trinity of life, liberty, and property, and both stressed literacy as a fourth pole of sound public policy in a federally organized democracy. Like Chase in his compilation of Ohio's statutes, Lincoln, for example, praised the Northwest Ordinance from which both their states had sprung, especially its admonitions against slavery and support of race-blind public education.

Illinois was as racist as Ohio. As daring in matters of race as freshman attorney Chase, in 1832 beginning lawyer Lincoln had told Illinoisans that education was society's "most important subject" and that he desired "to see the time when education . . . shall become . . . general." In 1857 Lincoln criticized Taney's distortions of history in *Dred Scott,* arguing that the Declaration of Independence embraced "all men." The next year, when campaigning against Douglas for his Senate seat, Lincoln repeated his arguments against the *Dred Scott* decision and quoted resolutions of the legislature of Vermont, Douglas's former state, "that liberty is a right inherent and inalienable in man and that herein *all men are equal.*" And like Chase, Lincoln asserted consistently that although no federal authority existed to diminish slavery in states where it existed, the nation possessed authority to contain—that is, exclude—it wherever federal jurisdiction prevailed. The two antislavery attorneys agreed also, in Lincoln's phrases, that "no more slave states be admitted into the Union" and that the federal government "ought to return to its ancient policy, not to extend, nationalize, or encourage, but to limit, localize and discourage slavery.*

Another frequent correspondent of Chase's and Lincoln's, Cassius Marcellus Clay, lived across the Ohio River from both Ohio and Illinois, in slave-owning Kentucky. Clay's activities further illuminated for Chase and Lincoln both the corrosive effects on democracy of the lawlessness that slavery engendered even for a bearer of that hallowed family name, Clay, and yet they also revealed the potentialities for redemptive antislavery activism even in a slave-owning state, or at least in one like Kentucky. Antislavery sentiment and associations had long existed there, but proslavery laws and unpunished mob violence kept them anemic. Many antislavery white Kentuckians like Birney had felt it safer to emigrate to free states. An exceptionally stubborn and courageous individual, Clay dared openly to fly antislavery banners in that northernmost slave state east of the Mississippi, a state as much slavery's exposed flank (or, from Chase's point of view, intrusive salient) as Missouri west of that river.

Like Lincoln a birthright Kentuckian and close to him and Chase in age, Clay retained lifetime Kentucky residence. Further linking him to Chase but marking him off from Lincoln, in matters of education Clay was an 1832 Yale graduate who also enjoyed the elite social status deriving from his relative, the revered Henry Clay. Long Whiggish concerning internal improvements, Cassius Clay was converted by Garrison to militant antislavery views. In 1845 Clay began publishing an abolitionist newspaper, the *True American,* in Lexington. Vigilantes drove it from there, then Louis-

*Roy P. Basler, ed., *The Collected Works of Abraham Lincoln,* 8 vols. (New Brunswick, N.J.: Rutgers University Press, 1953–1955), 1:8, 2:390–91, 3:127.

ville, then other locations. Clay suspended his persistent efforts when he enlisted to fight in the Mexican War. Ironically, his battlefield bravery helped to open the way for slavery to expand to the Pacific.

Returning to Kentucky, the bemedaled military hero revived his abolitionist newspaper. Despite his martial luster and family connections, Clay's outspokenness as he lectured, sermonized, and otherwise politicked around Kentucky exposed him frequently to violence. Often joined by or even incited by local peace officers, proslavery mobs assaulted him. Whereupon Clay, the author of a popular manual on hand-to-hand fighting, unsheathed his huge Bowie knife, cocked his brace of loaded pistols, and primed his portable cannon, aiming his weapons at unruly audiences. Ruffians almost always fell silent.

Both Chase and Lincoln applauded Clay's resistance to violence. It attracted welcome publicity that counteracted the John Brown stain on antislavery efforts. But antislavery results more enduring and widespread than Clay's required systematic, sustained efforts such as those Chase and Lincoln were making to form coalitions of state political organizations embracing their legal, constitutional, and moral views. A brave solo crusader, Clay became isolated from the main currents of race policy. Beginning in 1861, those dynamic currents, undammed by the war, swept the nation toward antislavery shores only dimly imaginable in prewar politics or law.

Still another of Chase's correspondents of the 1840s and 1850s, Pittsburgh attorney Edwin McMasters Stanton, enlisted under antislavery banners when war began. Born in 1814 in Ohio of cash-poor but upwardly mobile parents, Stanton, like Chase, enjoyed an elite higher education at Ohio's Kenyon College. Determined to become a lawyer, Stanton also followed Chase's mode and apprenticed himself as a clerk to Steubenville practitioners. Moving to Pittsburgh in 1836, he hung out his shingle.

Becoming peripherally interested in the increasingly acrimonious question in national politics of the extension of slavery into the federal territories, Stanton attended lectures by the abolitionist and race-equality advocate Theodore Dwight Weld and was welcome at the home of his early law partner, Judge Benjamin Tappan, whose brothers were major financial backers of the American Antislavery Society. Intent on achieving professional success, like many other ambitious lawyers, Stanton avoided publicly criticizing slavery. Though privately opposed to its extension, until the 1860s Stanton insisted publicly that he was no abolitionist, a straddling position close to Chase's and Lincoln's on that point. Instead, during the 1850s Stanton was active in backstage Democratic party politics, quickly achieving both wealth and recognition as an unusually well-connected party regular.

Like Chase and Lincoln whenever they could, Stanton served the legal needs of substantial businessmen and early industrial corporations. In their service this indefatigable, inventive lawyer traveled widely through the machine-hungry and litigation-rich Middle West, in one memorable instance snubbing Lincoln, his junior among counsel in the McCormick Reaper patent case. Like many of Chase's clients, most of Stanton's opposed antislavery agitation as unwelcome threats to trade. Stanton accommodated these concerns and, overtly at least, those of the increasingly testy southerners who dominated the Democratic party's national councils. For these reasons, in earliest 1861 Pres. James Buchanan, also a Pennsylvanian, in his lame-duck months appointed Stanton to be attorney general of the United States. When Stanton took office the Deep South's states had already seceded and the remaining northern tier of slave-owning border states from Virginia westward were teetering on the brink of secession.

The Republican party's nomination of Lincoln as its 1860 presidential candidate, then his election and his choices of cabinet members, triggered the Deep South's states' dramatic serial outgoings from the Union during the half-year before his March 1861 inauguration. Meanwhile Lincoln cobbled together his cabinet. Beyond traditional considerations of regional balance, he chose several members from among the party's most influential competitors for the presidency, Chase among them, whom Lincoln appointed treasury secretary. Chase's experience in Ohio's banking policies as governor and his deservedly high reputation among lawyers for effective representation of client banks convinced Lincoln so to recognize his competitor for their party's leadership.

New York's William Henry Seward, Chase's co-counsel in earlier antislavery litigations, was named secretary of state. Despite his "irrepressible conflict" rhetoric, Seward's politically ambitious but, in the antislavery spectrum, conservative goal was of a restored Union with as few changes as possible and perhaps none concerning slavery except for federal guarantees for its protection where it then prevailed. Another would-be party leader, Maryland's Montgomery Blair, a member of a conservative political dynasty potent in both that slave-owning state and in contentious

Missouri, was appointed postmaster general, and, like Chase, exercised powerful patronage. Indianan Caleb Smith and Missourian Edward Bates were named interior secretary and attorney general. Lincoln named New England newspaper publisher Gideon Welles, a recent Democrat and persistent conservative, as navy secretary, and, displeasing Chase, Pennsylvania's Simon Cameron as head of the War Department. Cameron was a notorious spoilsman in Chase's opinion, and his corrupting hold on Pennsylvania's politics did not make his relatively minimal antislavery credentials respectable.

Apologists for the southern states' exit stressed the allegedly antislavery radicalism of Lincoln and his cabinet choices. "The appointments of Seward, Chase, Blair . . . & the like has extinguished the sentiment of loyalty to the [federal] government . . . that remained in the Southern States," Alabamian John A. Campbell, a former U.S. Supreme Court justice who resigned in order to follow his state from the Union, reported to Jefferson Davis from Washington in April 1861, a week after Fort Sumter surrendered.* Actually, the cabinet nominees included no Garrison-Weld spokesmen. Only Chase represented antislavery's mildly left-of-center spectrum. Always proud of his isolation, Chase saw reason in his cabinet situation to be the Republican party's moral monitor over the president and as many other Republican officeholders as possible.

If too timid for Garrison in 1861, Chase nevertheless envisaged a significantly swifter pace for slavery's containment than Seward, Blair, or even Lincoln. Until 1861 Chase's position had been that the nation should hold itself aloof from slavery. The federal government had no constitutional duty to protect owners' property rights in the slave states, to return runaways who reached free states, or to allow the law of slavery into the federal territories. Chase's warnings that the *Dred Scott* decision foreshadowed nationalized slavery were among the most forthright that Republicans uttered. Yet he respected all states' centrality in the Union, even those with slavery. Still, in lawyerlike manner he gave priority to the shared duties of the nation and states to protect all state-defined private property rights, including free labor's right to acquire property, thereby harmonizing constitutional law and moral law. By so doing, he increased the Republican party's

---

*Lynda L. Crist et al., eds., *The Papers of Jefferson Davis*, 8 vols. to date (Baton Rouge: Louisiana State University Press, 1971–1992), 7:117–18.

{ *The Reconstruction Justice of Salmon P. Chase* }

appeal for midroad antislavery businessmen, farmers, urban workers, and ministers, and thus Lincoln invited him into the cabinet.

Spanning the Republican party's origins and its members' purposes, these erstwhile Whigs, Democrats, Know-Nothings, Anti-Masons, and Free-Soilers were linked primarily by their antipathy to slavery. This shared moral judgment led Chase among its champions to see the Constitution as a permissive authority for curbing, if only by the inaction implicit in Chase's freedom national concept, slavery's further territorial expansion and other vexing advantages. The Republicans' sense of the Constitution as an adequate, adaptable source of authority for beneficent purposes, more than of *Dred Scott*-like constrictions continued to attract into that new party's ranks advocates with other, eclectic, sometimes clashing social and economic goals, including protective tariffs, national banks, federally subsidized internal improvements, public education, and rural homesteads. Adding power to the mix, Republican legal pundits including Chase would soon build upon their positive perception of the Constitution's authority to cope with all needs that the Civil War would impose, including the administration's extraordinary expedients: suspension of habeus corpus, state reconstruction, banking, and emancipation.

Concerning emancipation's future, by abolishing slavery and involuntary servitude nationwide, not merely containing it, the Thirteenth Amendment transformed radical abolitionist visions into America's constitutional law. And to their credit, both Chase and Lincoln helped to create this evolution, though at differing paces. Then in 1867 and 1869, Chase, as chief justice, when deciding *In re Turner* and *Texas v. White* among other lawsuits, would comment on the recently amended Constitution.

As prewar antislavery activist and as wartime treasury secretary, Chase helped greatly to bridge the gulfs between Matilda's, Van Zandt's, and Dred Scott's failing legal appeals and Elizabeth Turner's and Texas' successful ones. Therefore it is in order to retravel the long roads connecting the Lincoln administration's installation in April 1861 with Chase's response to *Turner* in 1867 and to *Texas* in 1869.

Of Lincoln's first cabinet choices, Chase, Seward, and Bates had contested the 1860 Republican presidential nomination. In light of the successive one-term weak presidents since Jackson, the dreams of each man about his own presidential prospects in 1864 were reasonable. Seward soon recognized Lincoln's qualities and abandoned competition, Bates fell from contention, but not Chase. His political ambitions remained as intense as Lincoln's. Chase's recurring belief was that he could do the job better than its incumbent. His presidential itch fed also on his doubts about Lincoln's antislavery commitment, doubts deriving from the fact that Lincoln had led a secession-winter retreat from pure freedom national principles.

Chase's misgivings originated when, during winter 1860–1861, the southern states' unopposed secessions unleashed pressures for another sectional compromise like those of 1787, 1820, 1833, 1850, and 1854. Resisting these pressures but seeking somehow to halt secessions, Lincoln and other leading Republicans including Chase, aware of the Lemmons' appeal looming in the Supreme Court, publicly supported a proposal for a thirteenth constitutional amendment unamendably guaranteeing slavery in the states where it existed. This proposal, Chase would later insist defensively, harmonized with his freedom national doctrine. It "opposed the extension of Slavery beyond State limits, and proposed to afford it no Governmental support within the sphere of exclusive National jurisdiction." In 1860–1861 he, like most Republicans, "regarded Slavery within [its present] State limits, as beyond that sphere."

But Chase's freedom national position always viewed the Constitution as mutely tolerating slavery through inaction, if at all. Then, at Lincoln's behest in early 1861, Chase had sanctioned the proposed thirteenth amendment although in almost *Dred Scott*-like terms it overtly constitutionalized slavery, made the nation its perpetual protector, and thereby foreclosed all ultimate freedom national goals. By the proposed amendment's terms, posterity could never through moral persuasion and ordinary political procedures eradicate slave owners' state-defined property rights in the states then sanctioning bondage.

Even as incongruities became apparent in 1861 between Chase's freedom national ideas and the proposed thirteenth amendment, the latter became a casualty of the Confederate bombardment of Fort Sumter. When proposed, the amendment ploy had seemed to Chase, intellectually at least, to be a bearable price of Union, albeit one that countless generations of blacks would pay. But in Chase's later, more emotional, and, perhaps, more politically purposeful view, Lincoln's countenancing of the unamendable amendment and the linking of Chase's name to it raised the secretary's doubts about the purity of the new president's purposes compared to his. As a result, even before Lincoln's inauguration and Chase's installation as treasury secretary, the latter's disgruntlement included impatience with

Lincoln's secession-winter flaccidity, resentment at having been passed over for the 1860 presidential nomination, and his presidential ambitions for 1864.

Insights that hindsight—but only hindsight—allow, suggest that Chase, like many contemporaries, in 1861 monumentally misjudged Lincoln's probable performance as president. Ever a fond prisoner of his own prejudgments, Chase assumed that Lincoln, an undistinguished one-term former congressman without experience in managing large enterprises, could not work effectively with the Republicans then controlling Congress, discipline upstart generals, or control his cabinet choices. Yet Chase proved to be less educable than Lincoln about complexities in American society that the war magnified. Anxious to gallop toward salvational results inspired from battlefield sacrifices, Chase fretted impatiently because Lincoln kept him to a slower, steadier pace toward reunion and antislavery.

Expressing his awareness of their discordances in the barnyard imagery that irked Chase, Lincoln likened himself to a farmer driving a fragile wagon, the Union. Threatening its rupture, three semitrained Republican horses hitched in tandem proceeded forward toward reunion and some yet-unclear antislavery goal but in dangerously unsynchronized manner. The "radical" horse galloped, the moderate trotted, and the conservative walked deliberately. But, tied to the wagon's rear, its legs deeply dug in, the adamantly antiwar, Union-as-it-was, reactionary Democratic horse opposed all forward motion.

This question of pace and the nature of peace became a further wedge between Lincoln and Chase. By early 1862 Chase's war aims were already drifting away from colonization schemes for free and freed blacks and from freedom national containment positions and moving toward slavery's nationwide abolition and the continuing coexistence of blacks and whites on terms other than, and far better than, slavery, extending even to political rights for blacks. Lincoln would advance to Chase's new and more radical goals, but not until early 1865. Their differing paces and responsibilities kept rasping the sensibilities of these two remarkable men. In the midst of the mushrooming Civil War, Lincoln, a proved campaigner, had to govern. He headed a greatly diverse national political party's representatives in the cabinet and Congress, whose members needed to retain the support of a majority of constituents. Chase headed only the Treasury.

Performing his narrower yet essential duties, Chase implemented successful, or at least adequate, wartime fiscal policies including a resort to paper money issues unbacked by specie. Chase was moving toward constitutional radicalism about ending slavery. But concerning economics he remained a hard-money conservative who abhorred the Union's desperate paper money fiscal expedients that he himself had to implement. Yet he did implement them because, he hoped, they advanced the nation toward antislavery war aims. Reciprocally, those goals were unreachable without the nation, which suggests that Chase so ardently detested secession because its disintegrating effect might well be unstoppable. What in the future would deter any state, county, or city from seceding should a public policy irk its majority, if the outgoers of 1860–1861 did so successfully? Were the cords of Union so flaccid as to permit such a travesty of federalism? Then anarchy was entrained, society's constraints smashed, law, order, and property mocked, violence let loose, public and private debts repudiated, and religion, morality, and ethics relegated to history's dustbin along with federalism, progress, and democracy. None could survive without the lawfulness and order symbolized by every state's acquiescence in the verdicts of the elections prescribed by the Constitution.

Chase's fantasies about a wholly free and reunited nation possessed of fiscal rectitude constituted his revised grand vision. He reconciled his new total abolitionism with his profession's reverence for state-defined private property. Redefining slavery not only in freedom national terms, as extra-constitutional and immoral, Chase characterized it also as the immoral source of disloyalty, thus later justifying the voiding of owners' legal rights to own humans.

Slavery excepted, Chase remained, however, a laissez-faire economic thinker and anti-institutional constitutionalist, perhaps partly because pre-war federal and state authorities and many of the public institutions had been unresponsive or even hostile to his antislavery views. He entered the Lincoln cabinet in 1861 as he would the Supreme Court four years later still possessed of these attitudes. Though pressured by patriotism to sanction unprecedented wartime government interventions, he tended to view all official entities suspiciously. These attitudes contributed to the many paradoxes visible in the latter career of this multifaceted individual.

By his own monocular lights Chase was ambitious less for power than for realizing the single antislavery purpose, one paired with patriotism. Half steps, slow steps, or diversions were anathema. Although he was a political animal, Chase, unlike Lincoln, ever convinced of his own rectitude, was incapable of weighing policies in terms of their wider effects on always-imminent elections. Lincoln, as ethically sensitive as Chase, never forgot the need to weigh.

Chase's personal relationships with Lincoln became more brittle than the ties the president enjoyed with Seward, Welles, or Stanton (who succeeded Cameron as war secretary in early 1862 and quickly became Chase's staunch antislavery ally), none of whom were interested in contending against Lincoln in 1864. But despite their famous, frequent, and sometimes furious confrontations over policy and patronage, Lincoln kept Chase running Treasury operations for four years. He did so partly to balance the increasingly radical Chase with the conservative Seward, but chiefly because both men performed so well.

CHAPTER 5

Civilizing America's Civil War

As treasury secretary during most of the Civil War, Chase became increasingly sensitive to the many uncertainties persisting about the legal statuses and constitutional rights of individuals and states in the federal system. He believed that these uncertainties had caused the prewar decline of law and order that in turn had led to secession and civil war. After Appomattox Chief Justice Chase looked back across America's "war gulf." Vexed that these corrosive uncertainties had survived the war, he tried, in *In re Turner* and *Texas v. White* to lay them to rest.

Like all Republicans during the Civil War and for the first several years after it, Chase was confident that the nation possessed adequate constitutional authority militarily to suppress the Confederacy and to set reasonable conditions for restoring its states to the federal Union. Sharply differing opinions existed about the definition of reasonable, however. When the war started Chase still defined reasonableness in familiar freedom national terms: no further extension of slavery into the federal territories but also no interference with it in the states where it prevailed in 1860. Yet by 1864, with the Radical Republicans he was insisting that slavery must be abolished.

With patriotism as the flux, for Lincoln, Chase, and millions of other Americans the war welded abolition onto antislavery. But Chase's oscillation seemed to validate critics' judgments then and since that he was an opportunist who shifted his views in order to win the White House for himself. Without minimizing his itch to be president—one shared by Lincoln, several cabinet officers, and many congressmen and governors—it appears, however, that consistency existed between Chase's prewar freedom national stand and his postwar opinions in *In re Turner* and *Texas v. White*. The war forced him to amend but not to abandon his core concept.

Chase was ever a lawyer, but he was also the secretary of the treasury and hoped to be his party's next presidential candidate. Lawyers detested popular attacks on any private property as leading to anarchy. Chase perceived early a need for legally bearable, militarily relevant, popularly acceptable, and morally impregnable war aims that might encourage the return of the seceded states to the Union. Pressured relentlessly by his antislavery past, by the war itself, and by his inner goads, by midwar Chase helped to make war aims first of partial emancipation and then of the total abolition of slavery.

Yet the demise of slavery nationwide failed automatically to produce the pacific federal Union of Chase's law-and-order imaginings. In them each state, without compulsion, would provide equal race-blind legal rights to all its residents, black and white, even to females, because once slavery ended all persons were free. No halfway statuses existed except for felons, minors, mental incompetents, and apprentices. But because his assumptions and hopes were denied by events after Appomattox, Chase tried to realize them by broadcasting in his *Turner* and *Texas* opinions his message that all Americans were entitled to equal justice under state laws.

His message in the two cases reflects remarkable consistency. Though unavailing, his arguments in the 1830s on behalf of runaway slaves and their abettors and his speeches in the Senate in the 1850s expressed this theme of the essentiality of equalized justice. Despite all prewar setbacks and wartime vicissitudes, Chase remained confident that substantially decent law-and-order procedures would moderate man's tendency toward anarchy.

Chase's confidence in equal justice under law as the sovereign prescription for most of the nation's ills was unshaken by prewar reverses. His enormous correspondence suggests that his faith in this secular solution reflected his certainty that he was on the side of the godly. To Chase proof existed in the fact that although he lost his pleas for indigent clients like Matilda and Van Zandt and that as governor and senator he failed to imbed antislavery principles into public policies, he had also become wealthy by representing moneyed merchants, corporations, and banks.

Nevertheless, the states' secessions during the 1860–1861 winter and the Confederacy's initial battlefield successes shook Chase's confidence. Would a nation exist for him to serve as president in a future election? Could law or order survive this war?

As noted (p. 10), the Civil War was the Western world's longest, bloodiest, and costliest armed conflict between 1815 and 1914. Civil wars, especially those involving race or religion, evoke not dependence on law but combatants' brutally arbitrary behavior that fundamentally destabilizes already-riven societies. Americans were to avoid that abyss. With doleful exceptions Union and Confederate authorities warred in a relatively restrained, often highly legalistic manner. At the apex of Union government, Lincoln, Chase, Seward, and other accomplished attorneys, along with those in Congress and the federal courts, learned quickly the need to moderate interactions between Union troops and civilians, in part by substituting legal and quasi-legal procedures for a civil war's far commoner violent alternatives.

Chase encouraged legal policies and procedures; Union soldiers gave him the opportunity to do so. From the war's early days territorial contraction became the Confederacy's central theme. Confederate troops rarely ruled Union communities more than temporarily and felt no need to administer governments they had displaced. By contrast, federal troops occupied southern areas, and, staying, had to govern individuals, communities, and, eventually, whole states.

Chase was deeply excited by the unprecedented presence of national soldiers in the South for purposes other than to protect only slave owners' property rights. This veteran antislavery activist, former Ohio governor and U.S. senator, as secretary of the treasury quickly expanded his vast prewar correspondence network. Many antislavery colleagues entered the Union army. Others staffed numerous private religious, welfare, medical, legal, and educational associations long committed to antislavery goals and that served also the needs of Union soldiers, their homefront dependents, and white and black refugees in and from the South. Association spokesmen quickly educated Chase to the fact that in civil wars differences between battlegrounds and homefronts are illusory.

By early 1862 bluecoats controlled significant enclaves in Virginia, Kentucky, Tennessee, Florida, Missouri, Louisiana, and offshore Carolinas. Meanwhile, Congress repealed the fugitive slave law, imposed high duties (taxes) on imports, and enacted confiscation statues that, upon convictions in federal courts, penalized convicted individual rebels with the loss of slaves and other assets. These measures, among other derivative issues involving Chase's concerns about restoring law and order, raised certain questions. How could Treasury tax collectors, attorneys, judges, and jurors be found to implement federal statutes in occupied southern areas who without perjury could swear to their past and present loyalty to the United States as Congress also required? What was the legal status of slaves freed by Confiscation Act convictions? And, soon, in far greater numbers, of those freed by Lincoln's Emancipation Proclamation? Lincoln's proclamation could hardly come soon enough for an impatient Chase. Encouraged by his correspondents in the army and in welfare associations, inspired by patriotism, and aware from his Treasury duties how close national bankruptcy lurked, Chase shifted leftward to advocate as a premier war aim the nationwide abolition of slavery.

In prewar decades Chase's antislavery position was antigovernment because since 1789 federal authorities had protected slave owners' property rights and punished antislavery activists. This attitude was implicit in his freedom national credo, that by inaction of the government slavery might be containable inside its existing boundaries. But in 1861 Chase began to realize that the Union's armies in the South were outpacing his freedom national stance and making a casualty of inaction on slavery. At that point the restoration of the prewar Union with slavery intact became too modest a war aim for Chase.

As was common among the highly individualistic members of the antislavery vanguard, not everyone even among old activist comrades made the same shift, or, making it, did so at the same speed. Lincoln, for example, was just as sensitive to the moral imperatives that moved Chase toward abolitionism. But from larger concerns Lincoln hesitated to join Chase until early 1865. As their paces diverged, the long prewar concord between them began to sour.

Never patient or generous about moral choices other than his own, Chase carped often and publicly about Lincoln's slower pace. Chase misread it as evidence of the president's merely tentative antislavery commitment and insensitivity to the enhanced possibilities the war offered to end slavery's degrading effects on the nation's morality and its deadening effects on the economy. Serious frictions resulted. Still, Lincoln kept Chase in the cabinet to balance Seward's and Blair's standpat positions on slavery and to exploit Chase's banking skills.

Bankers were essential to the nation's fiscal needs and policies. No central bank had existed since Jackson's time. Vast sums were needed to finance the war. Frighteningly soon after becoming treasury secretary in 1861 Chase was almost in despair about the Union's prospects for survival because almost no private bankers were any longer giving specie on demand in exchange for the government's instruments of indebtedness.

Historically, such reluctance by private bankers reflected a government's severe fiscal distress, foretelling even its repudiation of public debt, that is, the equivalent of bankruptcy. The Union's imminent bankruptcy made time the Confederacy's not-very-secret weapon. Propositions were heard that in order to avoid repudiation the Union should strike a deal with the Confederacy to end the war on its terms because, if the Union persisted in the war, debt repudiation was probable. If the government was unable to meet contractual obligations to suppliers, interest payments for holders of federal bonds (a foretaste of *Texas v. White*), or the salaries and pensions for civil servants, soldiers, veterans, and their heirs, the nation must halt its war effort. Either way, the slave-owning Confederacy would emerge permanently independent.

To Chase, as to most lawyers and bankers, repudiations of public debts were as immoral and anarchically destructive of law and order as slavery and secession. His equation between this unholy trinity also had prewar roots. During the depression-afflicted 1850s major repudiations had occurred, especially in commercially ambitious northern states and localities. Exploiting prevailing legal theories of plenary state police power, theories southerners exploited in an exaggerated manner to protect slaveowners' property rights, northern communities tried to attract settlers, trade, and industry by issuing municipal bonds to subsidize canals, turnpikes, and rail facilities. Some issuers exceeded their communities' taxable resources, failed to meet interest payments owed to bondholders, and repudiated the obligation, whereupon the next wave of state lawmakers and judges repudiated the repudiations. In Iowa this situation inspired lawsuits by debt-holders, and losers appealed to the U.S. Supreme Court. Its *Gelpcke v. Dubuque* (1 Wall., 175) decision about which Iowa laws and verdicts deserved honoring, was issued in the Court's 1863–1864 term.

This was a heady season for the Union, then celebrating the Gettysburg and Vicksburg triumphs. Earlier that year Lincoln had accelerated the recruitment of blacks into the Union's armies, and in December 1863 he formalized a lawyerlike Military Reconstruction procedure that included a much larger-scale emancipation than his earlier proclamation.

Mirroring Chase's detestation of debt repudiations, a Supreme Court functionary reflected not at all on those momentous matters. Instead, his report on *Gelpcke,* which soon circulated among American lawyers, bankers, and investors, stressed the fact that by repudiating Iowa's repudiation of its debt commitments, the justices had imposed "high moral duties... upon a whole community [which was] seeking apparently to violate them." This was the approach that Chase wanted to take for the whole South, indeed, for the entire nation.

Years later when deciding *In re Turner* and *Texas v. White,* Chase also imposed "high moral duties" on former slave-owning Maryland and Texas. In these decisions, Chase's concern about state wrongs North and South echoed those of the 1850s and early 1860s. It justified his asking in *Turner* and in *Texas v. White* who or what constituted a state, and what limits existed on a state's power adversely to affect individuals' economic (that is, civil) rights, whether those individuals were black female apprentices or white bondholding investors.

Beginning in 1861, Chase helped greatly to overcome the nightmarish fiscal obstacles hindering the Union's martial success. Both unilaterally and in close cooperation with the Republican–War Democrat Union party coalition in Congress, he ultimately contrived adequate financial policies directed toward that end. But as of 1861 revenue was needed quickly and in unprecedented amounts to avert an economic disaster that would vitiate every battlefield sacrifice.

Spurred by Chase's urgent lobbying, from 1861 through 1865 Congress taxed heretofore unburdened imports, incomes, and internal commerce, borrowed millions through sales of government bonds, and authorized Treasury issues of greenbacks wholly unsecured by specie. Chase was a hard-money fiscal conservative. He equated repudiatable paper money, including the new greenbacks, with governmental immorality equal to that of slavery and secession. While the war lasted, Chase's patriotism took precedence over his principles about fiscal ethics. But from 1861 through late 1864 when he left the cabinet, Chase confided in his journal that he feared "the abyss of bankruptcy and ruin which yawns before us. May God open the eyes of those who control, before it is too late!"*

Later, as chief justice, Chase helped to judge the constitutionality of the Treasury's wartime expedients associated with his tenure there. His *Turner* and *Texas* opinions dealt with matters superficially unrelated to greenbacks. But common to these lawsuits was Chase's war-heightened apprehensions

---

*John Niven et al., eds., *The Salmon P. Chase Papers*, vol. 1, *Journals, 1829–1872* (Kent, Ohio: Kent State University Press, 1993), 381.

about the ease with which officials degraded economic rights by misusing the nation's war and fiscal powers and the state's police powers. So misused or misguided, a state could deprive a black female apprentice (the complainant in *In re Turner*) and white bondholders (the parties in *Gelpcke* and *Texas v. White*) of their property due from labor or investment.

The fact that Chase never abandoned his ambition to be president fed rumors that he directed his every action toward that goal. Some rumors noted that beginning in 1861 Chase dramatically increased the numbers of Treasury field agents and Washington-based clerical staff without statutory authority. Stationed in Washington, at every port of entry, and in each congressional district nationwide, the number of Treasury tax collectors and support personnel soon soared into the tens of thousands. Granted, the new income and excise taxes, tariff rates, and currency-novelties laws needed staff to process the income that the government required so sorely. Nevertheless, many contemporaries judged that by ballooning the Treasury rolls Chase was crafting a patronage-fueled presidential bandwagon for himself in time for the 1864 nominating conventions and presidential elections.

Perhaps. But considering Chase's lust for the White House, the highly visible, unprecedentedly enlarged, and, as measured in the prevailing context of long-standing race and gender prejudices, exotically constituted work force that his orders brought into the Treasury Department's Washington bureaucracy was a strange way to satisfy it.

Chase hired as Treasury clerks thousands of women and men of both races, even assigning some black males to supervise white women. Ultimately huge in numbers, Treasury personnel in the nation's capital boasted relatively few politically influential persons or even many voters. Females could not vote and black males in only a few states. Chase's defiance of the city's deeply entrenched racial and gender bigotries inspired distrust among many employers nationwide because of the equal-pay-for-equal-work policy he also initiated for his Washington work force. In sum, Chase's hiring and workplace policies outraged reactionary and standpat Democrats, alienated many Republican party heavyweights, and generally irked white male voters, clearly not the way to win the White House in 1864.

An agile survivor of three decades of fractious party politics, Chase knew that the exotic mix that staffed the Treasury's labyrinthine Washington offices cost him significant popular esteem among both political movers-and-shakers and ordinary voters across the country. Ten years later, in 1872, an Ohio confidant still puzzled by Chase's idiosyncratic and politically counterproductive wartime personnel policy asked for an explanation. Aware that his own death was impending, Chase offered reasons.

One was his lawyerlike need for an orderly way to meet his official responsibilities. Upon assuming the Treasury portfolio he had sworn an oath to discharge the duties of that office to the best of his ability. By this test his duty to implement the new revenue laws effectively and quickly inspired him to reject many known placeholders that patronage dispensers hastened to nominate. Yet he had to increase greatly and immediately the number of Treasury staff in Washington.

The situation mixed Chase's need for a timely, better rationalized administration of the revenue laws with the unsparing goads of his moralistic inner voice. He reminded his correspondent that except for the new oath of past loyalty, no statute set standards for civil servants "when I introduced [white females and blacks of both genders] into the [Treasury] Department in 1861." But relevant traditions "sanctioned the employment of *persons* to do the work ... and did not exclude females" (Chase's stress on the word "persons" bears remembering in light of later landmark debates in Congress and in Supreme Court decisions about limiting the outreach of the Thirteenth and Fourteenth Amendments).

Chase explained further that from early in the Civil War, battles fought south of the Potomac River made Washington a haven, if an expensive one, for displaced and economically distressed whites and blacks, the latter including many runaway slaves. Additionally, large numbers of northern women moved to Washington. Many were soldiers' wives or widows. Others had come as unpaid volunteers for myriad private evangelical, educational, medical, and legal-aid associations serving soldiers and freedmen. Angry sermons and sensational newspaper accounts attributed the area's growth of prostitution, venereal infections, gambling, vagrancy, and public lewdness and drunkenness, all hurtful to Union soldiers, to the women's economic distress. "My action [in hiring females and blacks] was originally taken from motives of humanity ... [generated by the] many refugees and others ... deprived of livelihood[s] by the war," Chase insisted in 1872. "I gave them employment to be able to provide for themselves and their families."

In his 1872 recollection Chase noted that from 1861 to 1865 he had been responding also to concerns he had long felt about women's and blacks' inferior legal positions, which he had had no practical way to remedy until he became treasury secretary. Somewhat remarkably in light of Chase's neo-Calvinist religious upbringing, early in the Civil War he had concluded that the immoralities degrading the capital resulted not from women's character flaws derived from Eve, a common contemporary assumption, but from race- and gender-skewed marketplace inequalities.

Chase's near-deathbed reminiscence of 1872 invites consideration also in light of his *In re Turner* decision of 1867. Elizabeth Turner petitioned Chase for relief from her labor contract because Maryland's racially discriminatory apprenticeship statute approved conditions for her, as a black female, inferior to those white peers enjoyed. During the war years Chase, revolted by the tawdry immorality besmirching the capital, reinforced his convictions that the too-visible wartime degradations resulted from customs and laws that sanctioned inferior rewards from labor for women and blacks. Denouncing such laws and customs in *In re Turner*, Chief Justice Chase seized the opportunity Elizabeth Turner provided him, and through him, potentially all women and blacks, to apply to her apprenticeship contract the nobler standard of the Thirteenth Amendment and the Civil Rights Act, legal equality, a view he would repeat in his *Texas v. White* opinion.

And so in 1872 the dying Chase asserted to A. F. Boyle that "it is true . . . that I have always favored the enlargement of the sphere of women's work and the payment of just compensation for it."* Always is a long time. Nevertheless, Chase's innovations in hiring and promotion at the Treasury offices in Washington, when considered with his postwar judicial decisions in *In re Turner* and *Texas v. White,* suggest that his self-judgment of 1872 rings true.

---

*Chase to A. F. Boyle, Dec. 11, 1872, *Chase Letterbooks,* ser. 4 (Washington, D.C.: Manuscripts Division, Library of Congress), 121:15.

CHAPTER 6

Means and Ends in the Union's
Evolving War Aims

Granted that apolitical and humanitarian reasons inspired him, Chase alone among cabinet heads hired thousands of blacks and females as civil servants and even placed an impressive number of black males in supervisory positions over white females. Although defying exclusionary gender and race customs concerning federal employees in the Treasury's Washington offices, he never initiated comparably adventurous personnel policies in other major Treasury divisions. The Treasury's most important division consisted of the revenue collectors. Just as before the Civil War, during it the nation's tax collectors remained white, male, and heavily involved in national, state, and local politics.

This situation was nothing new. Although contemporary academic theoreticians of American history and government ignored the practice, it was common knowledge among politicians, public officials, journalists, and businessmen that the Treasury's numerous field agents had always been enormously influential and, often, decisive players in the politics of the state, county, and city where they were located. Their influence derived from the fact that, by definition, revenue agents collected large sums from taxes and, more recently, tariffs. The war's swelling expenditures increased concerns about government bankruptcy. New tax laws greatly accentuated the revenue officers' political clout virtually everywhere.

Federal laws required tax collectors to be stationed in every port of entry, both oceanic and riverine, and in every congressional district. None escalated more in political significance than the agents Chase assigned to each militarily liberated southern area, with orders from him to initiate collections swiftly. Chase tended to appoint southern Unionists, carpetbagging Union army veterans, and activists in the eclectic religious and lay private welfare societies who followed closely behind the conquering bluecoats. By mid-1862, in Union salients ringing the Confederacy from Virginia to Louisiana and in the inland slaveholding states drained eventually by the Mississippi River, Chase's Treasury agents reopened federal revenue offices and filled influence vacuums.

The newcomers' implementations of the increasing flow of revenue and confiscation statutes almost inescapably had political consequences. Judiciously depositing collected taxes with favored local bankers, shrewdly disbursing funds to local military suppliers, and cannily selecting candidates for both state and national offices, Treasury agents' "money machines" lubricated the reviving local, county, and, eventually, state political organizations.

Individuals with mundane and mendacious purposes exploited the opportunities for personal gain that these processes permitted. Corruption flourished in part because from 1861 through 1863 neither Lincoln nor Congress correlated the piecemeal policies on confiscation, loyalty tests for public officials, and military emancipation or prescribed a statutory procedure for resurrecting state and local governments in the occupied South. And for as long as possible both the White House and Capitol Hill avoided ultimate commitments on that sensitive matter, the status of the South's slaves and its free blacks. Thus certain Union generals, such as George B. McClellan, who detested emancipation, along with Treasury Secretary Chase, who favored it enthusiastically, took advantage of the absence of higher policy by implanting subordinates of like mind in offices in the occupied southern areas.

Early staffing became supremely important. Beginning in 1861 Union policymakers and voters assumed that, granting military success and no government bankruptcy, the seceded states would be returned to the Union as states. Advocates of reducing seceded states to conquered provinces or to territorial status never commanded important support. Still undecided was the pace of the states' returns and a politically acceptable definition of who constituted their citizenry.

However defined eventually, by tacit assumption that citizenry would elect local, county, and state lawmakers, executives, and judges and select congressmen and the president, even electoral college members, who, in contested elections, would determine the presidency. Therefore the Union's enclaves in the South were important from the war's first days. In those rewon areas, the soldiers and Treasury officials who were implanting policies and protégés in local governments and political party organizations were determining the shape of the nation's future.

Aware that all American politics are local, officials from Lincoln down attended closely to Chase's revenue operations, so essential both for the nation's fiscal survival and for the complexion of the states' revivals. For example, in 1861 Congress required Chase to license trade from occupied areas, especially in cotton. Some Treasury agents became involved in corrupt licensing schemes. Among Chase's cabinet colleagues, several who were more conservative on antislavery issues than he implied that he sanctioned the venal schemes in order to fatten his wealth and ready his bandwagon for the 1864 presidential race.

Such implications about Chase himself have not been reinforced by proofs. And the existence of selfishness did not exclude other, nobler purposes. Persons trying to achieve them used the existing, often sordid Treasury field operations, especially those in the South, in efforts to shape a different and even perhaps a better future. And the increasing evidence of mendacity among some of his field agents deeply troubled Chase. After all, he had recruited many revenue officers from among his vast array of antislavery correspondents and volunteers in the evangelical, medical, educational, and welfare associations concerned with both Union soldiers and abandoned or runaway slaves in the South.

In addition to controlling licensed trade, Treasury officials were required by Congress to administer Confederates' abandoned or confiscated property, including land, crops, and slaves. Following Chase's orders, first on the Carolina islands and then in Florida, Louisiana, and Texas, Treasury agents and welfare association members tried simultaneously and often cooperatively to revive agricultural production and to encourage law and order, the latter a major concern of Chase's.

To stabilize the slave populations loosed from their masters' controls, Treasury officials sometimes imposed antivagrancy penalties, adapted from northern states' labor codes, on black workers who wandered away from assigned tasks. More imaginatively, Treasury and welfare workers educated blacks about free persons' ordinary legal rights and responsibilities, including those in work commitments, marriages, rents, sales, and other civil relationships. Slavery had left blacks inexperienced in these workaday matters. But they learned, Treasury and welfare agents reported exultantly to Chase.

The speed with which southern blacks learned verified antislavery advocates' assumptions about the lack of knowledge concerning responsibilities that slavery had brought about among its black victims. Once its deadening hand lifted, Treasury and welfare workers needed initially to educate blacks about legal obligations and rights. But thereafter, Chase was advised, blacks would live as whites did or should, protecting their own legal rights and observing their lawful commitments through recourse to local law-and-order procedures and to welfare and justice agencies that Union military and Treasury officials were establishing.

Optimistic reports from Chase to the president helped to counter tenacious claims of blacks' allegedly innate inability to be responsible for legal obligations. Thereby Lincoln became less amenable to repeated suggestions that biracial coexistence on terms other than master-slave was unthinkable and that all freed blacks should be colonized somewhere abroad, in Liberia, Haiti, or Central America. Chase helped to convince Lincoln that mass deportations were un-Christian and unnecessary. Chase's years'-long argument was that once slavery ended, the states needed to reconstruct their constitutions and laws and to reform their customs. When all state residents enjoyed adequately equal legal rights and met their legal responsibilities, then the destabilizing prewar violence that had triggered secession and civil war would disappear from the reformed Union.

By early 1862 Chase was already proposing the abandonment of the colonization idea and the arming of black males, a shorthand for southern slaves, for relatively few blacks lived in the free states; by early 1864 Chase also was advocating political rights for blacks. Lincoln temporized on these points. They threatened to wedge apart the several factions of the Republican–War Democrat coalition.

In addition to his view of slavery as immoral, Chase shifted toward a perception of the need for biracial political and legal equality. Evidence from Treasury agents, army officers, and churchmen in occupied areas of the South convinced him that the Confederacy lived fundamentally on the basis of slave labor and that even where frank slavery was curtailed, few blacks broke the bonds of slaverylike involuntary servitude. As an example of his shift, in March 1862 Chase noted in his journal the visit to his office of a Baltimorean, the Reverend Richard Fuller, who owned plantations on the Carolina islands that were in Union hands. Fuller "asked advice as to the course he should pursue in regard to his plantations and slaves at Port Royal. He wished to know what were his [legal property] rights in respect to them. Told him that, as a loyal man, he was Proprietor of the *land*. How about the negroes? [Fuller] asked. They were free, I replied. He thought his right to them was the same as his right to the land. Told him opinions would differ on that point, but that, for one, I should never consent to the involuntary reduction to Slavery of one of the negroes who had been in the service of the Government."

Further irking the harassed president, Chase kept raising the level of the Union's war aims, noting in his journal on one occasion: "How much better would be a manly protest against prejudice against color!—and a wise effort to give freemen homes in America!"* Driven by deep moral imperatives, by the end of 1862 Lincoln accepted some of Chase's views, yet the warmth that had characterized their prewar encounters was not revived.

Chase continued nevertheless to advocate as a postwar alternative the possibility earlier viewed as improbable and undesirable. He envisaged nationwide biracial cohabitation on terms made wonderfully more decent than master-slave, terms achieved through the equalization of legal rights and even political rights. Before the war Chase had pioneered freedom national ideas as a defense against aggressive proslavery advocates. Since then, wartime patriotism, piety, and a new insight into blacks' capacities, garnered from the Treasury's social experiments in the Carolinas and elsewhere, inspired him to escalate his prewar concepts to advocacy of freedom-plus-equality in the laws of the nation and of every state. This position was not shrewd for an unpopular treasury secretary who wanted to weld the coalitions of power brokers needed to win a presidential nomination from either major party, much less to win an election or to regain Lincoln's trust in Chase's sense of good political timing.

A much stronger war secretary than Cameron, Stanton meanwhile preempted Chase's Carolina social experiments. From 1862 to 1865, however, confiscation and trade-control frictions flared up everywhere around the contracting Confederacy. Despite their differences about jurisdiction, Stanton and Chase remained personal friends and effective colleagues. Unlike Lincoln or Chase, the administration's "Mars" had no political ambitions. Stanton's abrasive homefront procedures against anti-Unionists incurred even more criticism than the taxes and inflation associated with Chase's Treasury operations. Far closer than Chase to Lincoln in personal terms, Stanton understood that public men were almost certain to have their words and actions misunderstood. Both men feared the horrible gulf of national bankruptcy. But Chase more than Stanton knew from the data crossing his desk daily the awful proximity of that chasm.

---

*John Niven et al., eds., *The Salmon P. Chase Papers*, vol. 1, *Journals, 1829–1872* (Kent, Ohio: Kent State University Press, 1993), 331, 362.

Burdened by the increasing weight of the Union's fiscal needs, Chase was keenly aware of the political consequences possible from every Union battle loss, internal security improvisation, inflationary tick, and change in blacks' legal, social, and economic status. Yet both in the cabinet and publicly, he preached persistently about the necessity to elevate the Union's war aims. As open-minded, morally driven, and politically ambitious as Chase, Lincoln would also shift, but more slowly than Chase, who hectored Lincoln repeatedly on the need for quicker and grander action and several times threatened to resign.

Resisting Chase's pace and importunity, not his premises, in 1863 Lincoln proclaimed emancipation for slaves, an amnesty for whites, and a standard reconstruction procedure for unsurrendered rebel states. This policy, and the effects of Lincoln's decision early that year to recruit blacks into the Union's armies, a step that Chase had advocated for a year or more, thereby opened, widened, and improved America's road to total abolition, at least potentially.

Chase understood that a major reason slowing Lincoln's commitment to nationwide abolition as a war aim was the unclear consequent legal status of millions of present slaves. States determined citizenship, both federal and state. Free states defined black residents as citizens. But slave states denied that status to all bondsmen and, in practice, to almost all free black residents or sojourners. No federal definition existed of the status or the privileges of national citizenship except the largely irrelevant 1823 *Corfield v. Coryell* opinion and the overwhelmingly disesteemed 1857 *Dred Scott* decision.

His Treasury responsibilities raised diverse questions for Chase about blacks' citizenship and derivative legal rights, and the status, rights, and duties of states in the federal Union, questions he would encounter in *In re Turner* and *Texas v. White* and for which his wartime experiences helped to ready him. For example, concerning early Union army–Treasury enclaves off the Carolinas, Chase complained in his journal (pp. 362, 391) that in August 1862 Lincoln had revoked Gen. David Hunter's order arming "disciplined loyal Southern men—black, to be sure, but good soldiers and true." Soon thereafter he reiterated the ancient legal axiom that allegiance deserved protection, asserting in his journal that "every real [southern] loyalist [was black,] a man and a citizen."

Congress' 1861 Confiscation Act concerning rebels' property and the revocation of the fugitive slave law had left unanswered many vital questions. Chase had therefore to deal piecemeal with uncertainties arising about runaways' legal status in the numerous labor contracts that Treasury field agents contrived for thousands of blacks, often en masse, with ostensibly loyal white landowners—sometimes the latter were the blacks' erstwhile owners. Elsewhere customs officers detained a New Jersey cargo ship skipper who, like many northern merchantmen, was black. No slave state included blacks, slave or free, as state citizens, and no national branch had yet defined national citizenship. Federal law restricted coastal licenses to citizens. Were such skippers and runaways citizens of the United States?

Desiring to escalate the issues, in 1862 Chase recorded in his journal (pp. 391, 467) that he "called on Attorney-General [Bates] about [the] citizenship of colored men." He asked also whether the privileges of national citizenship included the vote. An undistinguished lawyer and timid politician, a conservative antislavery Missouri Republican but not yet an abolitionist, Edward Bates was "averse to expressing [an] official opinion." Chase finally extracted a reply, however.

Bates answered Chase rhetorically: "Is a man legally incapacitated to be a citizen of the United States by the sole fact that he is . . . not a white man?" History provided no neat answer, and the attorney general offered an official opinion in which he asked,

> Who is a citizen? What constitutes a citizen of the United States? I have often been pained by the fruitless search in our law books and the records of our courts for a clear and satisfactory definition of the phrase citizen of the United States. I find no such definition, no authoritative establishment of the meaning of the phrase, neither by a course of judicial decision in our courts nor by the continued and consentaneous action of the different branches of our political government. For aught I see to the contrary, the subject is now as little understood in its details and elements, and the question as open to argument and to speculative criticism, as it was at the beginning of the government. Eighty years of practical enjoyment of citizenship, under the Constitution, have not sufficed to teach us either the exact meaning of the word or the constituent elements of the thing we prize so highly.

Still, Bates lectured Chase, "the thing we prize so highly . . . the naked, unassisted fact of [federal] citizenship," had never included the right to vote or to hold public office. Almost every state denied the ballot to blacks. Every state excluded women, minors, paupers, lunatics, felons, and career soldiers from voting, yet all, including blacks, might be federal citizens if

Congress so willed. The Constitution did not define national citizenship or, except for "the highest national functionaries," the qualifications for federal offices, and it left voting rights where the Framers had found them, "resting upon the fact of home, birth, and . . . the laws of the several States." The states had no "controlling [national] authority over them" in these matters, "no limit to their power . . . but their own prudence and discretion." Therefore states' denials of suffrage or office to blacks no more demeaned state citizenship than denials to "a white woman or child." Finally entering where Chase wanted him to go, however, Bates, again rejecting the *Dred Scott* majority position, concluded that every "member of the nation . . . [including] the child in the cradle and its father in the Senate . . . [are] politically and legally, . . . equally citizens of the United States," that every individual's allegiance incurred the "reciprocal obligation" of protection by the federal government.*

Chase imposed on himself a duty to sway Lincoln past even these mainstream Republican positions of 1861–1862 to nationwide abolitionism and legal and political rights for blacks. Issues Chase had been raising since 1862 about individuals' legal status and the character and significance of national citizenship in this federal Union of states, and about the legal status of the rebel states, would resonate past Appomattox and resound in *In re Turner* and *Texas v. White.*

Lincoln had taken a big step forward in Chase's estimation when on January 1, 1863, the president ordered that black volunteers and draftees be admitted into the Union's military. Midyear antidraft and antiwar riots in major northern cities were also blatantly racist and antiemancipation, a fact allowing Chase and other champions of abolitionism to underscore the brave battlefield record of black Union army regiments. Echoing points that Chase had been urging in cabinet meetings, Lincoln advised the public in late August 1863, on the eve of off-year elections, that blacks were earning legal equality through their patriotic service and that since the preceding January the Union army, reinforced by black units, was dealing severe blows to the Confederacy. Chase agreed that arming blacks, especially slaves, was a great triumph for antislavery forces. But it still fell short of Chase's heightened war aim, a Union of race-blind legal rights in every rebellious state, perhaps also one day political rights in every state.

By late 1863 Chase was edging toward a position that at least in the re-

---

*U.S. Attorney General, *Official Opinions of the United States Attorneys-General* (Washington, D.C., 1791–), 10:383.

conquered states the nation should allow no halfway legal status to exist between servitude and equality. Once allowed, racial bigotry, like a toxic weed embedded in legal and economic relationships, would poison freedom's healthy fruits and thereby deny his basic proposition that a free society was intrinsically more moral than one with slaves or with anything less than full freedom, the latter defined as legal and political equality. State reconstructions, Chase asserted, needed more than deletion of formal slavery clauses from their constitutions, the requirement Lincoln stipulated in his December 1863 executive order on that process. To Chase this repudiation of formal slavery excised a primary state wrong. But Lincoln's scalpel did not cut deeply enough to satisfy Chase. Truly repentant residents of the occupied, reconstructing states should be required to excise from their constitutions statutes, case law, and marketplace customs, the slaverylike vestiges that in immoral ways demeaned free labor.

To Chase, Lincoln's reluctance to make the Union's war aim the total abolition of formal slavery and of involuntary servitude's demeaning remnants was overly timid irresolution. Both men suffered from accumulated fatigue. Then in earliest 1864, possibly but improbably without Chase's knowledge, would-be president-makers among his supporters published a circular opposing Lincoln's renomination and extolling Chase. In June 1864 he and Lincoln clashed over a relatively minor Treasury patronage appointment. Pushing too hard, Chase tendered his resignation, as he had done several times earlier. This time Lincoln accepted it. Chase had failed to realize that since early in the Civil War the scandals in Treasury field operations that he had neglected to prevent or control were muddying his reputation for morality on which his ability to influence events depended.

Meanwhile, uncertainties increased about what constituted an American state: its geography or its residents? If the latter, what minimum legal rights did states' residents enjoy by virtue of the end of slavery? What category of residents forming a state should the Union trust to run it—overtly repentant Confederates, consistent Unionists, or federal officials, including the now-maligned Treasury officials? In part because licensing and patronage scandals curtailed his political clout, Chase had to wait until the *In re Turner* and *Texas v. White* cases for opportunities to answer such questions in a manner generous enough to include blacks in states' politics. For the remainder of the tumultuous year 1864, Chase, his own supporters easily flattened by the Lincoln steamroller at the Republican nominating convention, observed events from the policy sidelines but kept himself well informed about shared concerns by congressmen, Treasury insiders, and antislavery (now abolitionist) comrades.

Although Lincoln's laggard pace toward nationwide abolition and equal legal and political rights for blacks had troubled the militant Chase, pace there was. Indeed, while still toying with colonization schemes, Lincoln had secretly lessened differences between him and Chase, edging toward votes as well as freedom for slaves.

In spring 1864, writing to Louisiana Unionist Michael Hahn, soon to be Lincoln's choice as governor of that showpiece wartime Reconstruction state, Lincoln had dared "barely [to] suggest for your private consideration whether some of the colored people may not be let in [as voters]—as for instance, the very intelligent, and especially those who have fought gallantly in our ranks." Prophetically, Lincoln suggested to Hahn that even token black voters might help "in some trying time to come, to keep the jewel of liberty within the family of freedom." But the president stressed, "This is only a suggestion, not to the public, but to you alone."* Hahn referred Lincoln's daring idea to Louisiana's Unionist legislators, who rejected it.

Almost as if to balance disappointments at this rejection and a similar one by supposedly reconstructed Arkansas lawmakers, the jewel of liberty flared with sudden brilliance because, as a prominent New York lawyer, George Templeton Strong, recorded in his diary in late 1864:

> The Hon. old Roger B. Taney has earned the gratitude of his country by dying at last. Better late than never. . . . Even should Lincoln be defeated [in the 1864 presidential elections], he will have time to appoint a new Chief Justice, and he cannot appoint anybody worse than Taney. Chase may very possibly be the man. Curious coincidence that the judge [Taney] whose opinion in the Dred Scott case proved him the most faithful of slaves to the South should have been dying while his own state, Maryland, was solemnly extinguishing slavery within her borders by voting [approvingly] on her new anti-slavery constitution. . . . Two ancient abuses and evils were perishing together. . . . "Maryland, my Maryland," . . . has undergone an organic change of structure. . . . The Confederacy will have nothing to say to Maryland as a free state.†

---

*Roy P. Basler et al., eds., *The Collected Works of Abraham Lincoln*, 8 vols. (New Brunswick, N.J.: Rutgers University Press, 1953), 7:243.

†Allen Nevins and Milton H. Thomas, eds., *The Diary of George Templeton Strong*, 4 vols. (New York: Macmillan, 1952), 3:500–501.

But Chase would, in *In re Turner*, for Maryland's new antislavery constitution and apprentice law triggered that case.

In December 1864 Lincoln named Chase to succeed Taney. Soon after Chase donned his judicial robes in earliest 1865, he administered the prescribed oath of office to Lincoln, the first second-term president since Jackson. With tenure until March 1869 and with a Congress dominated by their party supporters, Lincoln's second term would be defined, it seemed, by the new, then-pending Thirteenth Amendment, a commitment delighting Chase. Nationalizing freedom by destroying slavery far transcended their earlier shared freedom national views of containing bondage. As the viable base for the nation's postwar agenda once slavery died, that amendment, Lincoln stated publicly in early 1865, was "a King's cure [that is, a total solution] for all . . . [the nation's] evils . . . a very fitting if not indispensable adjunct to the winding up of the great difficulty," the still-unclear status of the South's states and of black Americans. Most of the latter were already free because of the effects of his 1863 emancipation and reconstruction orders and, Lincoln predicted, all would be free once the Thirteenth Amendment gained formal ratification.*

In December 1865 the requisite number of states did formally ratify the pending amendment. But as Lincoln and Chase acknowledged, tens of thousands of black Union soldiers had contributed essentially to the event nine months earlier, at Appomattox. The amendment's real ratification was the Confederacy's dissolution.

As excited as the president, Chase was subsequently further delighted by reports of Lincoln's April 11, 1865, address to a crowd that gathered outside the White House, celebrating the happy imminence of the Confederacy's surrender. Instead of his secret recommendation to Hahn of a year earlier, concerning only Louisiana, Lincoln advocated publicly for all the states North and South what Chase had been urging, that literate blacks and black Union army veterans vote and that all states educate residents' children, white and black. John Wilkes Booth equated this proposal to "nigger citizenship" and, three days after the president's happy, impromptu April 11 speech, saw adequate reason to murder Lincoln and to try also to assassinate Seward and perhaps Grant.

*Basler, *Collected Works of Abraham Lincoln*, 8:399–405.

Lincoln died at the height of his successes, precisely when the nation was realizing the war aims toward which Chase had been urging him. Chase's reputation suffered then and since both because of the scandals in some Treasury operations in the South and because he had criticized Lincoln and in 1864 had even dared to try to supplant him in the White House. Considering Lincoln's overwhelming mastery of the Republican party's 1864 nominating convention and of the subsequent election campaign, Chase's competition with him was more presumptuous than irreverent.

Our knowledge of events since Appomattox allows certain insights. Much evidence from our own time suggests that like the wars they succeed, postwar periods spawn complex problems for the winners as well as for the losers. But in spring 1865, Chase, like Lincoln, was optimistic that the Thirteenth Amendment was a cure-all for the ills that had ailed the nation.

He was optimistic, not naive. Optimism governed in Congress also but had not precluded a nagging concern on Capitol Hill that future Taneys or Calhouns might resurrect *Dred Scott*-like arguments, denying the nation authority to implement the amendment's bans against slavery and involuntary servitude. Therefore Congress had included the amendment's implementation clause.

Then, in spring 1866, in wholly unanticipated circumstances, Congress, with its pioneering Civil Rights Act, found it necessary and proper to spell out in detail the amendment's brief yet universal prohibitions against any individual or any authority on any level of the federal system holding any other individual in situations amounting to slavery or involuntary servitude. *In re Turner* soon would result from these situations and *Texas v. White* would not wait long in the wings. In deciding those cases and others, Chase tried to lay to rest the unforeseeable but recurring uncertainties that in the decade after Appomattox brought forth two more amendments to the Constitution, Military Reconstruction, and several antivigilante laws.

In spring 1865, however, as Chase readied for his duties as chief justice, he was both optimistic about the near future and pleased by his accomplishments. His deftness in money matters had helped to make the government's credit far firmer in 1865 than in 1861. In addition to providing at least adequate fiscal resources for the Union's increased military requirements, Chase was proud of the fact that he had been a central player in the extended efforts to make abolition the price of reunion. As Chase and other slavery-focused reformers saw matters, slavery had linked the Civil War's causes, aims, and results, thereby justifying the Union's extraordinary wartime expedients. Energized by antislavery activists such as Chase, the nation's armies and governing institutions had made both Appomattox and the free, orderly, better future possible that Chase had been seeking for decades.

Optimism like theirs echoed in countless speeches, sermons, commencement addresses, and judges' charges to juries in 1865. A central message was that measures needed to cope with peace would be easily provided by existing government institutions or by a very few new ones that could be created through familiar political processes. A later critic of these views, Charles Francis Adams, Jr., recalled a conversation soon after Appomattox with an Illinois farmer-legislator. In response to Adams's prophecy that legal, constitutional, and political difficulties awaited states then contemplating the regulation of railroad rates, the Illinoisan replied: "Difficult! Why I don't think I should have any trouble in drawing up an act in half an hour which would settle the whole thing."*

Yet the "whole thing" involved in government's efforts to promote race-blind equality still remains unsettled in the sense of an agreement about means, if not ends, over 130 years after Appomattox.

*Charles Francis Adams, Jr., *Remarks on a National Railroad Commission* (1882), 4.

CHAPTER 7

Matters Momentous and
Mundane in Reconstruction

Although "Negro Suffrage was a thing to speak of with bated breath and with many a shudder," shrewd journalist Whitelaw "Agate" Reid reminded *Cincinnati Gazette* readers on July 23, 1865, Lincoln had at last committed himself to that goal, not least because Chase had been pressuring him toward it, the newsman concluded. Even while mourning Lincoln, Chase shared in the optimism that suffused the northern states through the remainder of 1865. It sprang from the prevailing confidence that the nation possessed both the appropriate institutions and constitutional authority for realizing at once the pacific future that would inevitably be far better than the slavery- and secession-shrouded past.

Sharing in this benign mood Chase relaxed more than he had in years. He lived in a grand home in Washington with his daughter Kate and a large staff. Indefatigable Kate made it a social center of the sort that he, before apprenticing for Wirt, had hardly dreamed of entering, much less owning. Married to a wealthy Rhode Island senator, Kate devoted her time to him and her father as social hostess and political amanuensis. Her beauty and relentless pursuit of the presidency for her father alienated many people, including Mary Lincoln, which distressed Kate not at all.

Like the restored but war-weary nation it served, the Supreme Court that Chase joined in early 1865 needed badly to enjoy a recuperative interval. Its term extended only until March 1865, and its docket dealt with relatively minor hangover wartime matters and business contentions whose parties enjoyed Supreme Court jurisdiction only because of their interstate situations. Although during that term the Court did declare unconstitutional a section of a very minor federal statute concerning the still-infant U.S. Court of Claims (*Gordon v. U. S.*, 69 U.S. 561), it remains accurate to conclude, as did eminent scholar Charles Fairman, that "never again would there be a [Supreme Court] term wherein so few [significant] questions were answered."* This hiatus surprised persons who, with glee or fear, in part because of his espousal of votes for blacks, had predicted that once heading the Court, Chase would try immediately to push that institution toward new, radical frontiers of racial equality.

Not so. A Supreme Court justice may lust, as Chase did, after the presidency, but even a chief justice must consider the issues in litigation before him. In 1867 *In re Turner* allowed Chase to rule on a black female's federally protectable legal rights as affected by her state's racially discriminatory apprenticeship statute. Then in 1869 *Texas v. White* gave Chase an opportunity to link *Turner* implications about individuals' rights to large issues of states' responsibilities and to lift both to the Supreme Court level. The *Texas* litigation involved another moral issue that was sacred to Chase—that social order required the inviolability of all debts, private and public. He seized the *Texas* opportunity, therefore, to lecture the states about their obligations to honor contracts, a topic not disassociated from *Turner*.

Events intervening between 1865 and 1869 brought Chase to both those positions. In spring 1865, odds seemed high to Chase that Lincoln's successor, the Tennessean Andrew Johnson, would begin his administration from the policy height of black suffrage that Lincoln had reached. Chase signaled his own symbolic adherence to racial equality under law by admitting to practice before the Court a black protégé of Sen. Charles Sumner's, John Rock, an unprecedented action that satisfyingly mocked the *Dred Scott* decision. In Ohio, news of Rock's admission inspired racist doggerel in the far-right *Columbus Crisis* (January 15, 1865):

> Chase on de bench,
> Nigger at de bar,
> Go away white man,
> What you doin' dar?

But Chase intruded no other blacks to alter the complexion of the Court. Indeed the unending flow of humdrum lawsuits much like those any state judge handled bored Chase. The resulting doldrums, however, did let him and the associate justices take each other's measure.

*Charles Fairman, *Reconstruction and Reunion, 1864–1888: Part One* (New York: Macmillan, 1971), 133.

Ranked by party lines, the Democrats included Georgia's James Wayne, Pennsylvania's Robert Grier, Maine's Nathan Clifford, New York's Samuel Nelson, and Tennessee's John Catron (who was dying as Chase joined the Court). Although less confrontationally than Taney, these men had criticized Lincoln's wartime executive orders and Congress' crisis legislation, especially the measures on what today would be called internal security. Besides Chase, Lincoln's five appointees were Californian Stephen J. Field, a War Democrat turned Republican, and the relatively old-guard Republicans David Davis of Illinois, Ohioan Noah Swayne, and Iowa's distinguished Samuel Miller. Their discordant personalities and variant views on constitutional aspects of major public policies would soon involve the justices in contentions as fierce as any that were to consume congressmen and President Johnson.

During the quiescent atmosphere of the Court that year, Chase took time to deal with his own title. Using his quick-study talents to master the Court's intricate customs and procedural rules, he was troubled that his new position had traditionally been titled chief justice of the Supreme Court. Wanting further to obliterate the *Dred Scott* stain of favoring any one section of the nation and symbolically to underscore the reunifying results of the war, Chase stipulated that henceforth he be called chief justice of the United States. As quickly as the general public had accepted his earlier decision when treasury secretary to have "In God We Trust" added to all minted coins, the altered style rooted quickly in the nation's legal communities. Thereafter, each day of the Court's session, at eleven o'clock in the morning, a functionary cried out: "The Honorable Chief Justice and the Associate Justices of the Supreme Court of the United States!" Everyone rose as the chief justice and associates marched solemnly into the ornate Court chamber located in the Capitol's basement beneath the Senate. The justices bowed to the attorneys standing at the bar waiting to be heard, and the lawyers returned the courtesy, whereupon the crier completed the brief but impressive ceremony by uttering another phrase that to Chase was the law's necessary component: "God save the United States of America and this Honorable Court!"

Among the justices Chase was less a king than a baron among barons. A chief justice governed but did not rule. Chase administered Court business, but his vote in cases was equal only to that of any justice. He could admit Rock, specify his own title, partially set the Court's docket, and, except as a justice specifically asked to initiate judgment on a pending lawsuit, assign cases. But Chase could not control the speed at which his colleagues proceeded to decisions, or, of course, the decisions themselves. Unlike the two famous preceding chief justices, John Marshall and, in lesser ways, Roger Taney, on many momentous matters of public policy Chase would only rarely be able to convince testy fellow justices to bend their views to his own.

The unquantifiable effects of a personality like Chase's are made the more impenetrable when factored in with the similarly craggy attitudes of several of the other justices. He had achieved success in elective politics essentially by exploiting a single moral issue, slavery, on which, over decades, he had shifted only marginally, which meant that he was expert in sermonizing congregations of voters. But as a lawyer he had rarely been equally successful in his numerous court appearances on behalf of runaway slaves and the people who aided them.

As chief justice, Chase assigned circuits to the associate justices, a traditional duty that received his high priority. Few civil and criminal lawsuits ever reached the Supreme Court. Instead, the great majority of complainants ended their pursuit of federal justice in a district court. The small percentage of cases that escalated to a circuit court were heard by a two-judge panel consisting of the sitting district judge and a peripatetic Supreme Court justice assigned by the chief justice to serve several districts, usually in or near the associate justice's home state. His job, Chase confided to a correspondent, J. D. Van Buren, on March 28, 1868, early taught him that "it is only as a Circuit Judge that the Chief Justice, or any other Justice . . . , has, individually, any considerable power."*

His view was too modest. Chase's circuit included the states of reclaimed Virginia and formerly slaveholding Maryland. Issues reaching him for adjudication during the first postwar years became virtual dress rehearsals for *In re Turner* and *Texas v. White.* Deriving from the uncertain status and rights of blacks in the former Confederate states and from the standing of those states in the federal Union, in 1865 those issues were already dividing President Johnson from his wartime political allies, the Republican–War Democrat Union majority in Congress, even as Chase began traveling his first postwar circuit.

Chase Letterbooks, ser. 4 (Washington, D.C.: Manuscripts Division, Library of Congress), 114:339.

The circuit took him into Virginia, the defunct Confederacy's keystone. Early in the war bluecoats had aided antisecession Virginians in gaining control of the state's westernmost counties and in setting up there a West Virginia state government loyal to the Union. At a time of sharp reverses for the Union almost everywhere else, the reclamation of even this relatively small pocket of rebeldom and its transformation into a militarily strategic loyal state lifted northerners' morale. But the process of statemaking involved in the birth of West Virginia was of doubtful constitutionality, for the Constitution's Article 4, Section 3, stipulated that "new States may be admitted by the Congress into this Union; but no new State shall be formed or erected within the Jurisdiction of any other State; nor any State be formed by the Junction of two or more States, or parts of States, without the Consent of the Legislatures of the States concerned as well as of the Congress" and Article 5 added that "no State, without its Consent, shall be deprived of its equal Suffrage in the Senate."

In an effort to cloak the proceedings with a semblance of procedural regularity, a puppet Union government in Virginia approved the secession of its western counties. But legal, constitutional, and political questions persisted. Was West Virginia a state? Who should decide? The paramilitary diminution of a parent state's territory and creation of an offspring state was unique in America's history. Only the Court's 1849 *Luther v. Borden* decision (48 U.S. 1 [1849]), resulting from Rhode Island's Dorr War, seemed to be at all relevant. The Court had preferred then to duck the burden of choosing which of two contenders was the legitimate government of a state. That was a "political question," the justices had declared and had passed the choice on to Congress.

In 1865 most members of Congress had been elected on war issues in November 1864. A relative unknown, President Johnson was a former Democrat turned Union Republican. His selection by Lincoln to be his running mate in 1864 reflected the Tennessean's antisecession stance in 1861 and his subsequent service as the military governor of his state.

Even as the war wound down in early 1865 party alignments were shifting. Destined to be rejoined by the president within a year, hard-and-fast northern Democrats welcomed news from the South that party organizations were reviving quickly. Soon northern and southern Democrats would again coalesce on terms that, though recognizing emancipation, were otherwise of a nature that Calhoun might have approved.

Boiled down, those terms drawn from the far right of contemporary alternatives envisaged the South's states as bottom-weighted dolls springing up immediately after Appomattox to full statehood. No penalties, no further confiscations, no disfranchisements or exclusions of former rebels from federal or state offices, and no federal stipulations about blacks' legal status—these demands formed the common chorus. Federal aid to the South was welcomed but no diminution of states' rights was admitted.

For their part, far-left Radical Republicans feared the loss of zeal among supporters now that peace was won and secession and slavery were both defunct. Radicals and moderate Republicans alike were keenly aware of the fact that abolition of slavery meant that the Constitution's three-fifths clause (Article 1, Section 2), which since 1789 had given southern whites a disproportionately loud voice in the House of Representatives, was now as defunct as slavery itself. But this meant that southern blacks would count as whole persons in determining the number of their state's delegations to Congress. An increase in political power to losers in a civil war was unique in history. To balance the numbers, Radical Republicans, echoing the point that Chase had urged on Lincoln, insisted in 1865 that blacks should also vote in their state elections as a federal right.

Whole galaxies of fluctuating intermediate positions existed in both parties and among factions, often depending on transitory circumstances. To Chase, in 1865 the positions of both far-right Democrats and far-left Republicans were little connected to the real-life situations facing millions of blacks and whites in the southern states. The Treasury agents' wartime social experiments in the South and the related work there of numerous private welfare agencies had given him intimate familiarity with the level of distress. Further, Chase's new judicial duties presented him primarily with issues of individuals' economic wants and legal rights. Unsurprisingly, therefore, Chase's immersion in these concerns was misperceived as a diminution of his commitment to race-blind political rights. He did give that matter less priority. Yet he did so only because he gave higher priority to the practical enjoyment by both races of decently level legal and economic playing fields.

And so as Chase grappled with his new work he was comfortable with the midroad Republican consensus that the South's states remain in the "grasp of war" until a new national policy emerged. One was needed because in formal terms none had survived Lincoln's death. No one knew, however, when a viable Reconstruction policy would emerge. And to Chase time was an enemy of law and order.

He worried less about the several hardening theories then circulating about postwar Reconstruction than he did about immediate contentions, some of which were already flaring into firefights. For example, private parties in Virginia and West Virginia were disputing the ownership of assets. In legal theory states defined private property and confirmed titles to its ownership. Some Virginia claimants denied that West Virginia existed. West Virginians wanted the Court's implicit recognition of the new state's separate status by providing it a federal circuit distinct from Virginia's. Chase was anxious to transform into lawsuits the threatening violence about the large economic, social, and political interests affected by Virginia's bifurcation.

Accordingly, on January 7, 1865, his first day as chief justice, after consulting his new colleagues, all of whom concurred (except for one who was ill), he announced that West Virginia was indeed a state for the limited but important administrative purpose of assigning to it the federal district and circuit court facilities and services that all states deserved.

Overeager Democrats and excessively excited journalists misconstrued Chase's pragmatic administrative ruling on West Virginia as favoring the Democrats' notions of instant, completed Reconstruction. Not so. The postwar period was only beginning, not ending. Nevertheless, implications existed in Chase's 1865 ruling on West Virginia that deserved and received attention. Could or would federal judges conjure up analogous rulings for other former Confederate states? Such rulings might bridge or widen the increasing gap in politics between the Republican left and the Democratic right.

Equally mundane matters needed fixing first if social order in the South was to be preserved. Briefly, what worried Chase most was the legal condition of the multitudes of ordinary civil relationships that residents in those states had effected during the war years. At a time when concepts of the sanctity of contracts were hardening into a kind of legal ideology, it was abhorrent to think that every private contract, marriage, birth, death, divorce, sale, purchase, deed, lease, partnership, or professional license occurring during four war years in the seceded South was invalidated by the disappearance of the Confederate authorities who had issued or recorded them. What of court decisions by Confederate judges? Was every imprisoned felon and vagrant automatically freed, every private debt dishonored, every tax law abrogated, every public institution, including schools, asylums, and hospitals, immediately to close because deprived of formal legal status?

If all wartime civil relationships were voided by the Union's triumph, then, Chase feared, like slavery in the past, vast legal uncertainties, monetary injuries, and social unrest must result everywhere in southern society and from there contaminate the rest of the nation. As a moralistic antislavery activist he had condemned slavery for decades, in part because the system of servitude produced generations of bastards; that is, the slaveowning states had not allowed slaves to enter into any civil contracts, including that of marriage. Chase was incapable of spreading to millions of whites the moral taint blacks suffered from widespread illegitimacy. In order not to play the role of a Typhoid Mary, however, Chief Justice Chase had to choose not among Reconstruction theories but rather between two contemporary legal interpretations of the consequences of wars.

One construal that was attracting Radical Republicans was that losers in a civil war lost everything. A second view favored by spokesmen for conservative Democrats generally and for southern Democrats nearly unanimously was that the Civil War was a war between two nations. Therefore, the total Union triumph left nonwar private legal relationships, obligations, and rights undisturbed.

In 1861, the Supreme Court, its members still essentially those of *Dred Scott* notoriety, had decided the *Prize Cases* (67 U.S. 635 [1863]). By a narrow majority the justices had sustained Lincoln's early emergency measures, including those that initiated naval blockades of southern ports and seizures as "prizes" of hostiles' waterborne property. In effect the justices sanctioned a middle view: that the Civil War partook of the characteristics of both a war between nations and one wholly domestic.

Chase, like Lincoln, was greatly relieved by the Court's *Prize Cases* straddle, and in Chase's opinion the justices further redeemed themselves by their *Gelpcke v. Dubuque* decision that stabilized municipal debts in particular and the obligations of all public debts in general. Chase's actions suggested that after 1865 he mixed the *Prize Cases* view that the Civil War was one of dual nature with the *Gelpcke* view that governments on every level of the federal system, as well as all private persons, were required morally, legally, and constitutionally to honor their contracts, including those on apprenticeships and debts, but to do so with all cards on the table.

Although in Chase's opinion the justices had partially redeemed themselves by their *Prize* and *Gelpcke* holdings, other wartime decisions by the Court were less pleasing to the overburdened treasury secretary and less attractive to the new chief justice. Those precedents, those decisions of 1863 and 1864, left doubtful the validity of diverse federal improvisations aimed at apprehending active anti-Unionists and barring potential ones from holding public offices, whether elective or appointive, or, among other rights or privileges, from practicing law in federal courts. As of 1865 these wartime decisions by the Court implied uncertain validity about Chase's implementation of the Confiscation Acts and assignments to blacks of lands and other property abandoned by refugee masters.

Thus, whole galaxies of uncertainties accompanied Chase in his circuits and in the Supreme Court's full-bench proceedings. Were the wartime exclusionary loyalty requirements still in effect? If so, then the complexion of the South's postwar state and local officialdom would indeed be redefined, for the great majority of white males could not so swear. If these requirements were no longer in effect, would recent Confederates who were state judges, attorneys, and jurors by reason of President Johnson's pardon-and-amnesty executive orders beginning in March 1865, give blacks and white Unionists equal justice? And, in light of Chase's emphasis on the uninterrupted obligations of private contracts, what of uncompleted or partially completed private contracts for the purchase, lease, or sale of slaves?

In his circuits beginning in 1865, Chase heard and decided hundreds of private claims, including Elizabeth Turner's, in which the parties' interests and responsibilities depended on judges agreeing that wartime civil commitments survived into the postwar years, and other claims that the minor Confederate officials deserved insulation from damage claims for reasonable actions taken under orders. When deciding *In re Turner* in 1867 and *Texas v. White* in 1869, Chase had the great satisfaction of stabilizing a more decent legal status for black Americans and of defining usefully the nature of a state in the federal system.

But he was destined to live too long. As years passed he observed the perversion of those opinions by his fellow justices. Over Chase's unavailing dissents they greatly eroded whites' thin commitments to race-blind equal legal rights under law. And in 1873, shortly before Chase died, the justices mocked his earlier emphases on the uninterrupted obligations of nonwar civil contracts by sustaining the present obligations of prewar contracts for the sale of slaves.

In 1865, however, Chase held his circuit courts, confident that America's history and law provided sure guides for public policies and private conduct. Perhaps with an eye cocked on a future run for the presidency, he decided not to let his circuit court rulings slide into oblivion. Instead, he contrived ways to keep the bench and bar as well as the general public aware of his rulings, for he was proud of them. Beginning with his administrative order on West Virginia, Chase had his rulings reprinted in the nation's premier legal periodicals. By this device he hoped to preview for the bar and the public issues of political concern that were likely to reach the Supreme Court's docket and implicitly to buy time by indicating to impatient antagonists such as individuals on the Virginia–West Virginia border that federal justice was on its way.

Further to spread those tidings, Chase had at his command another channel of communication to attorneys nationwide, the reporter of the Supreme Court. That official edited, published, and sold the texts of the justices' decisions and opinions to subscribing lawyers across the country. But the justices had little respect for the incumbent reporter, John W. Wallace, partly because he larded the *Supreme Court Reports* with his own estimates of the quality of the justices' decisions and those of the state judges, whose rulings losing parties appealed to the high court.

No consistent reporting of federal circuit decisions existed then. If circuit decisions appeared in print, they surfaced often in inaccurate, truncated, or biased form, in local bar publications or even in obscure county-seat newspapers. As he would in *In re Turner,* Chase anticipated that after initial decisions in the federal circuit courts, momentous matters would be appealed to the Supreme Court. Therefore accurate records of his circuit proceedings were desirable, perhaps invaluable. Such records would provide the whole Court with a full report, reestablish Chase's legitimacy among the old antislavery leadership who had criticized some of his wartime policies on black labor, and be available also for exploitation by his supporters if in 1868 he dared a run at the presidency.

To these ends Chase recruited an unofficial reporter for his circuit, Bradley T. Johnson, a Virginia lawyer and former Confederate army officer whom President Johnson had pardoned. Johnson served Chase as circuit reporter from 1865 until the latter's death in 1873, while simultaneously practicing law in the same court. This relationship invited conflicts of interest that would be impermissible today but that apparently raised no eyebrows then.

Chase and Johnson educated each other. The latter accepted Chase's positions in *In re Turner* and *Texas v. White*—that the war had altered federalism, leaving it free but still essentially state-centered on ordinary civil relationships and criminal justice yet with the federal rights of the nation's citizens cloaked in the judicial protections of the Thirteenth Amendment and, soon, of the 1866 Civil Rights Act. Perhaps to build political strength in the South and among conservative northern Democrats, but also from his own convictions, Chase, though continuing to emphasize racial equality in law when it was a factor in cases before him, accepted Johnson's views on other, nonrace and nonwar matters of vital importance in workaday civil relationships, including marriage, divorce, wills and estates, and purchase and sale contracts, except for those involving slaves. In 1876 Johnson published Chase's circuit court opinions as a tribute to the deceased chief justice, because, Johnson asserted, they had afforded the nation a sure basis for rapidly recrystallizing the foundations of civil society in the South.

Yet efforts were neither sure nor rapid. Most events of 1865 and 1866 were far outside Chase's ability to control or even to affect. Exceptions included such matters as the West Virginia–Virginia dispute and the legitimization of nonwar private contracts entered into during the war. More momentous events outran Chase's purposes, however, events that were triggered in the White House and that inspired dramatic responses in the South.

Away in their home districts until December 1865, most congressmen, like Chase on his circuit or in Washington, watched those events closely. President Johnson chose not to call a special session of Congress. Instead, through the army he ruled the South unilaterally, except as federal judges, including Chase, were once again about their district and circuit court duties. Moving far more immediately than was possible for Chase or any other federal official, Johnson recrystallized southern society in ways that encouraged superior legal positions for white residents instead of the equalized legal status that Chase had envisaged for whites and blacks. Employing hangover "grasp of war" constitutional theories for his authority, President Johnson superseded Lincoln's wartime state apparatuses and ended the remnants of Chase's social experiments in the South (resettling displaced slaves on rebels' abandoned or confiscated lands), suspended further confiscations, and ordered the army to organize a dozen new "provisional" state governments, over each of which he appointed "provisional governors." These officials initiated constitutional conventions whose delegates recommended popular ratification of the Thirteenth Amendment, a step that voters in some southern states sanctioned only with notorious reluctance. Every provisional governor, convention delegate, voter, and state and local functionary was white. Most were former Confederates or known prosecessionists or both whom Johnson had pardoned, as were the men elected to be those states' U.S. senators and representatives. This swift, presidentially driven rejuvenation of the southern states had immense consequences. Their delegates to Congress realigned quickly with the shifting northern Democratic party. Constitution-bound Republicans, such as Chase and others of the antislavery vanguard with whom he maintained a vast correspondence, began to assert that the prospective augmentation of southern whites' voting strength, which would result from black co-residents' lack of voting rights, justified a more cautious pace in state restoration. It also called their attention sharply to blacks' actual situations, which had more weight than theories about Reconstruction.

From their shared Senate years President Johnson knew Chase's consistent antislavery states' rights constitutional position, one implicitly underscored by the latter's ruling on West Virginia. Aware also that Chase spent weeks in mid-1865 touring much of the South and assuming that he favored admitting the newly reconstructed southern states immediately to representation in Congress, Johnson asked him to report on conditions there.

The president had misjudged the chief justice. As was true of other informed commentators, Chase, in a manner resembling his technique in prewar equity pleadings of quickly mastering impressive amounts and kinds of evidence, using the texts and effects of their own new constitutions, civil and criminal statutes, and justice procedures amassed telling proof against the swift readmission of southern states. Less driven than Chase by a lifetime of moralistic and legalistic antipathy to slavery and of political and legal attempts to curb it, Johnson apparently thought that Chase's well-known ambitions for the presidency would result in a report on the South favorable to Johnson's actions, thus gaining his support for Chase's presidential bid in 1868. By then again a Democrat, Johnson coveted that honor for himself but was unable to win it. American politics has no lower index for a sitting president than inability to control the nominating convention of his own party.

To President Johnson's displeasure Chase concluded that most southern whites were unregenerate and that most southern blacks were oppressed by unobstructed bigotry. Neither they nor white Unionists enjoyed practical legal remedies in the amended state constitutions or in the U.S. Constitution for wrongs committed against them by state officials or private persons.

The calm persisting in the Supreme Court's ornate basement chamber contrasted to the excitement that broke out in December 1865, one floor above, when Congress began its first postwar session. Partisan storms about the legal status of the southern states wracked both Senate and House when, through parliamentary devices, Republican majorities, enraged by the same kinds of evidence that had repelled Chase and apprehensive about the renascent political clout of the reunited Democratic party, first excluded the southern states' delegates-elect and then considered the next steps for the South and the nation.

Those next steps built on evidence accumulated by Congress' new Joint Standing Committee on the Restoration of the Southern States (commonly known as the Reconstruction Committee). Confirming the essential points Chase had made in his report to Johnson, that evidence led to bills extending the life of the Freedmen's Bureau, creating a Civil Rights Act, and proposing a Fourteenth Amendment to the Constitution. Debates on these intimately interwoven measures reflected supporters' convictions that individuals clearly needed some practical federal remedy for outrages committed by states, outrages that were perpetuating black residents' civil and criminal inequalities and leading to involuntary servitude. Illuminated by debates attending these measures, uncertainties proliferating over means and ends and about the status of individuals and of states in laws and constitutions were moving *In re Turner* and *Texas v. White* from prologue to action.

CHAPTER 8

Freedom's Meanings:
States' Wrongs and Citizens' Rights

Former slave Frederick Douglass warned American Antislavery Society members in May 1865 that "all of us had better wait and see what new form this old monster [slavery and slavelike involuntary servitude] will assume, in what new skin this old snake will come forth next" before Congress readmitted the former Confederate states to representation or before the society ended its oversight of events in the South. Douglass's advice that the society's members not relax or disband circulated in its publication the *Liberator* (May 26, 1865). Although resignations from this single-interest private association slowed, they did not end.

By resigning from the Antislavery Society, departing members celebrated the fact that it had achieved its primary goal. They agreed implicitly with Lincoln that the Confederacy's defeat and the impending ratification of the Thirteenth Amendment cured the nation's primary ills, thus fittingly rounding out four decades of antislavery agitation. Since Lincoln's December 1863 amnesty and reconstruction order, with Union army help white residents of the overrun southern states had since renounced the Confederacy, held new, all-white elections, and rewritten constitutions and laws that renounced slavery. Lee's surrender was imminent when Douglass spoke. And Lincoln intended to impose additional conditions such as tax-supported education and limited black suffrage on the surrendering states, including Texas, from where *Texas v. White* would emerge. Further, Maryland, an unseceded slave-owning state, after fierce debates in early 1865 had abolished slavery, an event soon to make *In re Turner* possible.

Celebrations were appropriate, Douglass acknowledged, but causes existed also for continuing concern. Having ended slavery, the already-reconstructing states were continuing or had contrived new civil and criminal "black codes." Because their labor and contract sections sanctioned legal status too much like slavery, in the Thirteenth Amendment proposal Congress had included a ban on involuntary servitude as well as on slavery. In early 1865 Congress had created also a short-duration Freedmen's Bureau in the War Department, assigning to it welfare and justice duties, and even as Douglass spoke, bureau attorneys were trying to harmonize local and state laws with the proposed amendment.

Nine months later, in December 1865, Michael Hahn, the Louisiana Unionist important in Lincoln's efforts to reconstruct loyal state government there, spoke in Washington. Hahn was familiar with Chase's social experiments with blacks. In his lecture, "Manhood, the Basis of Suffrage," Hahn recounted how, since becoming president after Lincoln's death, Andrew Johnson had displaced him, impeded the efforts of the Freedmen's Bureau, and, using hangover "grasp of war" legal doctrines, initiated a new round of state reconstructions across the South. Each state drafted new constitutions that acknowledged the death of slavery and revamped their criminal and civil laws accordingly.

Hahn and many other South-watchers asserted that these revised constitutions and laws, especially those on crime and labor, disguised persisting race-based involuntary servitude that was close to slavery. The result, Hahn warned, was that Louisiana's black codes, like those elsewhere, mocked the Thirteenth Amendment, which was just then being ratified. Such accusations triggered swiftly politicized estimates about the nation's responsive duties, if any, under the amended federal Constitution, to protect victimized state citizens.

Agreeing with Chase's judgments in his midyear report to Johnson on southern conditions that the president had ignored, Hahn warned his listeners not to "mince matters, let us call [the black codes] by their right names." The black codes encouraged Louisiana's employers and officials to act in ways "which, in substance and reality . . . in all but name . . . revive all the features of . . . [slavery]." Therefore the nation must "secure the substance as well as the name of freedom."

Hahn complained that the racially bigoted southern officials Johnson had appointed were masquerading reactionary purposes behind states' police power regulations on crime, public health, and labor, thereby diminishing the real meaning of freedom. Legitimate exercises of state police powers were necessary, he acknowledged. The police power concept reflected government's practical need for a legal instrument useful in maintaining public order and protecting private rights to person and property. But in the former slave-owning states, police power regulations protected only a favored class of persons, principally former

Confederate whites. Disfavored categories, white Unionists and blacks, were harassed.

Their grossly discriminatory black codes disfranchised and otherwise penalized white Unionists and all blacks, including federal military veterans, relegating them to inferior legal status, Hahn continued. Those hastily revised civil and criminal statues accommodated the death of slavery. But to critics, they subordinated black residents to inferior legal conditions that, in employer-employee situations, for example, were describable as involuntary servitude. Several of the former slaveholding states (including Maryland) enacted apprenticeship laws that relegated black children to a status so like slavery as to make a distinction negligible.

Like other critical commentators on southern conditions, Hahn concluded that the overt means in state police regulations did not match their covert purposes. Entire sections of those states' revised civil and criminal laws were viciously unfair. For example, nominally with anticrime purposes, "sunset" statutes excluded blacks from transiting white neighborhoods after stipulated daylight hours, in effect permitting blacks access only as menials, under felony charges of arrest, fine, and imprisonment. Laws on mortgage foreclosures, rent defaults, and other uncollected debts virtually invited local authorities to harass blacks more than whites. States barred blacks from becoming peace officers, from serving on juries or in militias, from licensed trades and professions, and from voting. Among the black codes' race-based inequalities, rules for workers, including apprentices, and for vagrants and paupers inhibited or forbade mobility. Such laws lent themselves to criminalizing noncriminal behavior, and they applied to adult males, to minors, and to females, the last two becoming issues of *In re Turner.*

The black codes' criminal sections were the most obviously irksome. They commonly forbade interracial marriages, defined them as felonies, and punished blacks convicted of felonies more harshly than whites convicted of the same offenses. Though allowing blacks' testimony if adverse to white parties in litigations, black code provisions demeaned the value of black witnesses. Among the most viciously discriminatory of these codes, Alabama's provided for county commissioners to create "houses of correction" in which chain gangs, bread and water diets, and the hiring-out of inmates' labor to private contractors were included among "such reasonable correction as a parent may inflict upon a stubborn, refractory child." Aimed particularly at blacks who in large numbers were exercising their new-found luxury of mobility, Alabama defined a vagrant in a manner to entrap innocent freedmen in the coils of the criminal law, as one who behaved like "a stubborn or refractory servant; a laborer or servant who loiters away his time, or refuses to comply with any contract for a term of service, without just cause; and such person may be sent [by a sheriff] to the house of correction . . . [or] the common jail of the county" until a trial and conviction by "any justice of the peace," an official who was rarely a lawyer or possessed of any formal education at all. To Chase these codes were a perversion of freedom, a revival of slavery or of something so near to servitude as to mock his lifetime aspirations and the nation's recent sacrifices.

Commonly without indictments, evidence, opportunity for self-defensive testimony, or other minimal procedures usual in the North, southern justices of the peace, magistrates, and sheriffs, most of whom were recent supporters of the Confederacy, jailed delinquent debtors, most of whom were black. Many victims endured lengthy sentences at unpaid hard labor for creditors or county. Alternatively, at auctions disturbingly reminiscent of slave markets, counties leased the labor of convicts to private contractors. Too often, the contractors subjected their unpaid workers to harsh discipline, hazardous working situations, and subhuman living conditions.

No state was wholly free of statutory or customary race bigotry. But the former slave-owning states' black codes outdistanced all others in their layered diminutions of freedom. This situation raised for Chase both legal and ethical questions that, answered, threatened his political ambitions. Nevertheless, in *In re Turner* he considered whether the Thirteenth Amendment authorized appropriate federal justice remedies when improper exercises of a state's police powers violated individuals' personal and property rights. And in *Texas v. White* Chase answered the broader question, what was a state in the federal Union?

Undoubtedly Chase hoped for political gain from shrewd answers. His triplex worlds were always simultaneously those of a devout Protestant, a sophisticated attorney, and a political pro aiming at a presidential nomination. He had proposed to Lincoln, who, too late, accepted the idea that black suffrage in the South would allow the federal government to remove itself from direct coercive efforts on behalf of blacks. Instead, like whites, voting blacks could protect themselves by balloting. If votes failed to satisfy, then litigations were another remedy.

Lincoln's successor as president was wholly unsympathetic to Chase's strategy yet failed to curb excesses like the black codes. They repelled advocates of equal justice under law, especially those who, like Chase, throughout his adult career had equated justice's balanced scales with commandments humbling every individual before God. Like many antislavery militants whose stubborn devotion had defined the Republican party, Chase's urgent Christianity burned as intently after Appomattox as before, informing and justifying his positions on public policies. His theological lexicon had long twinned the immorality of slavery with secular anarchy. America's history proved to Chase that private rights, public morality, popular government, and law must fail when anarchy prevailed or even threatened. To him the states' secessions of 1860–1861 had eroded anarchically the Constitution's prescribed elections and the political and legal processes that made balloting meaningful and justice possible. Exclusions of worthy individuals from access to politics or law was equally dangerous in 1865.

He had valued company in these views. The influential minister George B. Cheever vilified the black codes as inimical to law and religion. In his *Petition and Memorial* (December 1865) Cheever prayed for Congress to suppress the black codes because they were "terrible examples of . . . illegal, unconstitutional, and tyrannical bills of attainder . . . [replete with] unusual pains and penalties . . . and forms of colored crime ingeniously constructed, with [criminal] statutes of forced labor for life, or imprisonment and sale [of prisoner' labor] as payment of jail fees." If let stand, the black codes would proclaim implicitly that the Thirteenth Amendment "may . . . with perfect impunity be nullified."

Conscience had long been at the heart of Chase's pleadings for equity, and, he had assumed, in the form of the Thirteenth Amendment it was now embedded in the Constitution. In the 1860s, as in the 1830s, he still sang hymns and recited New Testament passages from memory. Like Cheever, Chase understood equal justice in law to be required by imperatives both secular and divine. What God had wrought at Appomattox virtuous men had embodied in the Thirteenth Amendment. To Chase, as to Lincoln, it constitutionalized the equalitarian commandments of the Declaration of Independence and the Constitution's Preamble and reinforced secularly the Bible's requirement that every individual know the truth—read, the law—if freedom was ever to ring.

Despite his religion's premise that sin was more common than virtue, and his long career as lawyer and politician, to Chase the black codes' resurrections of slavelike involuntary servitude were shocking. Like many antislavery activists, Chase had a romantic streak. He had long accepted the idea that slavery was America's single, or at least worst, sin. Its abolition had not after all thwarted the serpent's venom. The black codes proved that though the southern states had stopped overt slavery, the poison of involuntary servitude was still lurking there.

Through 1865 and much of 1866 Chase was almost like a fatigued combat veteran who, after celebrating a hard-earned victory over a determined foe, finds the defeated antagonist suddenly challenging the verdict of battles. He was disequilibrated by the success of the antislavery crusade and by the reappearance of involuntary servitude too like bondage to be endured. Both confused him. He had won his war. But where was the secular community of the godly?

Perhaps it was still locatable if southern states replaced their black codes with relevant, and, to Chase, morally superior, portions of the northern states' criminal and civil laws, especially those on contract and labor. Chase's wartime treasury agents and Union army provost marshals had pioneered efforts in this direction. They had introduced labor contracts and detailed work directives that inhibited further wanderings by runaway and abandoned slaves and that, through favoring employers and landlords, nevertheless bound tenants, laborers, and employers to the obligations and benefits the contracts stipulated. Despite increasing obstacles imposed by President Johnson, the bureau persisted in this core phase of its work. Bureau lawyers found especially relevant the laws New England states had contrived to keep its numerous industrial workers productively on their jobs and those laws midwestern states had developed for migrant agricultural labor. Elizabeth Turner's bureau attorney was as well prepared to represent her as Chase was to judge the merits of her plea.

Chase's readiness resulted from his conviction that the nominally race-blind labor and contract laws of New England and the Northwest Ordinance states were better models for the South than the black codes. Southerners should rigorously excise from their labor, family, and criminal laws obviously racist elements like those that marred Maryland's apprenticeship statute and replace them with superior alternatives. Such excisions and substitutions would prove to northern voters that erstwhile slave owners were merely employers who, like northern factory owners, were full players in capitalism's games, itself the best proof to Chase of the South's redemption.

Abstract justice was not on Chase's agenda. Biracial access to capitalism's risky games was. Access was essential if individuals were to enrich both themselves and society through exercising their liberty to contract, a liberty already being deified by lawyers and businessmen. That liberty was Chase's benchmark of a worthy, progressive society. He wished to encourage in every state each individual's ordered liberty to practice a worthy work ethic in which a person contracted his or her labor, chattels, money, or talents in competition with any other tenderers and honored every contract commitment. Ever the patriarch, Chase identified as the essential social cement the discipline of family hearths and factory timeclocks, which, however stern, was infinitely superior to the erratic cruelties of slaveowners' whipping docks.

The legal commentaries Chase had devoured since the 1830s and still respected ranged from James Kent's *Commentaries* to James Schouler's *Treatise on the Law of Domestic Relations* (published in 1870 but circulated earlier in part). They gave employers disciplinary rights over workers, such as those rights husbands enjoyed over wives and children, guardians over wards, and—*In re Turner*—employers over apprentices. But in free labor law, employers also had to perform fully whatever they had promised when they contracted with a worker or apprentice.

It seemed obvious to Chase that southern legislators should abandon the black codes and implicitly exhibit repentance for the past by elevating black and white workers to a legal plane as high as that which northern whites enjoyed, meaning to the level of disciplined labor stability. Such uncoerced action in 1865 or early 1866 might well have silenced the region's critics and released the credit needed for its physical regeneration. But encouraged by the president, southern whites rejected the obvious.

Their rejection imposed on Republicans in general a task that acceptance might have made unnecessary. It was to explain to the lay public the intricacies of free labor law and the law of contract in time for the education to pay off at the polls in the fall 1866 congressional and state elections and, to Chase, in the 1868 presidential sweepstakes. Assuming this task, Republican spokesmen generally chose to attend first to freedom's most obvious antonym, slavery, now disfavored by history and constitutionally and legally prohibited. A diverse, innately local, and largely uncataloged array of life and labor situations, involuntary servitude proliferated between freedom and slavery. And freedom, like involuntary servitude, was much more difficult than slavery for Republicans to deal with, primarily because freedom was a largely unstudied congeries of pragmatic customs. White males enjoyed freedom, including the freedom or liberty to contract, largely without legal restraints except to find persons possessed of whatever seemed worth contracting for.

Free Americans' right to contract required that they enjoy access to areas where market exchanges were made. Legal theorists had dignified that practical need as the right of mobility. The purpose of mobility was not to encourage flights from the obligations of state-defined private contracts, including those on marriage, labor, leases, or debts. Such irresponsibility burdened local economies with abandoned families, vacant dwellings, unpaid rents, and uncompleted work. Orphans and paupers consumed capital better spent on investments. And vagrants, strangers in one's midst, too often descended to criminality. Rather, freedom-as-mobility existed as a right in order to encourage responsible individuals voluntarily to assume capitalism's risks and to honor resulting contract obligations. By honoring them, risk-takers enhanced personal wealth, and it in turn nourished and stabilized the larger society.

All private contracts were enforceable by the participants' state, the invisible third party in every civil relationship. Slaves were the only property banned nationwide. After the war, as before it, states exercised what contemporaries labeled innate police or municipal powers. Through them, states denied or limited the rights of mobility and contract to vagrants, paupers, felons, most married women, mental defectives, and, while bound to a contracted term of service, to apprentices. Elizabeth Turner's case linked the federal right of mobility to her state's right to sanction labor contracts.

As 1866 began Chase and other critics of these developments recalled that before the Civil War the Constitution's fugitive slave recapture clause and laws implementing it had bridged the federal system in the interests of slave owners. Could Congress now bridge the state-dominated federal system in a manner to diminish uncertainties fueled by the black codes about blacks' legal competency to contract? Once freed, did former slaves enjoy a federal right of mobility and a state-derived right to contract?

Anticipating uncertainties, in 1862, Chase, as noted, had asked U.S. Attorney General Bates to specify what benefits derived from national citizenship, and Bates had replied that, apart from mobility, no one knew. The "naked, unassisted fact," he reported, was that with few exceptions, such as mobility, only states' statutes and customs defined Americans' lives.

Neither then nor later did Chase quarrel with the fact that the states' side of the law of freedom, as measured by individuals' contract rights and obligations, was far larger, more intimate, and familiar to lawyers and laymen than the nation's. This was and should remain a federal system, he believed. It was appropriate that state constitutions, laws, and customs sanction mature individuals' rights to compete voluntarily by entering into enforceable private contracts, including those on marriage, housing, sales, debts, and all other legitimate mutual civil commitments. When constructively released, energies flowed from such private risks. By contracting to exchange obligations, talent, brawn, chattels, or capital, striving and supposedly equal individuals hoped mutually to profit and, according to the legal theory Chase favored, also benefited society. Therefore government should play only Adam Smith's passive, invisible hand, laissez-faire role regarding contracts, unless the parties were seriously unequal. Inventors of free labor contract theories concurred that inequitability resulted when in their precontract negotiations employer and worker, landlord and tenant, vendor and purchaser, and husband and wife were less than equally rational, responsible, informed individuals.

Chase had helped to imbed that legal theory in political fact. The 1856 Republican party's election-year platform glorified free labor theory. It was far more than a mere slogan to attorneys of Chase's generation. They revered free labor contract theory as vital to the social stability that, they believed, resulted from the acquisition and defense of private property, that guardian of every other right.

Capitalism and individualism were transcendentally important virtues to lawyers, including those who were antislavery activists. Chase qualified on both counts. He accepted wholeheartedly the premise that individual contractors had to stand on reasonably equal footing before the law if they were to be held responsible to fulfill their contracted obligations. Therefore, without objections from Chase, in this state-centered federal system, states' laws excluded or limited the rights to contract or to be mobile of felons, mental defectives, paupers, vagrants, children, and apprentices, persons the law deemed to be intrinsically incapable of assuming equal responsibility.

Legal theorists concurred also that every individual contractor had committed himself to mutually agreed terms only after a slow process. During it they supposedly deliberately studied, then carefully specified, every obligation and benefit they expected from exchanging goods, services, or money, plus every penalty for total nonfulfillment or partial completion. The theoretical slow pace in negotiations and the assumed rationality of every individual contractor justified government's punishing violators of agreed terms, if a case was appealed.

The need for disciplined social control over labor appears now to be incongruous with the cult of individual personality in private contracts then becoming dominant in the law. But if discerned at all, to Chase the incongruities were inessential. If marketplace behavior remained unstabilized and undisciplined, Chase feared that resulting class strains might erode American society in ways worse than the prewar proslavery lawlessness he had always deplored. Individuals must be as accountable in law as in religion. This message infused notable prewar free-state legislation and court decisions that imposed on injured laborers the burden of proving that no fellow worker had contributed to workplace injuries, for example.

Much in free labor contract theory was illusory. The theory added to the advantages that the possession of capital and political power gave to this generation of energetic industrialists, growers, and investors. Hirelings were rarely if ever equal to employers of farm and factory labor in their marketplace dealings. Few work contracts actually reflected meticulous examination of or agreement on every detail by equally weighty parties. At the request of employers, managers, or landlords, for example, police inhibited the mobility of striking workers and tenants by holding them to jobs or domiciles until work or leases were completed. Conversely, often withholding rents or salaries due for completed labor or tenancy, employers fired or dispossessed laborers or tenants for nonperformance of contract terms. Workers injured on the job who claimed that their employers had failed to provide safe tools faced the heavy burden of proving to unsympathetic judges that neither they nor a "fellow servant" had been negligent.

Beginning in 1865 such disparities between free labor legal theory and marketplace fact inspired northern industrial and agricultural workers, labels embracing also many small merchants and farmers, to organize as the Knights of Labor and the Patrons of Husbandry. Some spokesmen for both societies criticized free labor legal theory and practice. But members of both associations infinitely preferred life and labor governed by free labor hypotheses to the major American nineteenth-century alternative, Calhoun's version of master-slave relationships.

Notwithstanding the innate procapitalism of both the Knights and the Patrons, fears persisted that if misunderstood, free labor legal theory was encouraging rootlessness and lawlessness, a declension leading to an anarchy of classes rather than of sections. Social conservatives worried about the sudden upsurges in mass vagrancy among southern blacks, whose wanderings in search of long-scattered families had partly inspired or justified the black codes. In northern states, increased street beggary, rent and debt evasions, and industrial strikes evoked increasingly stringent policies punishing vagrants and favoring employers, landlords, and creditors. Proponents of these tougher policies justified them in part with arguments that by distorting the meaning of freedom the Thirteenth Amendment was destabilizing society.

Such assertions rose in a lawsuit decided in New York's prestigious supreme court in early 1866. The widely reported decision in *Tyler v. Herndon* (46 Barbour's Reports, 439) lent dignity to such counsels of fear. The litigation arose because, allegedly for good reasons, landowners ejected tenants before their lease expired yet claimed full rents. The tenants' lawyer challenged the claim, arguing that if his clients had involuntarily to pay for an unreceived service they and third-party subcontractors were reduced substantially to that newly constitutionalized offense, involuntary servitude.

This was an unanticipated use, or, in their opinions, abuse of the anti-slavery lawyers' hallowed arguments and of the treasured Thirteenth Amendment. Comforting Chase on this score but vexing him on other points, the New York high court ruled that the involuntary servitude argument was groundless because when two parties entered into any civil contract they mutually assumed detriments. Such obligations reduced no one to involuntary servitude. Any lesser interpretation, the unanimous opinion asserted, "sweeps away all contracts." Consequences of this shocking magnitude and destructive effect were never intended or anticipated by the amendment's framers and ratifiers.

Chase agreed. But then the New York judges squeezed together the meanings of slavery and involuntary servitude, stating that the amendment "was designed for one specific object, and no other, to wit, the abolition of personal slavery within the United States, the system of personal and involuntary servitude by which one person owned as property and could absolutely control the person and services of another . . . against his will and consent."

No antislavery lawyer Chase knew wanted to give the amendment such "a sweeping effect . . . [as] to destroy every contract . . . upon the ground that it was in effect a personal servitude." Chase's prewar and wartime experiences with theories and realities about free labor made him distrust a further pronouncement of the New York jurists about the Thirteenth Amendment, that in enacting it "no other object was ever suggested" than to end slavery. Slavery was indeed "the mischief to be remedied—the evil to be abolished—the end to be gained," as the New York court stated. But the only one?

Hard experience had taught Chase that except in its socially corrosive qualities involuntary servitude was not substantially synonymous with slavery. To be sure, both evils reduced their victims to conditions less than free. But compared to slavery's frank degradations, involuntary servitude was often imprecisely shadowy, hiding under scattered portions of states' civil and criminal portions of the southern states' black codes.

Although positions taken in this case by the New York judges irked Chase, his proentrepreneurial views were favored because the landowner in the New York lawsuit won. Chase knew that the real argument was between two contentious businessmen and had nothing to do with unrequited servitude.

Nevertheless, in the former slaveholding states the involuntary servitude taking root was a persisting residue from slavery, yet clearly not the same. Legitimized in the black codes, involuntary servitude explicitly altered the theory of contract in which two equal parties agreed to mutually binding terms. Because of race, the black codes assumed and institutionalized the inferiority of one party, thereby lifting white contractors to a privileged legal status and therefore vitiating the key to dynamic contract law, the theoretical equality of the parties.

Chase's political ambitions and his judicial responsibilities inspired close attention to these circumstances. His circuit lay in former slaveholding states, and his prewar insistence on states' rights for antislavery purposes made the postwar Democratic party increasingly attractive to him as a hunting ground for a presidential nomination. Unlike the Republican party, the Democrats lacked electable leaders of national stature, including the increasingly discredited president who had returned to their party. For Chase, the responsibility to define involuntary servitude involved the same inseparable legal, political, and moral concerns that had always commanded him. As 1866 advanced the president and Congress also weighed the problem of involuntary servitude on the nation's political scales. To them the problem was a chore; to Chase it was a challenge.

As it had since the 1830s, his need had persisted to repair the wrongs in America's past in order to craft a better future. Chase had given this need expression when in 1866 he described Lincoln's cabinet, in reacting to his decision to emancipate, as "thinking of what they had just heard, and the future it opens."

As free labor, Elizabeth Turner was part of that opened future, part of the necessary and proper but still only potential "recrystallization of society and reorganization of the social order" referred to by Chase's circuit court reporter, Bradley Johnson. To Chase's credit, free labor was color-blind and gender-neutral. A broadly inclusive category, it embraced anyone who contributively risked money, muscle, talent, and time to marketplace endeavors, not only white or black male workers. Free labor necessarily also involved employers (erstwhile masters) who hazarded property, capital, and labor in the mutual contract commitments that both fueled and disciplined the marketplace and stabilized the social order. Chase equated freedom from slavery with freedom to contract, and it in turn required open negotiations and earnest fulfillment of contract terms.

This evolving legal theory envisioned a nationwide community of state-defined free labor communities that encompassed manual labor and white-collar professions and trades. Whether explicit or implicit, free labor contracts reflected both formal requirements and customs. Concerning a profession, contracts could require educational minima or passage of examinations for mandatory state licensing. In the trades, when applied in work contracts, free labor legal theory required specification of wages and, sometimes, perquisites such as responsibility to supply tools, seed, and training. Employers benefited by the restrictions free labor legal practice allowed on workers. Commonly, these restrictions included coercions such as loss of pay for employees who quit (that is, who exercised mobility) before the contracted end of a work agreement. More comprehensive restrictions faced apprentices and orphans. And still tighter restrictions, edging into criminal law, constrained leased convict workers, vagrants, and beggars.

Chase had devoted his professional skills, religious commitments, and political energies far more to freedom national goals than to free labor's actualities. Gauged retrospectively, the often Scrooge-like advantages employers enjoyed in Chase's concepts of free labor meshed poorly with later generations' more inclusive meanings of the word "free." But Chase and his antislavery contemporaries thought that both freedom national and free labor ideologies were less harsh than any southern state's preemancipation ways with slaves or free blacks or postemancipation black-code derogations of freedmen.

Chase's pleasure in his *Turner* stand partly reflected his confidence that it destabilized only those private contracts that reduced a party unreasonably either to formal slavery or, in substance, involuntary servitude. Otherwise, employer-worker contracts were to stand and to be enforceable in courts. Free workers contracting with equally free employers constituted the only appropriate legal environment for political democracy, constitutional liberty, and state-centered federalism. Only an exceptional situation such as Elizabeth Turner's, in which it was argued that as a minor she was not a voluntary party to her apprenticeship obligation and that the statutory standards her state had set for her employment were so racially biased as to trigger the Thirteenth Amendment's bar to involuntary servitude, justified a judicial disavowal of her contract obligations.

For these reasons the wartime legal operations of the Freedmen's Bureau concerning contract labor had made sense to Chase. As treasury secretary he had encouraged the work of the bureau's predecessors in conquered southern areas. Then, because of the black codes and increasing violence in the South, in 1866 he agreed privately with congressional Republicans that the bureau needed a longer if still limited existence and that its meager budget warranted increase. A bill to that effect met President Johnson's veto, threatening the death of federalism, which Congress overrode.

Inextricably intermixed with arguments on the bureau, Congress also considered a civil rights bill. A global first, it generated even more passion than the Freedmen's Bureau. No longer was national citizenship to be a virtually meaningless status. In order to enforce the Thirteenth Amendment, among its provisions the civil rights bill defined national citizenship to include blacks. Passed over Johnson's ignoble, sometimes racist veto message, the Civil Rights Act greatly expanded federal courts' jurisdiction over new federal offenses. Its major provision, however, defined citizenship:

All persons born in the United States and not subject to any foreign power, excluding Indians not taxed, are hereby declared to be citizens of the United States; and such citizens, *of every race and color, without regard to any previous condition of slavery or involuntary servitude,* except as a punishment for crime whereof the party shall have been duly convicted, *shall have the same right, in every State and Territory in the United States, to make and enforce contracts, to sue, be parties, and give evidence, to inherit, purchase, lease, sell, hold, and convey real and personal property, and to full and equal benefit of all laws and proceedings for the security of person and property, as is enjoyed by white citizens,* and shall be subject to like punishment, pains, and penalties, and to none other, any law, statute, ordinance, regulation, or custom, to the contrary, notwithstanding. (14 *Statutes at Large* [1866], 27, italics added)

Convinced that by retaining each state's race-blind public laws as the definition of federal civil rights, the Civil Rights Act equaled "progress," as Chase told a Dartmouth audience in mid-1866. Though now publicly advocating political rights for blacks, Chase noted to a fellow federal judge that the Civil Rights bill "is as important to the prosperity of the whites as it is to the security of the blacks."* Chase spread this message as widely as possible. Meanwhile Congress also cobbled together a Fourteenth Amendment proposal and submitted it to the states for ratification (which would not occur until 1868, after Chase decided *In re Turner* but the year before the Court decided *Texas v. White*). Destined to spin off unending judicial and political controversy to our own time, among other complicated matters the Fourteenth Amendment constitutionalized the Civil Rights Act's citizenship definition and forbade states from depriving citizens of their "privileges and immunities" or "life, liberty, or property, without due process of law." This shorthand for the Civil Rights Act's more detailed list of state wrongs, combined with the enlarged jurisdiction of the federal courts, virtually invited judges themselves to determine when states violated the act or the postwar amendments.

Reinforcing (not repealing) the Thirteenth Amendment, Congress' historic 1866 package ennobled all citizens, not only blacks, as Chase stated. "The mischief to be remedied was not merely slavery but its [persisting] incidents and consequences," a later justice, Joseph Bradley, asserted when

*Quoted in David Hughes, "Salmon P. Chase: Chief Justice," *Vanderbilt Law Review* 18 (1965):577.

dissenting with Chase in the historic—and, for blacks, tragic—*Slaughter-house* decision (83 U.S. 36 [1873]). The dissenters would insist "also that among those hangovers from slavery was that "spirit of insubordination and disloyalty to the National Government which had troubled the country for so many years . . . , and that intolerance of free speech and free discussion which often rendered life and property insecure, and led to much unequal legislation."

Long before 1873, however, like so many of his compatriots, Chase began to exhibit uncertainty about how the nation should meet the unexpected need to continue to be concerned about the victims and perpetrators of states' wrongs and about the desirable limits to the nation's powers in crises. His unease contributed to the oscillating qualities of his positions on both the wartime and postwar issues that came to his Court beginning in its 1865–1867 terms, to his subsequent failure to infuse the whole Supreme Court with the spirit of his *In re Turner* opinion, and to his success as spokesman for the majority of the justices in *Texas v. White.*

CHAPTER 9

In Re Turner: Its Hour Come 'Round at Last

In October 1867, while on his circuit in Maryland, Chase heard Elizabeth Turner's petition. It was one of manifold proofs that Michael Hahn's concerns of 1865 and those of the majority of Republicans of 1866 and 1867 had been depressingly legitimate. When Chase responded to their concerns in *In re Turner,* he confirmed a view that Congress had already expressed in the 1866 Civil Rights Act, that the Thirteenth Amendment had redefined and elevated the legal status of every American to that of free persons, thereby limiting states' capacities substantively to impair that status, even in the guise of private employer/apprenticeship contracts. And even as Chase considered *In re Turner* while on circuit, he docketed *Texas v. White* for the whole Court to weigh in 1869.

Beyond the fact that *In re Turner* was pivotal in Chase's life and that he tried to make it central to Reconstruction's history, this obscure lawsuit is itself inherently interesting. *In re Turner* arose from a Maryland civil statute. It was not a result of martial law during the war by which soldiers punished disloyal civilians in both loyal states and in militarily reconquered former Confederate states. Nor did it result from the March 1867 Military Reconstruction Act, whereby bluecoats were again overseeing revisions to the southern states' constitutions and laws, this time requiring state ratifications of the Fourteenth Amendment and black suffrage. Unseceded yet slaveholding and fully represented in Congress, Maryland became the Lincoln administration's showpiece as a nominally self-reconstructing state, a situation opposite to Louisiana's, that seceded but reconquered slave-owning state so important to Lincoln.

In 1861 Maryland had not seceded largely because Union soldiers prevented it. If accomplished, Maryland's secession and linkage to the Confederacy would have isolated Washington totally by severing the essential intersection there of the New York Central and Baltimore & Ohio railroad lines, a situation that perhaps would have wholly discouraged the

Lincoln administration and antisecessionists across the sundering nation. Lincoln's extraordinary recourse to military arrests of Marylanders thought to be security risks had prevented these eventualities. But the arrests had provoked Chief Justice Taney to issue his spectacular, ahistorical, and ultimately unavailing 1861 *Ex parte Merryman* (Fed. Case No. 9487) circuit opinion, in Baltimore, denying the nation constitutional authority to survive, a view Lincoln rejected.

Thereafter Maryland Unionists had painfully pushed the state's legislators to end slavery. They accomplished this feat against tenacious Democratic party and racist opposition only in the war's last year. In early 1865 Maryland ratified the Thirteenth Amendment. The event inspired celebrations among antislavery whites and joyous blacks. They soon welcomed to Baltimore officials of the Freedmen's Bureau, among them the bureau attorney who two years later represented Elizabeth Turner.

Perhaps Chase's interest in Turner's situation was spurred partly because she, like Matilda, was also from Maryland and because he, like Turner, had also been an apprentice. In any event, Turner's situation was further evidence to Chase that Douglass's and Hahn's warnings of 1865 were valid; though forbidden, involuntary servitude did lurk stubbornly in the former slave states' black codes.

As symbolized by the complaining party, a black woman represented by a Freedmen's Bureau staff lawyer, from its origins to its conclusion *In re Turner* differed from almost every other case generated by the war whose results were heard by federal judges. It involved state-defined private contract rights deriving from the very recently amended federal Constitution and Maryland's constitution and laws—rights of inclusion, not exclusion; black civilians' rights to the fruits of their labor, not issues of military arrests of white civilians. Thereby Elizabeth Turner's petition illuminated numerous aspects of the evolving federalism that the Civil War had fueled. Chase implied in his answer to Turner's suit that in this dynamic federalism the nation's judges had constitutionally and statutorily explicit duties to sustain the rights of its newly defined nonwhite citizens, including females, to enjoy adequately equal state justice as well as other matters.

Elizabeth Turner was a "young person of color" who until emancipation was a slave of Philemon T. Hambleton of Talbot County, Maryland. When in winter 1864–1865 a new Maryland constitution abolished slavery and the state ratified the Thirteenth Amendment, "some local authority" had collected all the freed people of the county, among them Turner and her mother Betsey or Betty, and bound "the younger persons . . . as apprentices, usually, if not always, to their late masters." Elizabeth's birth year is unknown. She was almost certainly a minor in 1864. Her mother, also until recently Hambleton's slave (and perhaps his mistress), committed her daughter to serve their former master (who was also perhaps Elizabeth's father) by terms of an apprenticeship contract apparently "executed under the [newly revised] laws of Maryland relating to negro apprentices."

As 1866 ended, Elizabeth Turner appeared with an attorney before Chase, who was sitting as a federal circuit judge in the same Baltimore courtroom where, in the Civil War's first weeks, Taney had condemned Lincoln's orders to arrest pro-Confederate activist John Merryman. The coincidence of location and the polar disparities of the issues inspired analogies to Chase's more recent admission of attorney John Rock, a black, to practice before the Supreme Court bar where a decade earlier Taney had read his *Dred Scott* opinion.

Obviously Elizabeth was a brave young black woman. She needed courage to sue Hambleton, a local gentleman of substance and standing. Apparently Hambleton had owned numerous slaves, including Elizabeth, and though deprived of them, he still possessed substantial real estate and other property and, most likely, the political and social influence that usually attended ownership.

Henry S. Stockbridge, Turner's attorney, was also brave. He was white, for Maryland then licensed no black men and no women of any race in the professions. Stockbridge had Chase's respect as a fellow New Englander and as a graduate of Amherst College, an institution as elite as Chase's Dartmouth. Stockbridge had learned law as an apprentice-clerk in a practitioner's office, a fact perhaps inclining both men to sensitivity to Elizabeth Turner's situation. In prewar years Stockbridge had oscillated in terms of political loyalties, from early Whiggery to Know-Nothingism to the Republicans by 1856. In 1862 Stanton had appointed Stockbridge as a special attorney in the War Department. There he served with the important abolitionist Massachusetts lawyer, William Whiting, preparing defenses for Lincoln's unprecedented uses of executive war powers, including internal security arrests and emancipation, and for Chase's efforts to resettle and uplift runaway blacks. A prewar convert to Chase's brand of antislavery activism, Stockbridge was one of the many evangelists of equality under law that the Lincoln administration had recruited to cope with some of the legal problems generated by the wartime social experiments with southern blacks. Resigning his position in 1864, Stockbridge won election to the Maryland legislature, led the successful movement to call the constitutional convention that ended slavery in the state, then traveled across Maryland to win popular votes in favor of its adoption. Elected a Baltimore County judge, then in 1865 a state circuit judge, he lost his 1866 bid for election to the state's appeal court in the conservative resurgence of that year. Anxious to set the new Freedmen's Bureau and Civil Rights Acts into motion, Stockbridge accepted a position as state counsel for the bureau, his situation when Elizabeth Turner brought her problems to his attention.

Turner probably had saved no money during her slavery years. Few private attorneys anywhere offered pro bono services to indigents then; even fewer Maryland practitioners ambitious for profitable future careers in that former slave state willingly represented a black female laborer suing her white employer, the situation in Turner's instance. She was fortunate to gain the professional services of a lawyer who was intimately familiar with the problems that she and many thousands of other young black Marylanders experienced who were apprenticed under the state law. Stockbridge was professionally alert. Exploiting opportunities effectively to serve his client offered by the new Thirteenth Amendment and Civil Rights Act, he also took advantage of his personal history in Maryland's government in his equity plea to Chase on Turner's behalf.

Slavery's persisting residues substantively permeated provisions of Maryland's 1864 black code law concerning black apprentices, Stockbridge charged. Turner had never herself participated fully in the negotiations with Hambleton that led to her commitment to its terms. Now she wished to gain release from her apprenticeship contract that, in her name, her mother had made with him according to the terms of the equally new Maryland apprentice statute. Stockbridge wished Chase to issue a habeas corpus writ on Turner's behalf because the state's law created "manifest" (Chase's word) and substantial variances based on race between white and black apprentices, imposed only obligations on her, and skewed all rights to her employer-mentor.

For example, by terms of the relevant state law Hambleton enjoyed "property and interest" controls over Turner but not over his white apprentices. Maryland stipulated also that Hambleton teach white tutees, but not black ones, the basic skills of his trade and reading, writing, and arithmetic.

Employers could not transfer white apprentices' indentures to third parties. But without permission from black apprentices or their parents, employers could assign the apprenticeship contracts of black neophytes to third parties unspecified in the original agreement. And white apprentices also fared far better than blacks so far as the relevant law required minimal supplies of food, clothing, and domiciliary furnishings.

Before emancipation, Stockbridge granted, earlier Maryland laws on apprenticing whites and free blacks "had always preserved the broad line of demarcation between the white ruling race, and the black subject one." He acknowledged further that under Maryland's preemancipation laws "the free negro, while having no political rights, was entitled to civil or legal rights to a large degree, but not equally with whites." These racial differentiations prevailed when Hambleton and Turner entered into their labor contract, Stockbridge also allowed.

Then any misapprehensions that he was arguing for Hambleton rather than Turner vanished. The substantial effect of the many racially defined inequities stated with almost arrogant candor in Maryland's apprenticeship law reduced Turner to a legal status inferior to that of a free worker, a status equaling involuntary servitude, Stockbridge insisted. He intimated further that though both federal and state constitutions prohibited ex post facto laws, the prohibition did not apply to civil relationships like apprenticeship contracts. Conversely, although not yet ratified, the prohibition in the pending Fourteenth Amendment against states depriving citizens of their liberty and property without adequate legal process should apply in Turner's instance. Stockbridge argued further that because Turner's mother had committed her then-minor daughter to the apprenticeship contract, therefore Elizabeth had been bound to it involuntarily in violation of both the Thirteenth Amendment and the Civil Rights Act. Too long restrained of her liberty, she now deserved release from the contract.

Contrary arguments existed. Anxious to weigh them judicially, if only to condemn them, and anticipating perhaps that upon losing, Hambleton would appeal an unfavorable verdict to the Supreme Court, Chase waited eagerly for Hambleton's counsel or for Hambleton himself to appear. Meanwhile, as good lawyers should, Stockbridge and perhaps Chase prepared for possible rejoinders by Hambleton's counsel.

Potential rejoinders included a point of law long honored in most states that because Turner's mother had submitted her daughter to the apprenticeship adequate voluntariness by Elizabeth should be assumed to have existed in the contract. A similarly traditional response to Stockbridge's objections to Maryland's practice of differentiating between apprentices' races could have been that the clauses in the federal Civil Rights Act prohibiting such differentiations did not exist in 1864. As stated recently by Chase and the other dissenters in the *Test Oath* decisions (see p. 136), the traditional view was that the prohibition against ex post facto legislation applied solely to criminal matters. But the Court's majority had decreed otherwise. Therefore Hambleton's attorney could have argued that a voiding of Turner's civil contract of 1865 on the basis of subsequent public policies was substantively ex post facto. Substantive due process ideas were then circulating increasingly among lawyers and Supreme Court justices. Further, in 1867 the Fourteenth Amendment was still only a proposal awaiting the states' ratification. Its relevance to situations like Turner's was uncertain in 1867 and indeed would remain uncertain for decades. In sum, no generally acknowledged federal constitutional bar then limited the state's right to prescribe differential conditions for apprenticeships based on race. It was arguable that Turner's contract deserved judicial protection, not condemnation, and that she should not be released from her obligations.

Frustrating Chase, though undoubtedly delighting Turner and Stockbridge, no attorney representing Hambleton appeared in court so to argue. Chase still hoped to attract counterargument because of "the importance of the questions involved." He recessed his circuit court for a day. Still the respondent chose not to appear, personally or by counsel. Perhaps Hambleton found the notoriety distasteful or merely preferred to minimize or avoid lawyer's fees. If he was indeed Turner's father, it may have been that paternal sentiment governed his decision not to contest her plea for release from her legal commitment. Further disappointing Chase, no member of the Maryland bar volunteered to represent Hambleton's interests pro bono or as friend of the court. Chase's heavy circuit docket impelled him to put finis on the *Turner* case, and so, next day, he ruled.

His decision, "considered . . . with care, and an earnest desire to reach right conclusions," was to grant Turner habeas corpus "relief from restraint and detention" by Hambleton, who was in violation of the amended federal Constitution and the Civil Rights Act implementing it. Perhaps, as he did so often, in this instance Chase assumed that his views were unassailable. Therefore he offered only "a brief statement of . . . [his] conclusions, without going into the grounds of them. The time does not allow more."

Chase's "brief statement" presented "the following propositions . . . [as] sound law, and they decide the case":

1. The first clause of the Thirteenth Amendment to the Constitution of the United States interdicts slavery and involuntary servitude, except as a punishment for crimes, and establishes freedom as the constitutional right of all persons in the United States.

2. The alleged apprenticeship in the present case is involuntary servitude, within the meaning of the words in the amendment.

3. If this were otherwise, the indenture set forth in the return does not contain important provisions for the security and benefit of the apprentice, which are required by the laws of Maryland in indentures of white apprentices, and is, therefore, in contravention of that clause of the first section of the civil rights law enacted by Congress on April 9, 1866, which assures to all citizens, without regard to race or color, "full and equal benefit of all laws and proceedings for the security of persons and property as is enjoyed by white citizens."

4. This [Civil Rights] law having been enacted under the second clause of the Thirteenth Amendment, in enforcement of the first clause of the same amendment, is constitutional, and applies to all conditions prohibited by it, whether originating in transactions before or since its enactment.

5. Colored persons as well equally with white persons are citizens of the United States.

The petitioner must therefore be discharged.

The following order was entered: *Ordered by the court,* this 16th day of October, A.D. 1867, that Elizabeth Turner, be discharged from the custody of Philemon T. Hambleton, upon the ground that the detention and restraint complained of is in violation of the constitution and laws of the United States; and it is further ordered that the costs of this proceeding be paid by the respondent.

His statement illuminates Chase's deliberately inclusive definition of "all persons" to mean black males and females, among responsible, mature parties to civil contracts, with independent capacity to commit themselves to whatever conditions of labor and wages they wished. This aspect of *In re Turner* perhaps reflected Chase's innovative practice, unique among Lincoln's cabinet heads, of hiring large numbers of women during the Civil War as Treasury clerical staff. That wartime practice plus the *Turner* decision could have but did not erode the high legal walls that then and for many decades to come separated the working spheres open to females from those accessible to males, despite the Reconstruction amendments. On this score of including white and black persons of both genders as beneficiaries of the Thirteenth and Fourteenth Amendments, and, later, black males as beneficiaries of the Fifteenth Amendment, Chase was a pioneer. But as his dissents in *Texas v. White* and the 1873 *Bradwell v. Illinois* and *Slaughterhouse* decisions suggest, he clearly lacked adequate numbers of robed followers.

Chase was delighted that virtually every other federal and state judge who in the latter 1860s considered issues arising from the Thirteenth Amendment and Civil Rights Act agreed substantially with his *Turner* stand on civil contract matters, as they did with Justice Noah Swayne's opinion concerning race-biased criminal abuses in the *Rhodes* case (see p. 136). Chase knew also, however, that among lawyers concerns existed that the Thirteenth Amendment was too open-ended. Warnings proliferated that any party to any civil contract who regretted entering into it might allege Thirteenth Amendment grounds in order to win release. Therefore, the argument proceeded, freedom for blacks potentially foreshadowed multitudes of civil relationships in which neither slavery nor involuntary servitude was actually present but into which importunate attorneys might substantively infuse such innuendoes vigorously enough to confuse judges or juries. Lawyers had long concurred that services contracted for by the fictionally equal parties to every labor contract did not constitute "servitude" unless compulsions on one party made the commitment involuntary. Disguised compulsions, however, made mutuality implausible and warranted—no, required—judicial interventions to restore equity when and if a complainant sought this remedy. In short, to Chase the equality created by the death of slavery was primarily both a legal and a moral condition. Freedom involved legal rights and obligations as in family, work, and landlord-tenant relationships; it involved also limitations on employers and workers to produce and to pay for what was contracted for under preagreed conditions of life and labor. If voluntarily agreed to, such commitments were not servitude; if coerced, they created dependencies corrosive to freedom.

Thus the argument that excessive freedoms might result from exploiters of the ban on involuntary servitude did not impress Chase. He expected and wanted appeals from the loser in *Turner* and in the other related lawsuits to go to the Supreme Court. Always immodest, he perhaps assumed that the justices would accept his *Turner* principles and by applying them nationwide settle other socially disturbing public policy issues hanging over from slavery. Thereby, in addition to reaching a judgment he believed to be technically deserving and socially desirable, the Court would regain the commanding professional and moral authority that *Dred Scott* and some wartime decisions had cost it.

Chase meant *In re Turner* to clarify in concrete, workaday terms the ways that the Thirteenth Amendment and the Civil Rights Act had altered federalism. Those enactments had left inadequately specific the legal status and derivative rights not only of states but of all national citizens, a point he later stressed in the *Texas v. White* decision.

As the *Turner* case suggested, to Chase even a black female juvenile who as a slave had almost no legal rights was a national citizen, according to the Civil Rights Act. Did her altered and, to Chase, exalted status provide her with meaningful legal remedies through federal justice if state policies such as those explicit in Turner's apprenticeship contract degraded her situation? At least to his satisfaction, Chase's unstintingly positive answer to this question in his *Turner* decision resolved inarguably not only the issue of blacks' legal rights and status both in the former slave states and throughout the nation but also of all Americans' basic civil rights.

In sum, Chase, a man who once committed to a view rarely altered it, in 1867 and 1868 retained two of Lincoln's major constitutional positions. Lincoln had expressed the first in the 1860–1861 secession winter and frequently thereafter: secession by a state or a dozen states was inadmissible. And Chase stubbornly adhered to Lincoln's other view, iterated in April 1865, that the Thirteenth Amendment was the sovereign cure for every ill afflicting the nation.

Chase's total commitment to these two points as well as to the postulates of free labor ideology led him to conclude mistakenly that by incorporating them into the *Turner* and *Texas* cases he was all but closing Reconstruction's book, and decently, too. In 1868 and again in 1872 he assumed that because he had perceived a civilian alternative to Military Reconstruction he deserved the nation's gratitude and highest elective office.

Time's passage would reveal Chase as a poor prophet. But in 1867 he was far from alone in failing to foresee how scant and dilatory would be the attention that justices would thereafter pay to the Thirteenth Amendment except as the ending to formal slavery. To be sure the 1866 Civil Rights Act endured, and in 1867 Congress enacted an Anti-Peonage law also to enforce the Thirteenth Amendment. It forbade federal or state laws and customs and private contracts resulting in persons being held in service for debt and set penalties for anyone "who shall hold, arrest, or return . . . any person . . . to a condition of servitude." But implementation by officials and supportive lawsuits were destined to lag until after the century's turn.

Between the late 1860s and the early 1900s few appeals on Thirteenth Amendment grounds appeared on the Supreme Court's docket, partly because in revisions of the U.S. statutes in the early 1870s for unknown reasons the Civil Rights Act was broken into several separated parts, making its use by lawyers difficult. More important, whites' interests in blacks' conditions sharply diminished. As a result, except for only occasional reference to the Thirteenth Amendment when questions of convict and peon contract labor reached the Court, jurists—indeed, the legal community as a whole—ignored it and its early supportive case law, including *In re Turner*.

The kind of *Turner*-like lawsuit Chase expected to rise to the Supreme Court is suggested by one tried in 1869–1870 in Cincinnati, where he still maintained a law partnership and close connections with many residents. Among them were intimates who shared his belief that "liberty" involved religion and morality, that "property" required reliable and full performance of all marketplace contract relationships, that judges understood "due process of law" better than legislators, and that prayer be required in the public schools. Fireworks erupted, first in Cincinnati politics and then in lawsuits. After jousting inconclusively about proposing a federal constitutional amendment requiring prayer in schools, Cincinnatians concentrated on the city school board, whose members Roman Catholic residents were petitioning for tax support for parochial schools. Arguments arising from this petition attracted the largest crowds the city had experienced since the prewar antislavery controversies and the wartime patriotic assemblies. Debates proliferated on Darwin, the Bible, creationism, evolution, and the Constitution. In response to the petition, the Cincinnati Board of Education ruled that religious instruction and the reading of the Bible were prohibited in the common schools of Cincinnati and that the true object and intent of this rule was to allow the children from families of all sects and opinions to enjoy the benefits of the common-school fund. Defending the board's position in state court against a petition for an injunction requiring the board to reverse this policy, counsel Stanley Matthews, who knew Chase well, insisted, as Chase had in *Turner,* that legal equality was constitutionalized nationally. Once implemented, Matthews argued, this new dispensation "will bring into the full realization of the fundamental law that all citizens are absolutely, in all respects, equal before the law, in civil rights, in religious rights, in all the rights that spring from the possession of human life—in every thing which makes a man, a man."*

Despite this fervent plea, the Ohio judge enjoined the board from enforcing its rule, a decision the state supreme court sustained. Board members considered appealing to the U.S. Supreme Court. There, though Chase and his brethren were known to be pious Christians, they were "under oath to judge by the written Constitution," and, so judging, "must decide against the Bible," board members believed. Nevertheless, they did not appeal, thereby losing the place in history that the case might have enjoyed as the Supreme Court's first interpretation of the Fourteenth Amendment as connected to the First Amendment's denial to the nation of establishing a religion.

What inspired Chase's dramatically forthright *In re Turner* position? It imposed federal standards on private labor contracts sanctioned by a state and on behalf of a black woman. Thereby *In re Turner* was almost calculated to make Chase politically unacceptable as a presidential candidate in 1868 to white social conservatives in both parties, North and South, but particularly unacceptable to Democrats.

Answers to this question require a return to the first weeks of 1866 when it was becoming clear to Chase that slavery, so recently slain after so many decades of seemingly unavailing struggle even to contain it, exhibited a talent for resurrection as involuntary servitude that required his opposition. Chase perceived the Thirteenth Amendment as authorizing—no, commanding—that the substance of freedom be unalloyed. Confident that the then-proposed implementing statute for the amendment, the Civil Rights bill, was impregnably constitutional, in earliest 1866 Chase had readied to begin his circuit.

Even as he entrained, distressing news had flashed across the country of a bloodily suppressed race riot in Britain's Caribbean island of Jamaica. There, relatively close to the American South, in a society long dependent upon the slave trade, whites had freed slaves without a civil war in

---

*Charles Fairman, *Reconstruction and Reunion, 1864–1865: Part One* (New York: Macmillan, 1971), 1310.

1833. The riot shook many antislavery white Americans, and, in the sense of validating their dourest predictions, pleased those people who had opposed abolition that thirty years later racial tensions on that troubled island should still erupt in mutual savageries.

Then racial friction became almost epidemic in America's former slave states. Rarely punished by local or state justice authorities, individual and group vigilantes threatened and assaulted blacks and, increasingly, the whites who aided them, the latter including army and Freedmen's Bureau personnel and northern volunteer schoolteachers. An awful riot in which local officials joined the white mobs killing, beating, and looting blacks disgraced New Orleans. Similar events in other southern communities were distinguished from Louisiana's excesses primarily by their scale and duration. The disorders strengthened doubts about the depth of southern whites' repentance and the likelihood that President Johnson, cabinet officers close to him including the attorney general, or officials of the reconstructed states disrespected the Thirteenth Amendment's bar against involuntary servitude. And so in 1866 Congress had enmeshed itself in the voluminous debates out of which the Civil Rights Act and the Fourteenth Amendment evolved, and a year later it resorted wearily to Military Reconstruction.

Largely because of his disappointments and frustrations about early postwar Reconstruction, Chase, like many prominent Republicans, in piecemeal, unsystematic, and sporadic manner was beginning to lose some of his war-born secular faith in the ability of the nation's governing institutions to solve large-scale social problems by intervening. Seeking replacements for the assurance he was losing, Chase began reviving aspects of his prewar, state-centered, freedom national ideas, stressing the notion that especially in terms of coercive functions the federal government should have nothing to do with protecting slavery. Should it—could it—enforce freedom?

Many persons replying positively to this question were Chase's old comrades of the antislavery crusade. Yet their advocacy divorced them from people like Chase and other emancipationists who were also social conservatives. Except for slavery and the legally entrenched racial bigotries spinning off from slavery, immorally unsound paper money, and speculation-plagued banks, Chase yearned for a return to familiar prewar ways.

Unconcerned about asymmetries in his political affiliations, Chase was a deeply convinced dogmatist only about these few matters so fundamental to him. And he and other federal judges were on hand to protect those values. For example, he drew from his wartime Treasury service a conclusion that under certain circumstances, such as those in the *Gelpcke* situation, federal judges had to curtail state wrongs leading to fiscal instability. Indeed, federal judges must implement all constitutional guarantees and through law subdue lawlessness and stabilize both the society and the economy. And so, when questions deriving from slavery's remnants or currency issues infused constitutional lawsuits, as a federal judge Chase was predisposed to curtail these evils.

His predisposition to activism in these narrow spheres was all but irresistible. Unlike many other slavery-fixated holy warriors of the abolition crusade who opted out of activism once nationwide abolition was achieved, Chase perceived society as still needing his moral stewardship. As never before, equity procedures and substantive due process reasoning were providing opportunities for judges to infuse public policies with views that touched their consciences. Elizabeth Turner's situation caught Chase's conscience because slavery, though illegal, was regenerating under covert guises provided by states' black codes. Therefore as a judge he had a duty to stop these evil resurrections.

The justices' perceptions of evil were not uniform. Expressed in case decisions, their variant perspectives involved the active Court intimately in the political battles to define Reconstruction as it was lobbed between the White House and Capitol Hill, in addition to many other policy disputes. The eight years of Chase's chief justiceship, 1865–1873, saw judicial activism of an unprecedented nature but exercised for diverse beneficiaries. The Court's *Ex parte Milligan* decision (71 U.S. 2 [1866]), for example, signaled that whites' civil liberties enjoyed higher constitutional protections than blacks' civil rights. Though concurring with three other justices in the decision to free Milligan, Chase did so on differing grounds. He and the other concurrers sustained Congress' wartime right to authorize military trials of civilian anti-Unionists even in Indiana, noting that Congress' 1863 Habeas Corpus Act protected citizens by requiring the army to report its civilian prisoners. The military had failed to do so in Milligan's instance. Therefore he deserved release. Legal procedures to bar abuses of power were precious, Chase added, and he asserted further that where freedom was let ring each citizen's "zeal for public and private liberty" would result, presumably through lawsuits, in "official responsibility secured by law."

Many Republicans and blacks denounced the *Milligan* decision as a second *Dred Scott* defense only of whites' rights and called Chase untrustworthy. He welcomed the relative haven that his circuit duty afforded him, and he discerned in the *Turner* petition an opportunity to reassure his critics and perhaps himself of his unwavering commitment to racial equality under law.

Little wonder that Chase cherished proof that he was understood by a fellow justice, Noah Swayne, who, on circuit in Kentucky, decided that the state's black code provision barring a black woman's testimony in a criminal prosecution adverse to white vigilantes violated the Thirteenth Amendment and the Civil Rights Act. To be sure, Swayne stated, every federal judge owed respect to state statutes and precedents. But federal laws should command their first respect. Swayne insisted also that the Thirteenth Amendment forbade both formal slavery and involuntary servitude substantively close to slavery. For Chase the heart of Swayne's *Rhodes* judgment (Fed. Cas. No. 16, 151 [1867], 1309) was his colleague's pronouncement that the Thirteenth Amendment "throws its protection over everyone, of every race, color, and condition." Unless federal judges condemned present "mischiefs complained of or apprehended," the Amendment–Civil Rights Act combination was "a phantom of delusion." But then Chase had to vote in the so-called "*Test Oath*" *Cases, Ex parte Garland* (71 U.S. 333 [1867]) and *Cummings v. Missouri* (71 U.S. 277 [1867]).

Both *Test Oath Cases* involved not blacks' but whites' civil rights—an early forecast of the emphases most justices preferred during the ensuing century. The *Test Oath* lawsuits were dilemmas for Chase. He had built his legal and political career and expressed his religious ethic by opposing the exclusions of millions of slaves and free-state blacks from whites' ordinary pursuits. Now these lawsuits involved the exclusions of millions of whites, potentially, from the prospect of acquiring property through federal and state public employment, the practice of licensed professions, many other positions of trust, and voting. The government's attorneys argued that the necessities imposed by crisis justified the exclusions, that the ex post facto prohibition applied to criminal, not to civil, matters; that the exclusions were from privileges, not rights; and that the oath tests were a job qualification requirement like any other for would-be officeholders, professionals, and, in Missouri's instance, balloters. Underlying these arguments as they progressed to the Supreme Court were sharply variant visions of America's near future. Whatever their merits or faults, the federal and state oath requirements were also manipulable tools for redistributing political, economic, legal, and even social power.

For a bare majority of the Court, Justice Stephen Field declared the federal oath law, as extended by Congress to apply to attorneys seeking to practice in federal courts, and Missouri's law, to be unconstitutional. They barred from professions everyone refusing to swear, thereby depriving them of property. Chase was torn between his basic agreement with Field's views about property and his own intimate knowledge of how the oath tests could alter communities' power structures practically and, so doing, reshape society's futures. Reevaluating his own imperatives was never easy for this proud man. Though ambivalent because he was tied to the idea of individuals' progress through unfettered liberty, Chase, still the newest boy on the block, joined the other three dissenting justices who sustained the validity of the federal and state oath tests.

The *Milligan* and *Test Oath* decisions cast doubt on the national government's right to use the army to speed southern Reconstruction. Nevertheless, in March 1867 Republican congressmen enacted a Military Reconstruction bill over Johnson's veto, and soldiers used test oaths of past loyalty to enroll biracial voters and to exclude unfit candidates from state and local legislatures and offices.

Lawsuits from southern states and from individual white residents of those states alleged the unconstitutionality of Military Reconstruction. Speaking for all the justices (*Mississippi v. Johnson*, 71 U.S. 475 [1867]), Chase denied jurisdiction when Mississippi sought to enjoin the president from implementing the Military Reconstruction law that he had vetoed. Then Georgia sought from the Court an injunction against War Secretary Stanton and General Grant (*Georgia v. Stanton*, 73 U.S. 50 [1868]). Again unanimously, the Court, speaking this time not through Chase but through Justice Nelson, the senior associate, denied Georgia's plea.

The Military Reconstruction Act generated still another lawsuit alleging its unconstitutionality, this time in the form of a habeas corpus appeal from a Mississippian, William McCardle, a profoundly unreconstructed and fiercely racist newspaper publisher. His "incendiary and libellous" articles threatened public order in Vicksburg, according to the soldiers who arrested him. The Chase Court opted not to decide McCardle's case, and the justices, speaking through Chase, contented themselves instead with denying the Court jurisdiction conformably to a recent act to that effect by Congress (*Ex parte McCardle*, 6 Wall. 318 [1868]).

In light of Chase's hopes that his *Turner* decision would gain immediate nationwide attention, its timing could hardly have been worse. In addition to the Court's activism, other seemingly disparate proceedings involving Chase dominated the public's attention, consumed his energies, and ruined his chances for a presidential nomination. One of the most spectacular of these proceedings was the long-drawn-out impeachment of President Johnson for "high crimes and misdemeanors." A second was the Virginia grand jury that was considering an indictment for treason against Jefferson Davis.

Hardly had Chase returned to Washington from his circuit, on which he decided the *Turner* case, when in late February 1868 the House impeached Johnson. From then through May, when Johnson escaped conviction by a single senator's vote, impeachment news and rumors completely buried *In re Turner*.

The Constitution required the chief justice to preside at a president's impeachment trial, and this was the nation's first one. Controversy persisted over whether Chase had the high authority of a judge in a court or only a parliamentarian's humbler power. Chase decided that when so presiding he was a judge. Hurtful to Chase, old comrades of the antislavery crusade berated him for his scrupulously neutral conduct during the impeachment. His relative evenhandedness at the trial not only helped to kill his chances to be either party's 1868 presidential candidate, but it also affected Americans a century later. Because Chase chose to function as a judge, not as an umpire, impeachments have remained almost illusory remedies for presidential misconduct in office.

In the second front-page judicial proceeding over which Chase presided, he demonstrated further his distaste for military rule over civilians, including even Jefferson Davis. A prisoner since Appomattox, Davis languished in an army prison in Virginia, in Chase's circuit. A common perception was held that Chase had pressured federal attorneys to indict Davis and then to try him for treason.

Such critics forgot that Chase's mentor in the law, William Wirt, had prosecuted Aaron Burr for his assertedly treasonous misdeeds. Chase had studied the Burr trial intently. Though Chase believed that Davis deserved punishment for treason, by his deliberate inaction the chief justice helped to thwart a trial for that premier offense, for Chase refused to conduct his Virginia circuit while the area was under army rule. In his absence, in May 1866, a Virginia grand jury convened by the sitting federal district judge

{ *The Reconstruction Justice of Salmon P. Chase* }

indicted Davis for treason. Although Chase resumed his circuit duties, no trial followed. In November 1868, Davis's counsel moved that Chase and the district judge dismiss the prisoner, claiming that the only allowable punishments for high Confederate officials were those specified in the Fourteenth Amendment's third section. Chase agreed, but the district judge did not. They reported ("certified") their division to the Supreme Court, which, Chase concurring, in early 1869 dismissed the case.

Through the rest of the decade and the early 1870s, Chase's Supreme Court colleagues would concern themselves not with blacks' civil liberties but almost exclusively with those of whites. Indeed, *In re Turner* represented a peak for those years in judicial commitment, except for Chase's, to the federally mandated racial equality goals of the Thirteenth Amendment and the Civil Rights Act.

CHAPTER 10

Texas v. White: National Motto or Final Solution?

Sometimes, as eminent constitutionalist Charles Fairman reminded readers of his encyclopedic *Reconstruction and Reunion,* "A sentence uttered by the Court is important quite apart from what has been decided." The Supreme Court decided *Texas v. White* in 1869. It is remembered 130 years later largely because of one sentence in Chase's opinion: "The Constitution, in all its provisions, looks to an indestructible Union, composed of indestructible states." Chase's epigram "has become a national motto," Fairman concluded.

Chase would probably have been delighted to know not only that his telling phrase was immediately famous but also that it speaks from his time to ours. Yet he might well have been disappointed that his *Texas v. White* bequest has become merely a "national motto." He intended it to be far more, perhaps even a final solution for untying Reconstruction's knots and an attempt at netting a presidential candidacy for himself in 1872. Such motives suggest the wisdom of Fairman's further counsel about *Texas v. White:* "To appreciate its significance in 1869 one must recall the context."*

An important element in that context, Chase's first-impression decision in *In re Turner* confirmed the availability of the Thirteenth Amendment and the Civil Rights Act as federal judicial remedies for redressing the economic wrongs Turner suffered from her state-sanctioned racially skewed private labor contract. Chase's *Texas v. White* decision ruled that those remedies were available also to innocent bondholders deprived of their property by a state claiming to have seceded from the Union. Transcending this large point, Chase, in *Texas v. White,* answered incisively a recurring question in America's history: what *is* a state—its geography? officials? or, as his *Turner* opinion implied, all its people?

*Charles Fairman, *Reconstruction and Reunion, 1864–1888: Part One* (New York: Macmillan, 1971), 628, 630, 642.

{ 140 }

Chase meant all its people: whites, blacks, males, females, former rebels, and consistent Unionists. He had perceived a policy triad consisting of race- and gender-blind equal civil rights, a recommendation for universal male suffrage, and total amnesty for former Confederates. Such a policy might end the need for the vexing black codes, test oaths, and Military Reconstruction yet avoid a need for a decision on the constitutionality of the last and for other exclusionary or punitive policies and thereby diminish sectional tensions. Surely his doctrine of inclusions rather than exclusions would result in his grateful countrymen making him president. Seen through this lens, Chase's 1867–1868 circuit rulings supplement his *Turner* opinion and lead toward *Texas v. White*.

While circuiting, Chase dealt with the large property interests that had become uncertain if parties to lawsuits were considered to have been wartime traitors. Charges to this effect by litigants raised again, by declension, arguments about the nature of the Civil War left unresolved since the Supreme Court's 1863 *Prize Cases* straddle, a matter still unresolved years after Appomattox. Like Chase's *In re Turner* ruling in its subject arena, his circuit decisions in *Shortridge v. Macon* (1867) and *Keppel's Administrators v. Petersburg RR* (1868), for example, were the initial impressions by a federal judge about the ways nonwar private contracts and the official wartime acts of the Confederate national, state, and local governments affecting private property would be viewed. Were four years' worth of birth certificates, deeds, promissory notes, insurance, and business contracts including purchases and sales of stocks and bonds as void as the statutes of the Confederacy? If so, social and economic instabilities were imagined on a scale larger than had yet occurred. But if the Civil War was defined as a war between nations, then such consequences would be avoided.

As they did in other readmitted states, Texas' constitutional conventioners of 1866 ratified nonwar civil laws and derivative private contracts of the Confederacy's years. Chase's *Shortridge* and *Keppel* decisions came to the same conclusion. These decisions overshadowed *Turner*, as far as the South's businessmen, lawyers, bankers, and investors were concerned.

Chase dealt with the war's nature and the legitimacy of nonwar laws and private contracts much as Lincoln had done. Though Lincoln had refused adamantly to recognize the existence of the Confederacy and in most ways held to the position that what occurred was a vast rebellion, with respect to prisoners of war, the blockade, and other tinderbox issues he treated the conflict pragmatically as an international war between nations. So too did Chase.

Once more jumping party lines as he had so often before the war, in midsummer 1868 Chase, adhering again to his old states' rights doctrines, angled for a presidential nomination, this time as a Democrat. Apart from its prewar dedication to representing slave owners' interests and its opposition to every crisis policy of Lincoln's presidency, that party was his natural home. The judicial rulings that had cost Chase the support of many Republicans interested important Democratic party leaders in him as their top nominee. Some wanted him as the Democratic front-runner because he was a leading antislavery activist. With him heading the Democratic ticket, the party could advertise itself as purged of Copperheadism, a reformed and penitent new party.

Chase offered Democrats the chance to share his vision of the improved future that emancipation had opened. He combined this optimism with a way to exploit the swelling opinion he discerned even among important Republicans, that, while bypassing the issue of constitutionality, the nation should downsize or even end its militarized Reconstruction enterprise.

But in 1868 Chase and his supporters failed adequately to gauge the passion with which unregenerate Democrats viewed his antislavery past, wartime record, role in the Johnson impeachment, and postwar rulings on the legal status of emancipated blacks like Elizabeth Turner. Chase's personal history, culminating in his *Turner* ruling, made him vulnerable to attacks by the potent barons of a party that lacked an acknowledged head and sorely needed one. An activist on the bench, Chase failed to convey to the conventioners an implication in his *Turner* ruling that federal judges, not soldiers, were capable of implementing the nation's constitutionalized duty to defend the civil rights of "all citizens." To Chase this perception led to a conclusion that the nation had already won victory in Reconstruction without having basically altered the traditionally state-centered nature of the federal system.

Balancing his advocacy of gender-blind as well as race-blind access to state and federal justice, Chase proposed racially unfettered universal (that is, male) suffrage for amnestied or pardoned former Confederates and for blacks. Once these conditions prevailed, blacks, like whites, would protect themselves by voting and, like Elizabeth Turner, by lawsuits. Then with good conscience the national government could end its uncomfortably novel responsibilities in the South and pronounce the southern states full partners again in the federal Union, the central messages of both his *Shortridge* and *Keppel* circuit decisions and his impending *Texas v. White* opinion in the Supreme Court. His goal was "the complete recovery of the Southern states from the evils of the war," Chase emphasized; "their prosperity is the prosperity of the whole."*

Chase's famous 1869 opinion in *Texas v. White* encapsulated all these ideas. It asserted the constitutional indestructibility and equality of all states, including those of the South, a boon to Democrats. But his opinion also validated Congress' authority to impose Military Reconstruction laws on the former Confederate states. This duality was no way to win Republicans' or Democrats' hearts, financial contributions, or votes. In short, taken together, Chase's *Turner* and *Texas v. White* views were leaving him adrift in a political whirlpool.

It was swirling dangerously for Chase because, despite his correspondence network, through 1865 and 1866 he had not recognized that major elements in both political parties were adopting some of their adversary's constitutional positions concerning the nature and legal consequences of the Civil War. Democrats were adapting to their postwar needs Lincoln's wartime position that no secessions had occurred. Therefore, Democrats were now asserting that the South's states were valid members of the Union and deserved condition-free admission to representation. Responsively, some Republicans were resorting to Democrats' earlier extreme-right arguments that secessions had indeed occurred. Republicans added, however, that the Union had conquered the seceded entities and that therefore the Congress, not the Court, bore responsibility to define their present situations.

Chase received a forced-draft education on these matters during his 1867–1868 circuits when faced with the duty of deciding the *Turner, Shortridge,* and *Keppel* lawsuits and many others. His fumbled bid for the 1868 Democratic party presidential nomination, however, should not mask the fact that what he learned on circuit prepared him to cope with *Texas v. White.*

While on his 1867 circuit, Chase was already working on what became his *Texas v. White* judgment. The evidence suggests that his perceptions about the legal status of individuals in Turner's case nourished his ideas about Texas' constitutional status in the federal Union and the status of all the states, ideas he soon expressed memorably in *Texas v. White.*

Immediately famous, *Texas v. White* originated from postwar litigations

*Robert B. Warden, *An Account of the Private Life and Public Services of Salmon Portland Chase* (1874), 651.

initiated by the state to recover prewar U.S. government bonds that Texas' Confederate authorities had confiscated and then sold to third parties. In late 1865 the prominent Galveston attorney George Washington Paschal became Texas' agent in Washington for recovering the bonds for the state. Because he contributed to Chase's views on state-centered federalism as affected by the war, Paschal deserves additional description.

Paschal was a wise choice for his client, the state of Texas. Of Chase's generation, born in Georgia, he graduated from Princeton. Then, like Chase, he studied law as an apprentice. Paschal clerked for Joseph Lumpkin, later chief justice of Georgia's supreme court, a rare judge for this region and time who outspokenly criticized slavery and pleaded the South's need to industrialize. Just as Chase had enjoyed advantages while clerking for Wirt, Paschal benefited from the availability of Lumpkin's unusually complete law library. Paschal entered private law practice in Georgia about the time Chase did in Ohio, in the early 1830s. Becoming wealthy and politically prominent, Paschal was a consistent pro-Jackson Democratic party activist.

Even more a contrarian than Chase, Paschal married a Cherokee and with her trekked the infamous Trail of Tears to Arkansas after Georgia expelled her tribe. Attaining professional success in Arkansas, Paschal also served the Cherokees as their legal counsel and defended whites who had befriended runaway slaves, an activity even more hazardous in Arkansas than in Ohio. Then in 1849 Paschal moved to Texas. He set up shop in Galveston, then the state's largest city and busiest port, where he further paralleled Chase's work by compiling in a published digest Texas' laws, as Chase had Ohio's.

Outspokenly antisecession, from 1861 until Appomattox Paschal publicly criticized the Confederacy's harsh conscription and internal security policies. By then a lawyer of widely recognized ability and a staunch antisecession Unionist, Paschal suffered professionally and personally during the long Confederate dispensation of the state. He earned Chase's further respect when in 1862, during a brief Union army occupation of Galveston, Paschal alerted the treasury secretary to the fact that Texas' Confederate government was confiscating and reselling Unionists' assets, including U.S. bonds. Chase was able to stop payment on the securities. But Chase's successor at Treasury rescinded the order because President Johnson had pardoned the third-party purchasers.*

*Jane L. Scarborough, "George W. Paschal" (Ph.D. diss., Rice University, 1972), 99–124.

With Appomattox Paschal's loyalty paid off. Needing no presidential pardon, Paschal, a consistent Unionist, unlike multitudes of other southern attorneys, could and did subscribe truthfully to any loyalty oath required for practice in the federal or state courts. He represented the militarily reconstructed government of Texas in lawsuits seeking repossession of the controverted U.S. bonds. As the litigations made their way to the Supreme Court, respondents' counsel asserted on behalf of his former rebel clients that the state lacked standing to sue, in effect adopting the Radical Republicans' argument that by seceding the government of Texas had ceased to exist, the position concurred in by the Republican majority in Congress when imposing Military Reconstruction on the South's states.

Had Texas survived secession and total military defeat? Upon appealing to the Supreme Court, Paschal knew that he had to convince the justices not to sidestep the basic question, whether Texas had standing to sue, as the jurists had in *Georgia v. Stanton* and *Mississippi v. Johnson.* Paschal also had to show the justices a way to answer this question and yet avoid confronting Congress over the Military Reconstruction law's basic premise, that lawful state governments did not exist in the South.

He discerned an appropriate, Lincoln-like route, an approach that Chase had already perceived and sketched independently in his *In re Turner* opinion, as in those in the *Shortridge* and *Keppel* cases. That route led to concentration not only on the legal status of the state whose statute was in contention but also on the legal status and federally protectable rights of all individuals.

But Chase's opinion in *In re Turner* was a sketch, not a blueprint. Contemporary custom among justices when on circuit was to be brief in their rulings and to contain them to the issues and litigants presented to the judges. An assumption prevailed that almost all circuit judgments adequately settled the matter in dispute. If losers in circuit cases felt ill-served by relevant rulings they would appeal for rehearings by the Supreme Court of the points of law involved but rarely of the facts. Therefore when deciding Turner's fate, Chase had only outlined his perception of the factual impacts of the Thirteenth Amendment and the Civil Rights Act on the legal status of a black individual in an unseceded but formerly slaveholding state. Now, partly because Paschal cleverly tailored his brief for Texas in a manner to snare Chase's interest, *Texas v. White* presented the chief justice with a challenging opportunity. Chase could defuse the political mine-field that lay waiting because the legal statuses and affected assets of individuals and of the former Confederate states were still disputed years after Appomattox.

Chase had Paschal's brief with him during his 1867 circuit when he decided *In re Turner*. It impressed the chief justice, for in it Paschal shifted the issue from what Lincoln had called the "pernicious abstraction" of whether a state was in or out of the Union to citizens' rights. The latter had been Lincoln's primary topic in his last public statements of spring 1865 and was Chase's basic concern in Turner's case.

In his argument of alternatives, Paschal first disclaimed a need to worry whether any of Texas' several governments before and since Appomattox were legitimate. "Texas remained a State of the Union all the time," he asserted, "and Congress possesses the power to pass all necessary legislation to protect *every inhabitant in the United States in all his rights of citizenship in Texas*" (emphasis added). Then, paraphrasing John Marshall's *McCulloch v. Maryland* opinion, Paschal argued that Congress' possession of this power imposed on it a duty to "judge of the most appropriate means to guard and protect the powers committed to the Union."

The respondents' primary attorney was former Confederate general Albert Pike, another Arkansan. Since receiving a presidential pardon Pike practiced frequently at the Supreme Court's bar. Typifying the tendency of Democrats, at least when in court, to play some Radical Republicans' constitutional tunes, Pike denied that Texas presently was a state and therefore it lacked standing to sue in the Supreme Court. Its secession was a fact, he continued, not a legal fiction. The 1867 Military Reconstruction statute passed by Congress listed Texas as one of the "rebel States," meaning that it lacked equal status with those not listed. "There can be union only among equal States," he concluded. Not even the Supreme Court was competent "to declare that Texas is in law a State in the Union, when the legislative power has declared that it is not so in fact."

Issues the contending attorneys had raised touched the most sensitive political question since emancipation. The constitutional, legal, and political destinies of the former Confederate states, not only of Texas, hinged significantly on the Court's decision in *Texas v. White* about the status of those states since 1861. Merely by accepting jurisdiction, itself a step hotly debated by the adversary attorneys and by the justices, the Court implied that Texas existed. But speaking for the Court's majority, Chase ventured even further.

He assigned himself the writing of the majority opinion. It was a task that a truly driven would-be presidential candidate or mere placeholder probably would have preferred to dodge. But as Fairman concluded correctly, only Chase could have spoken with such authority on an occasion that required a definitive statement about attempted secession.

Why? As Fairman has noted, in preparing to speak for the Court's majority in *Texas v. White,* Chase exploited both Paschal's brief of 1867 and his own experiences as antislavery lawyer, cabinet officer, and federal jurist. Far longer than Paschal, Chase had been pondering the complex issue of the seceded states' legal status. To his own satisfaction, as in *Turner,* Chase had perceived connections between the legal status and rights both of states and individuals. In 1865, for example, Chase had advised an intimate that

> the pretended Acts . . . of Secession were absolutely null & all acts in furtherance of them . . . are equally null. . . . Precisely at this point comes in the error . . . of those who insist that the rights of suffrage . . . are to be ascertained by . . . the constitutions of the rebel States existing at the time of rebellion. Indeed it is difficult to see upon what ground of reason it can be asserted that the Constitution and Laws existing before the rebellion must [now] determine . . . citizenship & suffrage.*

By early 1865 Lincoln had also acknowledged these connections. Chase believed that had the president lived, by the close of his second term in March 1869 Lincoln would have transformed them into acceptable public policies, thus avoiding a need for the Court to settle *Texas v. White.*

Speaking for the majority of the justices in *Texas v. White,* Chase exhibited a hardliner's insistence on the permanent constitutional status of the state—any state—as the basis of the federal Union. He was as consistently firm as Lincoln about secession never having occurred, a point he stressed during his 1867 circuit when he championed equal legal rights for Elizabeth Turner. In his *Shortridge* opinion, for example, Chase had ruled that nonwar legal relationships such as marriage and ordinary business contracts entered into during the Civil War under the state's dispensation were valid and that the state's act of secession "did not effect, even for a moment, . . .

---

* Fairman, *Reconstruction,* 629–30.

[its] separation . . . from the Union." But though no secession occurred, state authorities' defiance of federal authority had led to the state's vulnerability to national emancipation and its Reconstruction sequels. They included equal legal rights for blacks and whites, Chase's central theme of *In re Turner.*

Chase had not stopped there. Well before 1865 he had advocated political rights both for black males and former Confederates. So far as blacks were concerned, in April 1865 Lincoln had publicly advocated that states extend voting rights to black Union army veterans and to literate non-whites. Since then Andrew Johnson had led the opposition even to that limited breakthrough. Chase's contemporaries attended closely to *Texas v. White,* partly to learn if he would dare to incorporate in his opinion his brave but politically hazardous support for extending voting rights in a color-blind manner. He dared.

Acknowledging first in his *Texas v. White* opinion that honest men differed on the present status of the rebel states, Chase offered a definition: in the Constitution the word "state" referred, variously, to territory, government, or people. Concerning its territory and people, Texas, notwithstanding its assertion of secession, remained a state in the Union. Because its government had been militarily hostile to the United States, Texas remained unrepresented in Congress. But both presidential and congressional Reconstruction policies had resurrected its government (Chase overlooked the fact that they were also successive governments) so that Texas enjoyed standing to sue in the Supreme Court.

As he had on circuit, Chase carefully separated the enactments of Texas' rebel authorities from the nonwar legal obligations that private individuals assumed during and after the war, except—and it was an exception of primary importance—for slavery and involuntary servitude, the issue of *In re Turner.* This exception brought Chase to enlarge on his stirring peroration about the indestructible Union of states. He added to it a prose hymn praising Lincoln's Emancipation Proclamation and the Thirteenth Amendment, then asserted that the Union's victory in the Civil War had done more than suppress the rebellion and end slavery. It had also redefined the people of each state to include blacks.

The "great social change" in the former slaves' legal status in their states of residence meant that the "new freemen necessarily became part of the people, and the people still constituted the State," Chase said. And so Texas endured as a geographical entity in which emancipation had redefined and greatly enlarged the number and racial character of its citizens.

Having dealt with Texas' territory and people, Chase considered the state's government. A provisional state government existed in Texas although the state did not yet enjoy representation in Congress. This situation would continue, Chase ruled in an expression of dominant Republican constitutionalism, until Congress, exercising the power and fulfilling its duty to do so under the Constitution's clause guaranteeing every state a republican form of government, admitted Texas to representation. Whether excluded or admitted, however, Texas and all the former Confederate states and all their residents were, nonetheless, "now entitled to the benefit of the constitutional guaranty."

It was up to Congress to determine when the Military Reconstruction Acts had worked their intended alchemy. Except by implication Chase refused to consider the constitutionality of the Reconstruction legislation. But he assumed its validity by concluding that the necessary evidence for Texas' full-fledged status would be a reformed state constitution conceived and ratified under Military Reconstruction. Such a Texas constitution should "conform its provisions to the new conditions created by emancipation, and afford adequate security to the people of the State," Chase concluded, in terms again essentially echoing his *In re Turner* opinion.

What shape should the rapidly recrystallized and reorganized social order assume in Texas and elsewhere in the South? Chase's *Turner* and *Texas v. White* decisions implied answers. They were based partly on his shrewd reading of northern public opinion that Reconstruction could not and should not last much longer. Although in the 1868 election year this perception failed to interest enough Democrats in Chase as a presidential candidate, he looked forward to 1872, when his message in both those cases, as in others, should win him support. That message was that better ways existed for southerners to shorten their region's subordination than semipermanent military government, exclusionary test oaths, and disfranchisements, or, worse yet, lawless vigilantism.

And so Texas' existing government had standing to sue, and, as the rightful heir of prewar state governments, it was the legal possessor of the U.S. bonds in controversy. On another level, one presumably deeply satisfying to Chase, his *Texas v. White* rulings convinced white Texans of the need at least formally to meet both his and Congress' minima.

Written and ratified in the wake of *Texas v. White*, a provision of Texas' 1869 so-called "black and tan" constitution mandated race-blind, equal legal rights for all its citizens:

[The] . . . adoption of any system of peonage, whereby the helpless and unfortunate may be reduced to practical bondage, shall never be authorized, or tolerated by the laws of this state; and neither slavery nor involuntary servitude, except as a punishment for crime whereof the party shall have been duly convicted, shall ever exist within this state.

Nevertheless, the word "ever" in Texas' reformed constitution and the principle of legal equality Chase stressed in both *In re Turner* and *Texas v. White* would live only briefly after 1869.

EPILOGUE

Fulfilled and Unfulfilled Pledges

Fortunately for his peace of mind Chase could not imagine how quickly his judgments in *In re Turner* and *Texas v. White* would be diluted. The pace of this dilution is suggested by the fact that in 1872–1873, the last full year of his life, Chase dissented from three Supreme Court decisions. One dissent was in the obscure *White v. Hart* (81 U.S. 646), one unrelated to *Texas v. White*, and involved a claim for payment—in 1872—on a pre-Thirteenth Amendment contract for the sale of slaves. His second dissent was evoked in the landmark *Slaughterhouse Case* (83 U.S. 36). It concerned white Louisianans' claims that their rights deriving from the Thirteenth and Fourteenth Amendments were violated because they were excluded from a state-authorized, private meatpacking monopoly. And the third, *Bradwell v. Illinois* (83 U.S. 130), resulted from that state's denial to a white woman of a license to practice law.

This trio of dissents was even more poignant because in 1870 Chase suffered what his physicians described as a nondisabling stroke. Back at work before the year ended, his fellow justices noticed a slurring of the precise speech of which he was so proud, a weary stooping of his former ramrod-straight carriage, and other evidences of physical or neurological impairments. Rumors circulated that Chase and Kate disguised the seriousness of his affliction in order not to diminish his presidential prospects in 1872. Returning to the Court, he resumed a full workload although he never recovered fully from the superficial effects of the stroke. His mental faculties unimpaired, however, Chase joined in considering lawsuits involving hangover wartime issues that were surfacing, along with newer matters of contention. By 1873, when expressing his disagreements to these three decisions, Chase was dying and knew it. And he knew that his dissents in the *White*, *Bradwell*, and *Slaughterhouse* cases were ineffective in resisting the swift erosion of his goals of *In re Turner* and *Texas v. White*, unavailing not only in the Court but also in the larger society. But

{ 151 }

probably he did not realize that he had contributed significantly if unintentionally to the dilution of the racial equality impulse that his dissents mourned.

Disappointed in 1868 that a presidential nomination eluded him, Chase was pleased that Grant's election promised both greater national stability and firmness on behalf of blacks' political and civil rights. Some wartime controversies resurfaced, including the Union's emergency monetary measures that he had shaped and implemented as treasury secretary. Although uniquely aware of the necessity of these expedients, Chase had been and remained uncertain about their constitutionality, especially of the Union's desperate resort to paper money issues. Ever fiscally conservative, his distaste for paper substitutes for hard money (that is, specie) surfaced in 1870. When deciding *Hepburn v. Griswold* (8 Wall., 603), Chase, speaking for a majority of the justices, sidestepped the basic question of Congress' authority to issue paper money. But he declared unconstitutional the wartime law mandating this substitute as legal tender when applied to private contracts requiring specie payment entered into before its enactment. That law violated the Fifth Amendment's ban on deprivations of property without due process of law and the Constitution's Article 1, Section 10 bar against states impairing contracts by substituting paper for specie, he ruled. Although the latter provision constrained states, not the nation, Chase bridged a gap in federalism by holding that the clause applied substantively to the federal government.

The decision was political. The majority justices professed their allegiance to the Democratic party. The minority judges were Republicans whose dissents echoed Chase's own justifications for the fiscal expedients of his Treasury years. A year later Grant appointed two new justices. A rehearing of the *Hepburn* issues resulted in their reversal, this time with Chase in dissent (*Knox v. Lee,* 79 U.S. 457), an oscillation that may have pleased him. He was on record against what he condemned as immoral paper money even though the Court had legitimized the nation's need for it during its greatest crisis, the Civil War.

Despite his deteriorating health, as the 1860s ended Chase again entertained hopes of his presidential prospects. He estimated reasonably enough that he had done a great deal to change the law in the direction of equality. And he had glimpsed, if only for too brief a time, the better futures that emancipation should have opened had the nation taken the directions he pointed to in his decisions and opinions in cases.

Still, his pride in his contributions to a greatly improved future was justified because by 1870 the Thirteenth, Fourteenth, and Fifteenth Amendments were part of the Constitution. Both civil and political rights were now race-neutral. To be sure, Chase regretted the omission of a specific gender-neutral provision, especially concerning civil rights, an omission he had tried to remedy in *In re Turner* and would fail to remedy in *Bradwell v. Illinois*. Nevertheless, in 1870 black Mississippian Hiram Revels took Jefferson Davis's former seat in the U.S. Senate. In 1865 Chase's admission of John Rock to the Supreme Court bar had symbolized the Union's military victory and the dethronement of *Dred Scott*. To joyous victors of the antislavery crusade Senator Revels's installation was Reconstruction's heady triumph. Recollections circulated in 1870 of the late Sam Houston's prewar reaction, that he would sooner be in hell, to a suggestion that a black might one day sit in Congress. William Gillette, an abolitionist correspondent of Senator Charles Sumner, Chase's political intimate, wondered if Houston was not now finding hell "heated seven times hotter . . . on actually seeing the hated, dreaded negro among you [in the Senate]? What a Revolution! How wonderful! We did not anticipate its advent so soon."[*]

Sharing in the excitement of Senator Revels's seating, Chase too cheered the "advent" of the Reconstruction "revolution," by which he meant also its substantial ending. Like Wendell Phillips, Chase believed that the pledges of the antislavery activists had been fulfilled. To him that revolution involved primarily federal responsibility to equalize the legal statuses of both the Union's states and their black citizens. Chase's major judicial rulings had helped to achieve this equality. As measured by his view of those rulings, Reconstruction was never a "fool's errand," as it was soon mislabeled; instead, it was a fundamental success. He was confident that his decisions on circuit and in the Supreme Court significantly had helped to lift millions of former slaves from legally irresponsible dependency, to validate the nonwar private legal relationships of multitudes of those states' white and black residents, and to ensure that the former slave-owning states no longer enjoyed a disproportionately privileged status in the federal Union. Therefore it was time for the nation to declare victory in its great crusade and to end it with amnesty for whites and suffrage for blacks, a formula he tried unsuccessfully to have the renascent Democrats adopt.

*Charles Sumner Papers, Houghton Library, Harvard University, 97:78.

Apart from the political, Chase's out-of-court postwar activities continued to involve him in many church-related evangelical, educational, medical, and legal-aid private associations with special interests in the South's blacks. He had become familiar with these groups during the war. Immediately after Appomattox he began to praise the fact that these private associations were self-supporting financially. Chase wanted responsibility for protecting blacks' civil rights through lawsuits to shift from government agencies and agents, including the Freedmen's Bureau attorneys, to lawyers retained by an appropriate private association.

He sought privatization largely because his chronic nightmares about the nation's war-eroded economy persisted after the war. Ever a hard-money man, Chase still feared that government insolvency and an economic collapse could lead to class violence worse than a civil war. By his cheeseparing standards of public finance, even the Freedmen's Bureau's inexpensive programs were too costly.

More than ever Chase had become anti-institutionalist. He remembered slave owners' prewar ability to manipulate government. Exposures of corruption in wartime government operations, some in his own Treasury Department, had outraged this hypercritical moralist. For crucial postwar years President Johnson had impeded Reconstruction implementations, commonly by misinterpreting relevant statutes and Supreme Court judgments. Indeed, Johnson, his complaisant attorney general, and other high officials had almost split the army into mutually antagonistic factions. In analogous situations abroad, when a nation's military took sides in civilians' political contentions classic coups d'etat followed. Johnson's impeachment had stopped his devious interferences, but it offered still another proof of the nation's need to untie its Reconstruction knots.

And so Chase was receptive to ideas favoring Reconstruction's privatization. Other long-faithful antislavery activists, including William Lloyd Garrison, Wendell Phillips, and Oliver O. Howard, the "Christian general" heading the Freedmen's Bureau, also agreed that reasons existed to retrench that paramilitary Reconstruction agency.

Many Republican congressmen agreed also that the Freedmen's Bureau should not be the only safe channel for benevolence. But they hesitated to close it altogether until Grant succeeded Johnson in the White House and evidence indicated that the white South was no longer unrepentant. Moreover, practical alternatives beckoned in the form of private associations' contributions of money and personnel. But Chase seemed oblivious of the fact that few lawyers like Elizabeth Turner's stepped forward to continue implementing race-blind legal equality on a pro bono or minimal-fee basis. Frederick Douglass's objection that if no bureau existed, blacks could not practically enjoy the equal protection of state laws as a right of federal citizenship was a better reading of reality than Chase's overly optimistic one.

Yet in advocating privatization Chase felt himself to be part of a new trend. The further advancement of millions of humans primarily by private rather than by government efforts would, he believed, prevent the nation's wards from becoming its permanent future dependents. He was imbued with a mixture of ideas derived from Christian evangelicals, Malthusian and Ricardian economists, Darwinian evolutionists, and American constitutional and legal commentators, including Jefferson, Kent, and Story, and from his own brand of free labor ideology, religious beliefs, and legal training. Ineradicably paternalistic toward blacks, insufferably so by present standards, Chase was far more concerned with their legal rights and moral uplift than with their actual lives. To him self-evident truths about Reconstruction were that only religious indoctrination and patient hard work for wages (shades of Bishop Chase) could teach recent slaves the social adhesives of discipline, thrift, self-control, self-reliance, and sturdy independency achieved by self-help.

Redress for wrongs lay in law and votes. Therefore equal legal rights for Elizabeth Turner, for example, were essential to her acquisition of these moral necessities and her contribution to society's stability. Unless the law ensured that employers would teach apprentices like her the trades contracted for, and unless workers like her were confident that their labors would bring the job skills contracted for and the wages needed to nourish stable families and to pay debts, both apprentices and journeymen would lose the incentive to work, to pay rent, and to fulfill all other contract obligations. Chase feared the alternative, that blacks would become not Jeffersonian yeomen but beasts of burden for employers (consider his *Turner* opinion) and political dupes (witness his emphases in *Texas v. White*). Instead, self-help by individual blacks, just as for whites, must replace the government's benefactions, guardianships, and interventions. As government receded, private associations' white teachers, ministers, physicians, and lawyers would provide temporary tutelage for blacks. Then, Chase

believed, blacks would soon defy racists' insistence that they were unimprovable beyond menial levels of work and education and irresponsible
in legal and moral relationships.

And so Chase advocated the privatization of Reconstruction. In 1867,
for example, he became president of the American Freedmen's Union
Commission, an umbrella organization for a coalition of private evangelical, education, welfare, and legal associations. On that occasion Chase urged
that they contribute funds and personnel to replace Freedmen's Bureau
officers. "We are endeavoring to carry forward a work begun by the government," he stated. Grass-roots private associations' services would outdo
government's "officious and intrusive interference with matters which
belong... to the [white] people among whom [blacks] live." Private welfare workers, missionaries, and lawyers, better than government officers,
could create "cordial and active cooperation with patriotic and Christian
men and women of the Southern States." Echoing next Tocqueville's notion that Americans best performed large public work through private
channels, Chase asserted that he had always thought it "true statesmanship to connect... the work of the government with the voluntary action
of the people." His fully reprinted speech evoked from the editor of Great
Britain's *Freedman,* on April 1, 1867, the wistful observation that "the true
statesmanship indicated by Chief Justice Chase" might have prevented the
bloody racial violence in Jamaica in 1865.

As ever a prisoner of his own perceptions, Chase misconstrued the
privatization of civil rights as the symbol of the ultimate Reconstruction
victory. He never doubted the morality, constitutionality, or success of the
prewar antislavery crusade that during the war he had helped to bring to
the far greater glory of abolition. Chase relished his role in elevating the
nation's initial war aim of reunion to reunion-plus-abolition. Concerning
postwar events, he was particularly proud of having carved middle ways,
as he saw them, in policy between reactionary racists such as Andrew
Johnson, who opposed all federal interventions on behalf of blacks, and truly
Radical Republican visionaries, who advocated extended, even perpetual
federal guardianship over the implicitly unimprovable freedmen.

Chase's middle way formula involved individuals protecting their own
legal interests and constitutionalized rights through racially equalized
access to the law's protections and through exercise of the ballot. In many
ways he exhibited an almost naive faith in the efficacy of such self-help by
free labor. He seriously likened the two and a half centuries of slavery to

the few decades of the Irish and German immigrants' entrances into America's political and civil mainstreams. So seriously did Chase credit this fantasy, rooted in his lifetime of dealing with legal abstractions rather than with the realities of race-defined poverty and other deprivations caused or perpetuated by racially bigoted state laws, that by 1870 he joined other veteran antislavery leaders who concluded that the nation had fulfilled its duty to black Americans. Thenceforth blacks could and should stand on their own feet as independent voters and responsible parties to free labor contracts bound by the laws of their states. Every legally responsible black created "testimonies . . . of the most practical kind, to the capacity of the emancipated and enfranchised blacks to take care of themselves," editorialized New York's *American Freedman* in April 1869. "The croaking prophecies that these people would be perpetual paupers, a burden alike upon the charities of the North and the pity of the Nation, receive in these facts a fitting refutation."

Unlike in 1868, in 1872 no publisher recruited a political journalist to write Chase's biography should he win a presidential nomination. Still, Chase's optimism about inevitable further progress was reinforced by the surge of legal treatises such as Thomas McIntyre Cooley's *Constitutional Limitations Which Rest Upon the Legislative Power of the States of the American Union.* Published first in 1868, Cooley's book sprouted new editions for a half-century to follow, quickly becoming the standard constitutional law textbook in the many new law schools then increasing in number and importance. An immediate runaway success, Cooley depicted a free and dual federalism in which nation and states functioned almost totally insulated from each other. It was a depiction close to Chase's freedom national doctrine, with the happy addition, as Chase measured matters, that Cooley assigned to judges frontline responsibility to resist excesses committed by legislators and voters.

In 1870 the Court, in *U. S. v. DeWitt* (76 U.S. 41), decided that Congress had overstepped by disguising as a revenue measure a prohibitive tax on the interstate transportation of naphtha, which when adulterated with kerosene was a popular but ferociously inflammable illuminant. For the Court, Chase held that Congress might regulate interstate commerce but not exclude from it even a hazardous substance. That policing duty was one that states only might perform if so impelled. Since the relevant states chose not to act and Congress could not, consumers enjoyed no protection.

Then in 1872 and 1873 the justices decided *White v. Hart, Bradwell v. Illinois,* and the *Slaughterhouse Cases,* the trio of lawsuits tragically significant to Chase in his last years. His peace of mind deriving from confidence that law led to individual and social justice was under attack. Chase lived to see the essence of his *In re Turner* and *Texas v. White* opinions turned back against him.

To Chase, slavery was the only exception to the truism that society's stability required sound property rights defined by contracts. Therefore, because of the immorality underlying its contract claim, *White v. Hart* deeply troubled him. The appellants, white Georgians and others in several states, demanded payment years after Appomattox for slaves sold before emancipation. They sought money and not, of course, the specific performance of again owning humans. Did the preemancipation property rights of buyers and sellers of slaves survive emancipation, Appomattox, the Thirteenth Amendment, and Reconstruction? The appellants' counsel relied on the federal Constitution's prohibitions against states impairing contract obligations and on the Fourteenth Amendment. The contracts involved in this lawsuit were clearly enforceable when made. But the Reconstruction constitutions of the appellants' states in some form denied the enforceability of preemancipation slave-sale contracts. Could Chase and the other justices reconcile two polar constitutional moral imperatives? One was the sanctity of private contracts, a lodestar of Chase's life. The other was the amended federal Constitution's prohibition against the only immoral private property, slavery, that his generation acknowledged.

To Chase's distress the majority of the justices decided that payment was required. To his further distress, the majority's reasoning, like the appellant counsel's brief, exploited his *Texas v. White* views about the states' indissolubility and his major circuit opinions affirming the validity of nonwar private contracts such as those in marriages and real estate conveyances. But though dismayed with his colleagues for sanctifying profits made by the purchase and sale of fellow humans, Chase's continuing physical weakness and declining morale quenched any possible fire in his dissent. It merely stated the fact of his disagreement.

Similarly, in the Court's immediately famous and enormously influential 5-to-4 *Slaughterhouse* decision of 1873, Chase was constrained by his feebleness merely to join in a dissent expressed by Justice Field. This lawsuit arose because in 1869 Louisiana granted a designated meatpacking company a lucrative twenty-five-year butchering monopoly for New Orleans, then the South's largest city. Louisiana's lawmakers granted the monopoly under the state's police powers, ostensibly in order to protect the public's health. During the Union army's occupation of the city, medical evidence had documented relationships between contagious illnesses and the unsanitary conditions prevailing in New Orleans' scattered and noisome abattoirs and markets. Centralization of butchering was needed in New Orleans in order to permit sanitary regulations to be enforced, as in other cities. Other reports were that the medical justifications camouflaged the fact that the coveted meatpacking monopoly went to the individuals who most generously bribed state lawmakers. Perhaps both arguments were true.

The justices, in weighing the appeals from earlier state and lower federal court judgments arising from the contested monopoly grant, chose to weigh the less sordid issues rather than the publicized claims and counterclaims about corrupted legislators. Exploiting points made especially by the appellant lawyers' briefs, the justices concerned themselves primarily with deciding whether the Thirteenth and Fourteenth Amendments and the Civil Rights Act had created federal rights against a state's excluding all but a designated privileged few from butchering, a state-licensed, private, for-profit trade.

Louisiana's attorney insisted that the Reconstruction amendments dealt exclusively with blacks' civil and political rights, not with whites' business corporations. In an undistinguished argument Louisiana's counsel emphasized the obvious point, that the state's police power justified the controverted policy. He denied that the Thirteenth Amendment had any purpose or effect other than to prohibit slavery and ignored the Fourteenth Amendment's imposition of minimal due process standards for exercises of state powers. Further, the American constitutional tradition held that a state's plenary police powers were up to the relevant state legislature to define and implement as it saw fit and that the legislative procedures implementing those powers were themselves adequate process. Louisiana's lawmakers had followed prescribed legislative procedures. In extraordinary situations that only legislators, not judges, could measure, private rights had to give way to the larger good.

In contrast to the state's counsel, the lead counsel for the complaining meatpackers sparkled. He was former U.S. Supreme Court justice John A. Campbell, an Alabamian who in 1861 had resigned in order to serve his seceding state and whose offense President Johnson had pardoned in 1865.

Conveying to the Court its members' first major encounter as a body with the Thirteenth and Fourteenth Amendments, in his arguments Campbell struck notes that harmonized neatly with those Chase had sounded in *Turner* and *Texas v. White.*

Campbell knew his former colleagues. Unaware that future jurists and constitutional commentators virtually would bury the Thirteenth Amendment under the Fourteenth, he afforded almost equal weight to both amendments in his argument. Arguing for the excluded meatpacking corporation, Campbell claimed that his clients, denied the right to practice their trade, were reduced to involuntary servitude because the state was depriving them of their property without due process of law. He insisted that the Thirteenth Amendment shielded his clients against such state's wrongs. Further hooking Chase's interest, Campbell noted that the 1787 Northwest Ordinance, which Chase's compilation of Ohio statutes had praised as the fount of midwesterners' liberty and prosperity, was the model for the Thirteenth Amendment's ban on slavery and involuntary servitude. That amendment had wider purposes than formally ending slavery for blacks, Campbell asserted. He then adapted to his clients' needs positions held by some Radical Republicans and by Chase in *In re Turner*, arguing that a law discriminating between any classes of persons, not only races, that deprived one class of freedom or property created an involuntary servitude. Further widening his definition, Campbell argued that Louisiana had reduced his clients to involuntary servitude by imposing "unreasonable obstructions" to their participation in butchering.

With his course set, Campbell steered his argument to the Fourteenth Amendment. The latter was "a more comprehensive exposition of the principles which lie at the foundation of the Thirteenth" because it forbade states from denying citizens "the more important and the most imperiled of the consequential rights" of life. Those broad basic rights were among the privileges stemming from federal citizenship, a status "of large significance, . . . [one] comprehended [of] great endowments of privilege, immunity, . . . [and] right . . . to cultivate the ground, or to purchase products, or to carry on trade, or to maintain himself and his family by free industry."

Thus, as in the earlier *Dewitt* case, the intrinsic issue in *Slaughterhouse* became whether the justices felt themselves empowered to peer behind lawmakers' stated intentions in enacting public policy. In *Dewitt* Congress' stated intention was to raise revenue; in *Slaughterhouse* Louisiana's stated purpose was to guard public health. The justices were faced with a need and, for some, an opportunity, again, as in the *Test Oath Cases*, to consider whether they could or should consider what lay beneath the stated intentions of state lawmakers about when and how to use state police powers. Was exclusion from an economic pursuit equivalent to the involuntary servitude forbidden by the Thirteenth Amendment? Had Louisiana denied nonlicensed meatpackers the equal protection of its laws, the same privileges enjoyed by the monopolists, and the same chances at potential property without due process of law? For a bare majority of his colleagues, Justice Miller replied negatively.

An antislavery Iowan of impeccable pro-Union credentials, Miller, to Chase's evident distress, rejected Campbell's broad interpretation. Without proof of personal servitude, much less slavery, no valid Thirteenth Amendment claim existed. The excluded butchers had only to use the procedures and facilities the state had specified in order to participate in the trade. Miller also defined the Fourteenth Amendment narrowly. True, it forbade states from abridging the federal rights of citizens. But two categories of citizenship, federal and state, existed. As Miller saw matters, it was impossible that the framers and ratifiers of the Fourteenth Amendment meant to transfer to Congress "the entire domain of civil rights heretofore belonging exclusively to the states."

In sum, the states retained authority over everything except a relatively narrow—indeed, traditional—range of citizens' federal rights, such as interstate mobility at home and protection when on the high seas or abroad. And so the majority justices recoiled from the too-drastically altered federalism Campbell envisaged, Louisiana's police powers remained undiminished, the excluded butchers stayed excluded, and millions of blacks were rent of federal protection.

Dissenting for himself and for Bradley, Swayne, and Chase, Justice Field discounted Louisiana's public health justification for the disputed statute. He charged correctly that Miller's narrow interpretation of the meaning of federal citizenship substantively diminished the Fourteenth Amendment's privileges and immunities clause into what Field called "a vain and idle enactment, which accomplished nothing, and most unnecessarily excited Congress and the people on its passage." Concluding in a manner to engage Chase's support, Field insisted that both the Thirteenth and Fourteenth Amendments aimed at realizing the rights stated as goals in the Declaration of Independence, "rights which are the gifts of the Creator; [rights] which the law does not confer, but only recognizes."

Chase agreed also with Justice Bradley's separate dissenting opinion. It echoed Chase's point in *Turner* that a result of the Thirteenth Amendment and a privilege of federal citizenship was to pursue a calling, "subject to such reasonable regulations as may be prescribed by law." What was "reasonable" the federal judges would determine because they had the "jurisdiction and plain duty" to repel states' diminutions of private rights to exchange one's skills or capital for gain in "whatever lawful employment he chooses to adopt (submitting . . . to all lawful regulations)."

Concluding, Bradley hit precisely on aspects of Chase's lifetime as an antislavery activist facing vigilantes and mobs as well as in his *Turner* opinion. Referring to the Thirteenth and Fourteenth Amendments, Bradley, enlarging on a phrase quoted earlier, stated:

> The mischief to be remedied was not merely slavery and its incidents and consequences; but that spirit of insubordination and disloyalty to the National Government which had troubled the country for so many years in some of the States, and that intolerance of free speech and free discussion which often rendered life and property insecure, and which led to much unequal legislation. The Fourteenth Amendment was an attempt to give voice to the strong national yearning for . . . that . . . condition of things in which American citizenship should be a sure guarantee of safety . . . and in which every citizen of the United States might stand . . . in the full enjoyment of every right and privilege belonging to a freeman, without fear of violence or molestation.

Chase, moved especially by Bradley's dissent, perceived accurately that *Slaughterhouse* consigned blacks to the mercy of their state governments so far as everyday economic realities were concerned. In the South, where the great majority of blacks lived, those governments were again controlled by their former masters and exploiters.

A few weeks after the Court decided *Slaughterhouse* it ruled on *Myra Bradwell v. Illinois* (83 U.S. 130). Like *Turner,* this lawsuit also involved a female but a white lawyer, not a black menial, a mature professional, not an apprenticed teenager. Yet both Elizabeth Turner and Myra Bradwell claimed federally protected rights under the amended U.S. Constitution against the adverse policies of their states.

Turner's lawsuit had evoked from Chase one of the first federal judicial definitions of the immediate relevance to blacks, beyond emancipation itself, of the Thirteenth Amendment, the Civil Rights Act, and the pending Fourteenth Amendment. Although Chase did not stress the matter of gender, his *Turner* opinion was also the first to shield women, including black women, even very recent slaves, under the protective umbrella of the newly amended federal Constitution. Because *Turner* was not appealed to the Supreme Court, his opinion affected only his circuit and then in limited ways. And a great deal had transpired between the *Turner* hearing in 1867 and Bradwell's in 1873.

Bradwell's lawsuit was the Supreme Court's first sex discrimination case, as it would now be described. It elicited from the justices their fateful initial ruling on the applicability of the Fourteenth Amendment to females. As in *DeWitt* and *Slaughterhouse,* the *Bradwell* litigation questioned the extent to which Supreme Court justices could or should monitor policies that states' lawmakers and judges had deemed to be necessary. And again as in *Slaughterhouse,* in deciding *Bradwell* the justices, Chase once more excepted, created another sharply delineated "two spheres," this time both of nation and state *and* of males and females. The result in *Bradwell* was similar to that in *Slaughterhouse.* The majority who decided *Bradwell* decided that the sphere of federal constitutional protections was small and certainly did not embrace a woman's wish to enjoy access to a trade or profession.

The woman at issue, Myra Bradwell, was forty years old in 1873, at least twice Elizabeth Turner's probable age in 1867. Bradwell had been editing one of the country's best law periodicals, the *Chicago Legal News,* for some years, meanwhile studying law under the tutelage of her husband, a regionally prominent attorney and later a judge. Illinois denied her a license to practice law. Not only was Bradwell female; she was also married. Her female nature and her married status assertedly made her incapable of keeping clients' interests confidential from her husband. Illinois law excluded married women from entering into contracts without their husbands' permission, and every representation of a client involved a contract.

Represented by U.S. senator Matthew Carpenter of Wisconsin, who had counseled litigants in several of the Supreme Court's landmark Reconstruction cases, Bradwell had appealed to the U.S. Supreme Court. Carpenter knew that several justices were upset by demands of women's rights advocates for the same constitutionally equalized civil and political rights that black men enjoyed. He skirted this minefield.

Shifting to points Chase had stressed in *In re Turner* and that were reiterated in his *Slaughterhouse* dissent, Carpenter emphasized that one meaning of emancipation was to open all vocations to every qualified person.

Although states retained authority to police the access roads to licensed trades and professions by setting appropriate qualifications, they could no longer exclude citizens for reasons of race from practicing licensed callings. Women were citizens and were entitled to the same privileges as men of protection against state discrimination.

Illinois did not bother to defend its procedures. And by its 8-to-1 verdict against Bradwell, the Supreme Court confirmed the accuracy of Illinois' reading of the situation.

To Chase's disappointment Justice Bradley, speaking for himself, Swayne, and Field, turned sharply away from his own earlier decisions in roughly analogous cases when on circuit. Bradley isolated Bradwell in the state sphere of the sharply separated constitutional galaxy the Court's majority had navigated in the recent *Slaughterhouse* decision. To be sure, Bradley stated, women were citizens under the Fourteenth Amendment's definition. All citizens' equal rights were constitutionally guaranteed. But that guarantee did not extend to all professions or callings, a point Justice Miller stressed in his concurring opinion. States also retained rights and duties in the federal system, Bradley continued. He heartily favored "the humane movements of modern society" that allowed women to advance themselves, but citizens' qualifications for different work varied greatly. The task of defining these qualifications was the prerogative of state lawmakers, who understood their local situations and who could best specify the qualifications for work involving special skills and total confidentiality.

Bradley granted that unmarried women could make contracts and that Bradwell was exceptionally qualified to be a lawyer. Nevertheless, her exceptional abilities did not warrant creation of an exception to existing legal doctrines. Society's fundamental duty was to maintain the stability and integrity of families. By practicing a profession, married women could become independent of husbands. Then society would erode, Bradley feared.

Bradley noted also the rigors of legal practice. Women's "timidity and delicacy" made them unfit for participation. Their "spheres and destinies" called for their protection by males, not for them to represent males as attorneys. In phrases now superannuated, Bradley insisted that "the paramount mission and destiny of women are to fulfill the noble and benign offices of wife and mother. This is the law of the Creator."

The majority opinion was antithetical to Chase's understanding of Christian doctrine and America's history and constitutional law. The only dissenter among the justices, he was too sick in body and spirit, however, to do more than record his disagreement. In effect, Chase stipulated by his dissent in *Bradwell v. Illinois* that he still stood on the far broader ground of race-free and gender-free access to life's opportunities, benefits, and hazards. Saddened that the Court's majority had drastically narrowed the dimensions of liberty in *Slaughterhouse* and *Bradwell v. Illinois*, on May 7, 1873, after suffering a second stroke, Chase died.

CONCLUSION

Chase died knowing that in 1862 he had been far too optimistic about the futures an end to slavery would open. A decade later, in failing health and reviewing in his mind's eye events since 1862, Chase awakened from a "singular dream" that he recorded at once in his journal (p. 695). As dreams do, his confused facts and chronology, mixing what had been possible with impossibilities. But Chase's dream perhaps mirrored his deepest yet repeatedly frustrated hopes for himself and for the nation and ideas he served.

In Chase's dream Union troops took Jefferson Davis prisoner at Appomattox. Yet somehow Davis almost at once succeeded Lincoln as president of the United States. Then repentant white voters in the former Confederate states selected only wholly admissible southern Unionists to represent them in Congress, its Republican majority delighted by evidences of the conciliatory sentiments prevailing among the defeated. Swift sectional reconciliation resulted when white residents of every southern state and community at once ratified the Thirteenth Amendment and conscientiously implemented it. To Chase, deep in his dream, the best evidence of southern whites' repentance for the decades of slavery and the years of civil war was their formalizing in their states' constitutions, laws, and customs the legal and political equality of blacks and whites, without resistance, much less violence. Therefore no Civil Rights Act, Military Reconstruction laws, Fourteenth or Fifteenth Amendments and their implementing statutes were necessary, no *Test Oath* or *McCardle* cases had to reach the Supreme Court, and no president needed to be impeached.

Confiding still in his journal the wishful phantoms of his imaginings, Chase recorded other pleasing consequences of mutual forgiveness. He wrote that with the "Constitution amended & slavery abolished . . . [and] Suffrage made universal—Davis resigned" as president of the United States and Lincoln was reelected. The resurrected Lincoln proclaimed "Universal Amnesty." Thereafter "general harmony" ruled across the United States.

And so at least in his dreams this mortally ill man wrapped himself happily in visions of a stable and prosperous nation populated by biracial communities whose members respected every American's legal rights and every state's autonomy. This to Chase was the future Lincoln had opened in 1862 with the prospect of emancipation; this was what should have emerged from slavery's eradication and the Confederacy's collapse, both later confirmed by the Thirteenth Amendment.

In his dream of 1872 Chase wrote finis to the nation's manifold problems created by slavery, secession, the Civil War, and Reconstruction. But like Abou-ben-Adam, he and the nation had to awake from his deep dream of peace—and face reality.

How well did he face it as chief justice of the United States? Predictably, upon his death dignitaries in their formal obsequies lauded his achievements and ignored his frustrations, failures, and faults. More perceptive opinions by contemporaries and by scholars over the years run the gamut from adulation to condemnation. Yet virtually all commentators recognize the need to survey Chase's whole career in order to understand his performance as chief justice of the United States.

A diary entry by George Templeton Strong, a prominent New York City attorney who during the Civil War was involved in freedmen's aid activities central to Chase's concerns, is typical of many contemporary estimates: "Died in this city, . . . Chief Justice Chase. . . . He leaves an honest record behind him, though in [public] office nearly all his days, . . . and was an anti-slavery man long ago when anti-slavery opinions seemed an absolute bar to all hope of social or political advancement."*

The nation faced its most wracking constitutional crises not only during the Civil War, though challenges then were fierce, but also during Andrew Johnson's impeachment three years after Appomattox. Chase presided over Johnson's impeachment trial because the Constitution required him to serve. He did so in a manner that diminished public anxiety about a rigged judgment either way and so fended off possibly recrudescing mob violence. In Chase's view mass violence and slavery were America's great failures.

Critics found evidence in Chase's several shifts of party allegiance of his allegedly opportunistic and unprincipled search for political advancement. Unquestionably a party-jumper, Chase had sought and won a number of local, state, and national offices, both elective and appointive. His Civil War services as Lincoln's treasury secretary had helped to initiate, energize, and sustain the national government's martial resources that ul-

*Allen Nevins and Milton H. Thomas, eds., *The Diary of George Templeton Strong,* 4 vols. (New York: Macmillan, 1952), 4:479.

timately dominated the seceded states. Nevertheless, his protestations of 1868 about his consistent dedication to states' rights rang true to the facts of his history.

For a tumultuous one-third of a century he was the antislavery crusaders' premier legal strategist. Chase's unswerving prewar preachment was that after 1776 all the states should indeed have been equal but were not. Constantly repeating this message in his political and legal sermons, Chase had opposed all national policies that favored one state-defined private property, that in slaves. His particular prewar targets were the federal fugitive slave rendition laws that he encountered during his years as "attorney general for runaway slaves." They intruded the laws of the slaveholding states into free states despite the contrary wishes of free-state majorities as evidenced by ballots, constitutions, and statutes.

The war years had never diminished Chase's prewar convictions that free states and communities best protected individuals' rights. While the nation's political and judicial institutions gave a priority of protection to slave owners' state-defined property rights, those institutions had been his enemy. Then nationwide abolition removed the causes of hostility while strengthening the state bases of the federal Union and underscoring the essentiality of morality in public policies. But the paradise he anticipated once slavery died never arrived.

On or off the bench, Chase was ever a political antislavery activist more than a profound student either of law or of the actual effects of slavery on its victims. Once he became chief justice, however, in a manner reminiscent of his study of Greek as an adolescent and of public finance as a cabinet officer, he applied himself successfully to mastering the intricacies of that malleable position. Chase, editorialized the *New York Nation* (May 15, 1873) on news of his death, "brought to the Court no store of legal learning, but . . . comprehensive views, considerable power of generalization, and a just sense of constitutional rights and judicial responsibility." The same might have been said of John Marshall or Earl Warren.

Concerning former slaves, Chase worried about their labor contracts as prescribed by relevant state law. But he never overcame his perception of blacks as white people with pigmented skins and salvageable, Christianizable souls. Thus Chase became an apostle of a kind of instant Reconstruction blessed by suffrage for all, amnesty for everyone, and quickly privatized welfare for former slaves.

His world, like ours, was filled with uncertainties yet often propelled by persons of passionate intensities. Chase tried to balance excess passion by affording the utmost possible freedom to responsible individuals. Much of his antislavery conviction stemmed from the fact that slavery and other involuntary servitude excluded responsibility.

At least this was the judgment of Chase's co-dissenter in *Slaughterhouse*, Justice Field, whose opinion for the majority in Bradwell's case so disappointed Chase. In the mid-1890s, aged and distressed by the widespread criticisms the Supreme Court was enduring for some of its current decisions, Field summed up Chase's life perceptively. He suggested correctly that so far as individuals' civil and political rights were concerned, Chase's constitutionalism was rooted in the Bible and the Declaration of Independence. To Chase (as to Field) governments existed "to secure these rights— not to grant . . . [or] create them." Irked because Chase was already being described even by scholars as an opportunistic trimmer, in part for his altering views in the *Legal Tender Cases,* Field insisted instead that Chase's shifts of both political allegiance and votes on the Court reflected "intellectual integrity." No public figure could face greater embarrassment than publicly to repudiate his own former policies, in this instance the Treasury's paper money issues, Field insisted. "He preferred to be the honest judge rather than the consistent statesman . . . [and so] decided against the constitutionality of the provision." Chase clearly preferred to be president of the United States rather than its chief justice, as Field acknowledged. Field surmised that had Chase won the office he most coveted, he "would have rendered great services to the country. . . . But there was enough fulfillment of great purposes in his career to satisfy the ambition of any one."

Perhaps. Such musings win only the Scottish verdict, "Not proved." But neither are they disprovable. And as Isaac Redfield, a former chief judge of Vermont, observed, Chase's "conservatism as a statesman, and his eminent qualities as a judge" deserve commemoration if for no other reason than "for the quality and character of his opposition to slavery" and its persisting incidents (see bibliographical essay, next page).

With that estimate, this history rests.

BIBLIOGRAPHICAL ESSAY

Aspects of Salmon P. Chase's several careers have attracted the attention of many historians, biographers, and other scholars whose interests in him reflected their specialized research concerns. But until recently only three womb-to-tomb surveys of his life existed. Two were published in 1874, only a year after Chase died: Jacob W. Schuckers, *The Life and Public Services of Salmon Portland Chase* (New York: D. Appleton and Company, 1874), and Robert B. Warden, *An Account of the Private Life and Public Services of Salmon Portland Chase* (Cincinnati: Wilstach, Baldwin, and Company, 1874). Both remain useful less as fully rounded critical biographies of Chase's life than as convenient printed collections of his correspondence and other relevant primary contemporary sources that specialist scholars have mined endlessly. In the third, Albert Bushnell Hart's briefer *Salmon P. Chase* (Boston and New York: Houghton Mifflin Company, 1899), the author offers keen insights into Chase's life; yet the book is neither a full-scale biography nor does it provide an adequate exhumation of any single facet of the subject's multifaceted activities. Many briefer biographical notices appeared soon after Chase's death, including Stephen J. Field, "Remarks on the Life and Character of Chief Justice Chase, Feb. 4, 1890," in *Some Account of the Work of Stephen J. Field*, ed. John Norton Pomeroy (1895), and Isaac Redfield, "Chief Justice Chase," *North American Review* 122 (April 1876):337.

Through the first half of the twentieth century, Chase, like many of Lincoln's closest wartime servitors including Bates, Blair, Seward, and Stanton, remained defined primarily by their official and personal relationships with the president. Hosts of researchers tracked Chase the better to pinpoint his location in the "Lincoln and" orbit. I have of course made copious use of Roy P. Basler et al., eds., *The Collected Works of Abraham Lincoln*, 8 vols. (New Brunswick, N.J.: Rutgers University Press, 1953–1955), and other Civil War–era politicians' papers, in manuscript collections and in print. Many scholars were unable in person to plow through Chase's mountainous arrays of letters, diaries, and journals held in several scattered depositories, especially the Library of Congress and the Historical Society of Pennsylvania. Such inquirers were helped by the printed partial selections in Edward G. Bourne et al., eds., "Diary and Correspondence of Salmon Portland Chase," *Annual Report of the American Historical Association, 1902*, vol. 2 (1903); and David Donald, ed., *Inside Lincoln's Cabinet: The Civil War Diaries of Salmon Portland Chase* (New York: Longmans, Green, 1954).

Until the 1990s, researchers' accumulated frustrations were only partially relieved by the availability of these essential yet attenuated printed accounts. Then John Niven and his able, indefatigable, and surely eye-strained editorial aides exponentially expanded the parameters of research on, about, or relative to Chase. Appearing annually in succeedingly weighty volumes, each exhibiting meticulous editorship over a universe of relevant monographic scholarship, *The Salmon P. Chase Papers*, vol. 1, *Journals, 1829– 1872* (Kent, Ohio: Kent State University Press, 1993), vol. 2, *Correspondence, 1823–1857* (Kent, Ohio: Kent State University Press, 1994), and vol. 3, *Correspondence, 1858–1863* (Kent, Ohio: Kent State University Press, 1996), all edited by Niven et al., and Niven's *Salmon P. Chase: A Biography* (New York: Oxford University Press, 1995), have substantially redressed the lack of emphasis on Chase.

Obviously, my book is not a full biography of Chase. Niven's very recent splendid one preempts that field, at least until major (presently unknown) documentary sources and unforeseen shifts in research interests justify another large-scale evaluation. Yet I do try to place these two of Chase's numerous judicial pronouncements, *In re Turner* and *Texas v. White*, into the context of his whole life. Therefore I happily and gratefully exploited Niven's edition of Chase's *Journals* and *Correspondence*. But I chose not to read his excellent biography until I had finished writing *The Reconstruction Justice of Salmon P. Chase*, and then not to amend the latter by alternative views expressed in the former.

The texts of these cases are in print. The brief Chase received of *In re Turner* was titled *Elizabeth Turner by her next friend Charles Henry Minoke, Ex Parte*. It was reported officially as *In re Turner*. Minoke was not her attorney. No case papers survive in the National Archives (Dr. Robert J. Plowman, director, National Archives, Philadelphia Depository, to author, January 24, 1995). *Texas v. White* is reported in 7 Wallace (74 U.S.) 700 (1869), the official text of U.S. Supreme Court actions in cases.

Activist politics, religion, and legal practice involving deprivations of individuals' legal rights defined Chase's life. Frederick J. Blue, *Salmon P. Chase: A Life in Politics* (Kent, Ohio: Kent State University Press, 1987), deals competently with his topic. Entrance into the life of the law as Chase lived it is available in Kermit L. Hall, *The Magic Mirror: Law in American History* (New York: Oxford University Press, 1989); Morton J. Horwitz, *The Transformation of American Law, 1780–1860* (Cambridge, Mass.: Harvard University Press, 1977); Horwitz's second *Transformation*, dealing with the period 1870– 1960 (New York: Oxford University Press, 1992); and William Nelson and John Phillip Reid, *The Literature of American Legal History* (New York: Oceana Publications, 1985). Insights into ways the law and constitutionalism mixed with Chase's devout religiosity are in George Hoemann, *What Hath God Wrought: The Embodiment of Freedom in the Thirteenth Amendment* (New York: Garland Publications, 1987); Victor B. Howard, *Religion and the Radical Republican Movement, 1860–1870* (Lexington: University Press of Kentucky, 1990); and David A. J. Richards, *Conscience and the Constitution: History, Theory and Law of the Reconstruction Amendments* (Princeton, N.J.: Princeton University Press, 1993).

In a special Chase Centennial Issue of *Northern Kentucky University Law Review* 21 (1993), scholars presented diverse multidisciplinary interpretations of his legal career. Further insights into that career are provided by James W. Ely, Jr., *The*

Guardian of Every Other Right: A Constitutional History of Property Rights (New York: Oxford University Press, 1992); Andrew Fede, *People Without Rights: An Interpretation of the Fundamentals of the Law of Slavery in the U.S. South* (New York: Garland Publications, 1992); and Peter C. Hoffer, *The Law's Conscience: Equitable Constitutionalism in America* (Chapel Hill: University of North Carolina Press, 1990). Robert J. Steinfeld, *The Invention of Free Labor: The Employment Relation in English and American Law and Culture, 1350–1870* (Chapel Hill: University of North Carolina Press, 1991), suggests why Chase feared that social instability was resulting from inadequate legal protections for individuals' property rights. Parallels to Chase's ideas are visible in David M. Gold, *The Shaping of Nineteenth-Century Law: John Appleton and Responsible Individualism* (New York: Greenwood Press, 1990).

Slavery-related legal matters central in Chase's prewar career are attended to by, among others, Stephen Middleton, *Ohio and the Antislavery Activities of Attorney Salmon Portland Chase* (New York: Garland Publications, 1990); Don E. Fehrenbacher, *The Dred Scott Case: Its Significance in American Law and Politics* (New York: Oxford University Press, 1978); Paul Finkelman, *An Imperfect Union: Slavery, Federalism, and Comity* (Chapel Hill: University of North Carolina Press, 1981); Aileen S. Kraditor, *Means and Ends in American Abolitionism: Garrison and His Critics on Strategy and Tactics, 1834–1850* (New York: Pantheon Books, 1969); Mark V. Tushnet, *The American Law of Slavery: Considerations of Humanity and Interest, 1810–1860* (Princeton, N.J.: Princeton University Press, 1981); and William M. Wiecek, *The Sources of Antislavery Constitutionalism in America, 1760–1848* (Ithaca: Cornell University Press, 1977).

On the eve of the Civil War, ideas like Chase's in circulation on slavery, freedom, and federalism are surveyed in Thomas D. Morris, *Free Men All: The Personal Liberty Laws of the North, 1780–1861* (Baltimore: Johns Hopkins University Press, 1974); Stanley W. Campbell, *The Slave Catchers: Enforcement of the Fugitive Slave Law, 1850–1860* (Chapel Hill: University of North Carolina Press, 1970); and Lewis Perry, *Radical Abolitionism—Anarchy and the Government of God in Antislavery Thought*, rev. ed. (Knoxville: University of Tennessee Press, 1995).

Concerning Chase and the Civil War, Horwitz, in his second book titled *The Transformation of American Law*, noted that he had ended his first volume with 1860 and started the second one with 1870. He explained that he had skipped the 1860 decade because "I believe that only a separate book can do justice to the profound significance of the Civil War in American legal history. I hope to write that book someday." This is a laudable intention from a scholar who is particularly well equipped to achieve it. As Horwitz knows, of course, an army of books, articles, and other scholarship helps to define though not to lighten his weighty but essential task. Probably the swimmers who survive in that decade's turbulent interpretive sea will have exploited James G. Randall's *Constitutional Problems Under Lincoln*, rev. ed. (Urbana: University of Illinois Press, 1951); Charles Fairman's *Reconstruction and Reunion, 1864–88; vol. 6, History of the Supreme Court of the United States* (New York: Macmillan, 1971–1987); Harold M. Hyman's *A More Perfect Union: The Impact of the Civil War and Reconstruction on the Constitution* (New York: Knopf, 1973); Hyman's and William M. Wiecek's *Equal Justice Under Law: Constitutional Development 1835–1875* (New York: Harper and Row, 1982); David Herbert Donald's *Lincoln* (New York: Simon and Schuster, 1995); and Phillip Shaw Paludan's *The Presidency of Abraham Lincoln* (Lawrence: University Press of Kansas, 1995).

Focus on Chase's wartime Treasury service and links to Congress is offered by Bray Hammond, *Sovereignty and an Empty Purse: Banks and Politics in the Civil War* (Princeton, N.J.: Princeton University Press, 1970); and Walter T. K. Nugent, *The Money Question During Reconstruction* (New York: W. W. Norton, 1967). Concerning Chase's evolution toward nationwide abolition as a war aim, in addition to the preceding titles, essential reading includes Herman Belz's *Emancipation and Equal Rights: Politics and Constitutionalism in the Civil War Era* (New York: Norton, 1978); Patricia Allen Lucie's *Freedom and Federalism: Congress and Courts, 1861–1866* (New York: Garland Publications, 1986); Eric Foner's *Reconstruction: America's Unfinished Revolution, 1863–1877* (New York: Harper and Row, 1988); and Earl M. Maltz's *Civil Rights, the Constitution, and Congress, 1863–1869* (Lawrence: University Press of Kansas, 1990). Each interpretation differs significantly from every other, yet all reflect the belated but appropriate assumption by scholars that Reconstruction began soon after the Fort Sumter surrender in 1861, not the day after Lee surrendered at Appomattox in 1865.

Michael Les Benedict's *The Impeachment and Trial of Andrew Johnson* (New York: Norton, 1973) is convenient and reliable on that topic. Matters essential to an understanding of Chase's positions in both *In re Turner* and *Texas v. White* are examined by Donald G. Nieman, *To Set the Law in Motion: The Freedmen's Bureau and the Legal Rights of Blacks, 1865–1868* (Millwood, N.Y.: KTO Press, 1979); Nieman's *Promises to Keep: African-Americans and the Constitutional Order, 1776 to the Present* (New York: Oxford University Press, 1991); and Nieman, ed., *The Constitution, Law, and American Life: Critical Aspects of the Nineteenth-Century Experience* (Athens: University of Georgia Press, 1992).

As I noted three decades ago in a biography of Edwin M. Stanton that I co-wrote, when at the turn of the century Lincoln's former secretaries John G. Nicolay and John Hay were planning their multivolume biography, they worried that their closeness to Lincoln would raise questions about their neutrality. In a letter (reproduced in William R. Thayer, ed., *Life and Letters of John Hay* [Boston and New York: Houghton Mifflin Company, 1915], 2:33), Hay advised his intended co-author:

> We must not write a stump speech. . . . We . . . ought to write the history of those times like two everlasting angels who know everything, judge everything, and don't care a twang of the harps about one side or the other. . . . Let us look upon men as insects and not blame the black beetle because he is not a grasshopper.

But Hay then allowed an exception to his admirable exhortation to objectivity: "We are Lincoln men through and through."

I am not a "Chase man through and through." Instead I am a historian with special interests in ways that laws, constitutions, and judges' decisions, such as Chase's in *In re Turner* and *Texas v. White,* illuminate the past and speak to the present.

Abolitionism, 6, 37, 40, 75, 86, 89, 135, 168
   antislavery and, 39, 72
   Chase and, 35, 70, 73, 88, 92–93
Adams, Charles Francis, Jr., 93
Adams, John, 18
Adams, John Quincy, 51
American Antislavery Society, 34, 64, 107
American Freedman (journal), on freedmen/poverty, 157
American Freedmen's Union Commission, 156
Angell, James, 20
Antigone (Sophocles), quote from, 12
Antikidnapping penalties, 45, 46
Anti-Masons, 30, 55, 67
Anti-Peonage law (1867), 131–32
Antislavery activism, 2, 10, 11, 22–23, 34–35, 37, 40, 47–49, 63, 69, 74
   abolitionism and, 39, 72
   Chase and, 35–36, 42–43, 46–47, 49–50, 61–62, 75, 83–84, 93, 101, 103, 105, 107, 111, 112, 125, 134–35, 142, 168, 169
Antivagrancy penalties, 83
Apprenticeships, 101, 113, 120, 123, 126, 128, 129, 155
   black children and, 109
   enforceability of, 6
   status of, 77–78, 127
Arnold, Isaac, 20
Attorneys
   partnerships of, 25, 28
   politics and, 25–26, 30
   work of, 26, 27

Ball, Flamen, 28
Baltimore & Ohio Railroad, 123
Bankruptcy, fear of, 75–76, 81, 82, 85

Barron v. Baltimore (1833), 48
Bates, Edward, 66, 67–68
   citizenship issue and, 87–88, 114
Beecher, Lyman, 28, 34, 35
Beecher Stowe, Harriet. *See* Stowe, Harriet Beecher
Betty's case, 60
Bill of Rights, 11, 41, 58
   slavery and, 43, 44, 48
   transformation of, 39–40
Birney, James G., 35, 63
   antislavery activities of, 40, 42
   candidacy of, 43–44, 51
   suit against, 45, 62
Birney v. State (1838), 45
"Black and tan" constitution, 150
Black codes, 33, 107, 109–10, 114, 120, 124, 126, 141
   Chase and, 111–12, 113, 135
   concerns about, 117
   disenfranchisement by, 109
   involuntary servitude and, 118
   Thirteenth Amendment and, 108, 111, 136
Blacks
   apprenticeships for, 109, 127
   citizenship and, 58, 59, 87–88
   as civil servants, 81
   harassment of, 109–10
   kidnapping, 45–46, 47
   legal status of, 61, 79–80, 84, 88, 102
   political rights of, 99, 148
   politics and, 89, 90
   property for, 102, 104
   social elevation of, 3
   as soldiers, 4, 5, 76, 84, 88, 91
   vote for, 91, 94, 95, 99, 105, 109, 110, 123, 142, 148, 153, 156
   See also Slaves

Blackstone, William, 20, 49
Blair, Montgomery, 65–66, 75
Bonds, x, 8
    paying on, 76–77
Booth, John Wilkes, 91
Boyle, A. F., 80
Bradley, Joseph, 161
    Bradwell and, 164
    Fourteenth Amendment
        interpretation by, 162
    Thirteenth Amendment
        interpretation by, 121–22, 162
Bradwell, Myra, suit by, 162–63, 164
Bradwell v. Illinois (1873), 130, 153, 162–63
    Chase and, 151, 157–58, 164–65
Brougham, Henry, 34
Brown, John, 54, 56, 62, 64
Brown v. Board of Education (1954), 56
Buchanan, James, 65
Burr, Aaron, 18, 138

Calhoun, John C., 51, 98, 117
    compact theory of, 58
    slavery and, 43, 46, 49, 55
Cameron, Simon, 66, 71, 85
Campbell, John A., 66
    Reconstruction amendments and,
        159–60, 161
Capitalism
    antislavery activists and, 115
    biracial access to, 113, 114
Carpenter, Francis B., 1
Carpenter, Matthew, *Bradwell* and, 163
Catron, John, 96
Charles River Bridge case, 18
Chase, Katherine Jane "Kate," 29, 94,
    151
Chase, Philander, guardianship by,
    13–15
Chase, Samuel Portland
    as anti-institutionalist, 154
    as chief justice, 91–94, 96–97, 100,
        101, 103, 104, 151–52, 161, 162, 167

children of, 29
    death of, 165, 166
    education of, 14, 15–16
    fiscal conservatism of, 77
    health problems for, 151, 152, 158
    legacy of, 10–12, 167–69
    legal profession and, 19–21, 25, 27, 28
    marriages of, 28–29
    political ambitions of, 30–31, 39, 78,
        86, 92, 94, 105, 118–19, 151, 152
    religion and, 2, 14–15, 22, 24, 29, 31,
        44–45, 111–12, 132–33
    teaching by, 16–17
    as treasury secretary, 65–69, 71, 72,
        78–81, 83, 89, 167
    youth of, 13–15
Chase & Ball, 28
Chase's Statutes, 28, 29, 33
Cheever, George B., on black codes,
    111
Cherokee Nation case, 18
Chicago Legal News, Bradwell and, 163
Chitty, Joseph, 20
Cincinnati
    Chase in, 27–29, 31, 32–33
    civic activism in, 33–34
    racism in, 54
    reputation of, 31–32
Cincinnati Board of Education,
    religious instruction and, 132–33
Cincinnati Gazette, 94
Citizenship, 114–15, 121–22, 146, 155
    blacks and, 58, 59, 87–88
    defining, ix, 58, 59, 120–21
Civil laws, 112, 141
Civil rights, 131, 141, 169
    black, 5, 135, 152, 154, 159
    employer/employee contracts and,
        7
    federal/state laws and, 10
    Fourteenth Amendment and, 161
    protecting, 153, 154, 156
    women and, 163

Civil Rights Act (1866), ix, 6, 92, 106,
    129, 166
  black codes and, 136
  Chase and, 121, 131, 145
  citizenship and, 121
  In re Turner and, 123, 126, 127, 128, 130,
    139, 140
  interpretation of, 159, 162–63
  provisions of, 103, 120–21, 132, 134
Civil War, 72, 73–76, 167
  constitutional law and, ix
  nature/consequences of, 143
  slavery and, 93
Clay, Cassius Marcellus, 55–56
  antislavery sentiments of, 63–64
Clay, Henry, 17, 63
Clifford, Nathan, 96
Cohens v. Virginia, 18
Colby, Abigail Chase, 39
Colby, Isaac, 39
Columbus Crisis, on Rock, 95
"Comity" clause, 57, 58, 59
Commentaries on American Law (Kent),
    20, 113
Commentaries on the Laws of England
    (Blackstone), 20, 49
Commonwealth v. Aves, (1836), 41
Compromise of 1820. *See* Missouri
    Compromise
Compromise of 1850, 56
Confederate states, status of former,
    7, 146–47
Confiscation Act (1861), 86–87, 102
Constitution, 60, 92
  Chase and, 2, 11, 62, 68
  citizenship and, 59, 88
  elections and, 111
  impeachment and, 138
  new state admissions and, 98
  slavery and, 37–38, 42–44, 47–50,
    54, 57, 58, 67, 70
  See also State constitutions,
    redrafting

Constitutional Law (Sergeant), 20
*Constitutional Limitations Which Rest
    Upon the Legislative Power of the
    States of the American Union*
    (Cooley), 157
Contract labor, Chase and, 120
Contracts, 104, 123
  civil rights and, 7
  equality of parties and, 118
  individuals and, 116
  nonfulfillment/partial completion
    of, 116
  right of, 113–14, 115
  upholding, 101, 102, 114, 128
Cooley, Thomas McIntyre,
  federalism and, 157
Copperheadism, 142
Corfield v. Coryell (1823), 48, 86
Corruption, problems with, 82, 89
Course of Legal Study (Hoffman), 20
Cranch, William, 20
Criminal laws, 110, 111
  rewriting, 109, 112
Cummings v. Missouri (1867), 136
Curtis, Benjamin R., *Dred Scott* and,
    59

Dallas, Alexander, 20
Dartmouth College case, 18
Davis, David, 96
Davis, Jefferson, 66, 153, 166
  indictment of, 138–39
Debtors, jailing, 110
Declaration of Independence, 161
  Chase and, 11, 35, 62, 63, 111, 169
  slavery and, 41, 43, 44, 48, 51–52
Declaration of Sentiments, 34–35
Democracy in America (Tocqueville),
    28
Democratic party, 31, 106
  accommodationists in, 43
  compromises by, 56
  emancipation and, 98

Democratic party *(continued)*
  leaders of, 118–19
  loyalty to, 30, 54
  racism and, 54–55
  slavery and, 67, 124
Disenfranchisement, 109, 149
Dorr Rebellion, 8, 98
Douglas, Stephen, 62, 63
Douglass, Frederick, 108, 124
  Freedmen's Bureau and, 155
  on slavery/involuntary servitude,
    107
Dred Scott v. Sandford (1857), 7, 67, 86,
    90, 92, 95, 101, 136
  Chase and, 56, 66, 68
  impact of, 56–58, 60–61, 88
  obliterating, 96, 153
Due process, 41, 48, 128, 132, 135, 152

Education, 62, 63
Eliot, T. S., quote of, 1
Emancipation, 3, 5, 7, 11, 22, 82, 86, 91,
    98, 148
  acknowledging, 149
  Chase and, 1, 67, 73, 152
Emancipation Proclamation, 2, 11, 75
  significance of, 3, 148
Equality, 73, 84, 89, 90, 136, 156
  blacks and, 102, 166
  Chase and, 95, 111, 133, 150, 152
  contract law and, 118
  legal/political, 85
Equity, 21–23, 42, 135
Erie Canal, 26, 27
Ex parte Garland (1867), 136
Ex parte Merryman (1861), 124, 125
Ex parte Milligan (1866), 135, 136,
    137

Fairman, Charles
  on Supreme Court, 94–95, 140
  Texas v. White and, 147

Federalism, 5, 9, 10, 11, 120
  Chase and, 22, 144, 152
  dual, 157
  secession and, 70
  slavery and, 50
Field, Stephen J., 96, 137
  Bradwell and, 164, 169
  on Chase, 169
  Fourteenth Amendment
    interpretation by, 161
  Slaughterhouse and, 158, 169
  Thirteenth Amendment
    interpretation by, 161
Fifteenth Amendment, 11, 153,
    166
  blacks and, 130
Fifth Amendment, 41, 48, 152
  slavery and, 59
  violation of, 58
First Amendment, 39, 133
Fort Sumter, 66, 68
Fourteenth Amendment, 106, 127, 128,
    166
  blacks and, 123, 130
  Chase and, 11, 79, 139
  citizenship and, 121
  civil rights and, 161
  impact of, 151, 153
  interpretation of, 133, 134, 159, 160,
    161, 162
  preemancipation property rights
    and, 158
  ratification of, 7
  women and, 163, 164
Fourth Amendment, 41
Freedman (journal), 156
Freedmen's Bureau, 106, 108, 124,
    126
  black codes and, 112
  contract labor and, 120
  problems for, 154, 156
  racism and, 134

Free labor contract theory, 9, 131
  Chase and, 118, 119–20, 155, 156–57
  marketplace and, 116–17
  social order and, 115, 119
Free-Soil party, 50, 55
  antislavery activists and, 62
  slavery and, 67
Fugitive recapture laws, 47, 48, 50, 51,
  57, 114
Fuller, Richard, 84

Gag-rule controversy, 51
Garniss, Catherine Jane, marriage to,
  28
Garrison, William Lloyd, 43, 44, 53,
  63, 66
  Constitution and, 42
  Declaration of Sentiments by, 34–35
  Reconstruction and, 154
Gelpcke v. Dubuque (1864), 76–77, 101,
  135
Georgia v. Stanton (1867), 137, 145
Gillette, William, on Houston, 153
Goodenow, John, 20
Gordon v. U.S. (1865), 94
Grant, Ulysses S., 91, 154
  black political/civil rights and,
  152
  injunction against, 137
"Grasp of war" constitutional theory,
  104, 108
Grier, Robert, 96

Habeas corpus, 45
Habeas Corpus Act (1863), 135
Hahn, Michael, 90, 91, 123, 124
  on black harassment, 109
  Freedmen's Bureau and, 108
  on Johnson appointments, 108
Hambleton, Philemon T., Turner
  and, 124–29
Harrison, William Henry, 31, 51

Henry, Patrick, 18
Hepburn v. Griswold (1870), 152
Historical Sketches of the Principles and
  Maxims of American Jurisprudence
  (Goodenow), 20
Hoffman, David, 20
Houston, Sam, 153
Howard, Oliver O., 154
Hunter, David, 86

Impeachment, 7, 138, 154, 167
Individual rights, protecting, 115, 168
In re Turner (1867), 3, 5, 16, 23, 37, 61
  Chase and, ix, x, 6–7, 10–11, 38, 39,
  44, 53, 67, 72, 73, 77, 80, 89, 91, 95,
  102, 103, 120–22, 128, 129–33, 136, 138,
  139, 141, 143, 145, 146, 148, 149, 162,
  163
  citizenship and, 88
  dilution of, 151–52, 153, 155, 158
  equality and, 150
  significance of, 9–10, 123–39
  slavery/involuntary servitude and,
  148
Invention of Free Labor (Steinberg), ix
Involuntary servitude, 6, 84, 92, 106,
  112, 130, 150
  abolition of, 4, 67, 89
  Chase and, 117–20, 169
  persistence of, 109–10, 113–14, 118–19,
  133, 160, 161
  Thirteenth Amendment and, 120, 134

Jackson, Andrew, 19, 23, 67, 75, 91
Jacksonianism, 23–24, 29, 30, 32
Jamaica, race riot in, 133–34
Jefferson, Thomas, 18, 62, 155
Johnson, Andrew, 96–98, 134, 145, 159
  black civil rights and, 148, 156
  Chase and, 95, 103, 104, 105
  Civil Rights Act and, 120
  executive orders by, 102

Johnson, Andrew *(continued)*
    Freedmen's Bureau and, 108, 112
    impeachment of, 7, 138, 154, 167
    Reconstruction and, 5, 104, 137, 154
Johnson, Bradley T., 103, 119
Johnson, Reverdy, 57–58
Joint Standing Committee on the
    Restoration of the Southern
    States, 106
Jones, Wharton, suit by, 47
Jones v. Van Zandt (1846), 47, 48, 50

Kansas-Nebraska Act (1854), 56, 58, 62
Kent, James, 20, 21, 28, 113, 155
Keppel's Administrators v. Petersburg RR
    (1868), 141, 142, 143, 145
Kidnapping, 45–46, 47
Knights of Labor, 116, 117
Know-Nothings, 30, 55, 67
Knox v. Lee, 152

Labor
    forced, 111
    social control over, 113–14, 116
Labor codes, 9, 83
Laidlaw, Sarah, marriage to, 29
Lane Seminary, antislavery activists
    at, 34–35
Lawyers. *See* Attorneys
Lee, Robert E., 107
Legal Tender Cases, 169
Lemmon v. . . . New York (1860), 61, 68
Liberator (journal), 107
Liberty party, 40, 43, 55
    Chase and, 50, 51–52
Lincoln, Abraham, ix, 26, 33, 56, 61, 64,
    82, 88
    abolition and, 90
    antislavery activists and, 62
    appointments by, 11, 65–68, 91
    assassination of, 91–92
    black suffrage and, 84, 94, 99, 110

    Chase and, 1, 13, 14, 16, 65, 69, 71, 72,
        83, 89, 166–67
    Confederate states and, 131, 141,
        147
    Dred Scott and, 62–63
    emancipation and, 2, 3, 11, 63, 67, 75,
        86, 148
    equality and, 111
    equity and, 22
    law practice of, 20, 30
    nomination of, 65, 91, 92
    Thirteenth Amendment and, 68
    war aims of, 1, 89
Lincoln, Mary, 94
Little Africa (Cincinnati), 32
"Little Gidding" (Eliot), quote of, 1
Locke, John, 62
Lovejoy, Elijah, 50
Lumpkin, Joseph, Paschal and, 144
Luther v. Borden (1849), 8, 9, 98

McCardle, William, 137
McCardle case, 166
McClellan, George B., 82
McCormick Reaper patent case, 65
McCulloch v. Maryland, 18, 146
McLean, John, 47, 59
"Manhood, the Basis of Suffrage"
    (Hahn), 108
Marketplace, contract relationships
    in, 116–17, 119, 132
Marshall, John, 18, 97, 146, 168
Marx, Karl, 49
Matilda (slave's daughter), 42, 48, 52,
    67, 73, 124
    defending, 40–41, 45, 46, 47, 50
Matthews, Stanley, 132–33
Merryman, John, 6, 125
Mexican War, 52, 64
Military Reconstruction, 7, 76, 92, 131,
    134, 141–43, 145. *See also*
    Reconstruction

Military Reconstruction Act (1867), 123, 137, 146, 149
Miller, Samuel, 96
    Bradwell and, 164
    Fourteenth Amendment and, 161
Mississippi v. Johnson (1867), 137, 145
Missouri Compromise (1820), 33, 56
    Dred Scott and, 57, 58, 60
Monroe, James, 33

Nelson, Samuel, 60–61, 96
New York Central, 123
New York Nation, on Chase, 168
North American Review, Chase in, 34
Northwest Ordinance (1787), 47, 59, 160
    Dred Scott and, 60
    Lincoln and, 62
    slavery and, 33, 41

Ohio Antislavery Society, 48
Ohio Colonization Society, 33
Ohio "Conscience" Whigs, 55

Partnerships, 25, 28
Party allegiance, shifts in, 54, 167
Paschal, George Washington, 144–45, 147
    Texas v. White and, 146
Patronage, 23, 30, 79
Patrons of Husbandry, 116, 117
Pennsylvania Supreme Court, Prigg and, 46
Peonage, 132, 150
Personal liberty laws, 45, 46
Petition and Memorial (Cheever), 111
Philanthropist (newspaper), 35, 39, 48
Phillips, Wendell, 44, 153
    Constitution and, 42
    Reconstruction and, 154
Pike, Albert, Texas v. White and, 146

Plundering Generation: Corruption and the Crisis of the Union, 1849–1861, The (Summers), x
"Political question" doctrine, 8, 9
Political rights, 169
    black, 152, 153, 159
    women and, 163
Practical Treatise on the Law of Contracts (Chitty), 20
Preamble, slavery and, 11, 44, 111
Prigg v. Pennsylvania (1842), 41, 47, 50, 57, 60
    impact of, 45, 46, 48
Private property, 8, 74, 75
    Chase and, 22, 24, 36, 39, 62, 66, 158, 168
    free contract labor theory and, 115
    slaves as, 6, 22, 36, 37, 38, 42, 43, 59, 158
    voiding, 21
Privatization, advocating, 154, 155, 156
Prize Cases (1863), 101, 141
Provisional governments, 5, 104, 149

Racism, 9, 10, 32, 85, 89, 105, 112, 133–34
    Democratic party and, 54–55
    fighting, 157
Radical Republicans, 72, 99, 146
    black civil rights and, 156
    Reconstruction amendments and, 160
    seceding states and, 145
    social order and, 101
Recollections of the Early Chicago and Illinois Bar (Arnold), 20
Reconstruction, 76, 91, 99–100
    Chase and, 10, 12, 100–101, 105, 167
    preemancipation property rights and, 158
    privatization of, 154, 155, 156
    See also Military Reconstruction

Reconstruction amendments, ix, 130
  interpreting, 159–60
Reconstruction and Reunion (Fairman),
  140
Reconstruction Committee, 106
Redfield, Isaac, on Chase, 169
Reid, Whitelaw "Agate," on black
  suffrage, 94
Republican party
  Chase and, 50, 53, 60, 88
  formation of, 59–60
  free labor theory and, 115
  Lincoln and, 65, 92
  slavery and, 62, 67
  See also Radical Republicans
Republican–War Democrat Union
  party, 77, 84, 97
Republic of Texas, slavery in, 52
Revels, Hiram, 153
Rhodes case, 130, 136
Rock, John, at Supreme Court, 95,
  96–97, 125, 153
Roe v. Wade (1973), 56
Runaway slaves, 33, 52, 66
  capturing, 45–46
  Chase and, 40–41, 125, 168
  defending, 22, 38–41, 45, 47, 49, 73,
  97
  rights of, 41–42, 54, 87
  Treasury Department and, 83
Rush, Richard, 21

Schouler, James, 113
Scott, Dred, 56–67, 67. *See also Dred
  Scott v. Sandford*
Secession, 68–69, 73, 98, 99
  Chase and, 70, 72, 131
  rolling back, 82, 89
Sergeant, Thomas, 20
Seward, William Henry, 47, 55, 74, 75,
  91
  appointment of, 65, 66, 67
  Lincoln and, 71

Sex discrimination, 162–63
Shaw, Lemuel
  Betty's Case and, 60
  Commonwealth v. Aves and, 41
Shortridge v. Macon (1867), 141, 142, 143, 145
  Chase and, 147–48
Slaughterhouse case (1873), 122, 130, 160,
  162, 164, 169
  Chase and, 151, 157–59, 163, 165
Slave owners, property rights of, 61,
  74, 75
Slave revolts, 33–34, 50
Slavery, 5, 117–18, 150
  abolishing, ix, 4, 67, 73, 89, 108–9,
  130, 168
  Chase and, x, 22, 32–35, 39, 52, 55, 61,
  70–71, 75, 84, 85, 89, 92, 97, 105, 133,
  135, 158, 167–69
  criticism of, 33, 38–39
  equity and, 42
  political parties and, 67
  property rights and, 6, 42, 43, 158
  states rights and, 41, 44
  in West, 56
  See also Involuntary servitude
Slaves
  legal status of, 6
  as private property, 22, 36, 37, 38,
  49–50, 58, 59
  Treasury Department and, 83, 84
  See also Blacks; Emancipation;
  Runaway slaves
Smith, Adam, contracts and, 115
Smith, Caleb, 66
Smith, Eliza Ann, marriage to, 28–29
Sojourners, 45, 57, 58, 86
Somerset case, 42
Sophocles, quote of, 12
Spoils system, 23, 30, 79
Stanton, Edwin McMasters, 64–65, 85,
  125
  injunction against, 137
  Lincoln and, 71

State constitutions, redrafting, 108, 149, 150
State debentures. *See* Bonds
States' rights, 8, 9, 42, 99
 Chase and, 44, 142, 167
 slavery and, 41, 44
Steinberg, Robert, ix
Stockbridge, Henry S., 125, 126, 128
 on apprenticeship/blacks, 127
Story, Joseph, 21, 28, 155
 Prigg and, 46
Stowe, Calvin, on slavery, 34
Stowe, Harriet Beecher, 13, 28, 34
 on attorneys, 37
Strong, George Templeton
 on Chase death, 167
 on Taney death, 90
Subcontractors, issues concerning, 117
Suffrage
 black, 142, 148, 153, 156
 extending, 29, 141, 148
Summers, Mark, x
Sumner, Charles, 55, 95, 153
Supreme Court Reports, Wallace and, 103
Swayne, Noah, 96, 161
 black codes and, 136
 Bradwell and, 164
 Rhodes case and, 130, 136

Taney, Roger B., 8, 91, 96, 97
 death of, 90
 Dred Scott and, 7, 58–61, 63, 90, 125
 Merryman and, 125
 military arrests and, 124
 "political question" doctrine of, 9
Tappan, Benjamin, 64
Tax collectors, appointment of, 81–82
Taylor, Zachary, 55
Temperance, 31–32, 34
Tenth Amendment, 44
"*Test Oath*" *Cases* (1867), 161, 166
 Chase and, 128, 136–37
Test oaths, 136–37, 141, 145, 149

Texas, 52
Texas v. White (1869), 3, 5, 16, 23, 37
 Chase and, ix, x, 7, 10–11, 38, 39, 44, 53, 67, 72, 73, 77, 80, 89, 95, 102, 103, 110, 121, 122, 140, 142–43, 146, 147
 citizenship and, 88
 dilution of, 151–52, 155, 158
 equality and, 150
 significance of, 9–10, 140–50
Thirteenth Amendment, x, 67, 110, 167
 black codes and, 108, 111, 136
 blacks and, 130
 Chase and, 11, 68, 79, 80, 92, 117, 118, 131, 145, 162
 citizenship and, 121–22
 convict/peon contract labor and, 132
 impact of, 5, 6, 132, 148, 153
 implementation clause of, 92
 In re Turner and, 123, 124, 126, 127, 130, 139, 140
 interpretation of, 159, 160, 162–63
 involuntary servitude and, 107, 120, 129, 134, 160, 161
 judicial protections under, 103
 preemancipation property rights and, 158
 problems with, 117, 151
 ratification of, 4, 91, 104, 124, 166
 slavery and, 68, 91, 107, 129, 160
Three-fifths clause, 99
Tocqueville, Alexis de, 28, 156
 on attorneys, 25, 26
Treasury Department, 82–83
 corruption at, 89, 92
 social experiments by, 85, 99
 staffing, 81–82
Treatise on the Law of Domestic Relations (Schouler), 113
True American (newspaper), Clay and, 63–64

Tucker, St. George, 20, 21
Turner, Betsey (Betty), 125
Turner, Elizabeth, 7, 9, 19, 67, 80
    apprenticeship of, 6, 120, 125,
        127–28, 131
    Chase and, 112, 135, 147
    equal rights for, 155
    Freedman's Bureau and, 124
    free labor and, 119
    habeas corpus for, 128
    mobility and, 114
    suit by, 123, 124, 126, 162
    See also In re Turner
Turner, Nat, revolt by, 34
Tyler, John, 51
Tyler v. Herndon (1866), 117

Uncle Tom's Cabin (Stowe), 47
Union Army
    antislavery goals of, 74
    blacks in, 4, 5, 76, 84, 88, 91
U.S. Court of Claims, 94
U.S. v. DeWitt, 157, 160, 163

Van Buren, J. D., 97
Van Buren, Martin, 31
Van Zandt, John, 50, 67, 73
    defending, 46–47, 48
Vesey, Denmark, revolt by, 33
Vigilantes, 92, 134, 149, 162
Virginia, bifurcation of, 99–100,
    104

Wade, Benjamin F., on Chase, 15
Wallace, John W., 103
War Department, Freedmen's Bureau
    and, 108
Warren, Earl, 168
Washington, Bushrod, 48
Washington, D.C.
    Chase arrival at, 16–17
    slave trade in, 51, 52
Watercourses (Angell), 20
Wayne, James, 96
Weld, Theodore Dwight, 64, 66
    antislavery activities of, 34, 35
Welles, Gideon, 66, 71
West Virginia
    assets for, 99–100, 103, 105
    formation of, 98
Whigs, slavery and, 67
White v. Hart (1872), 151, 157–58
Whiting, William, 125
Wiecek, William, 42
Wirt, William, 23, 26, 94
    Burr prosecution and, 138
    Chase and, 17–21, 27, 28, 30, 31
    equity and, 21
    legal profession and, 25
    politics and, 30
    writing of, 18
Women
    as civil servants, 81
    legal position of, 79–80
Wright, Elizur, 48